SF

I Was Invited

By the same author

Vision and Belief
Tunes of Glory
Brief Encounters

I Was Invited

The autobiography
of
Ian Mackenzie

ICS Books
Glasgow

First published in Great Britain in 2003 by
ICS Books
Institute of Contemporary Scotland
Suite 304B, The Pentagon Centre,
Washington Street, Glasgow G3 8AZ

ISBN 0 9546527 0 3

Typeset by Carrick Publishing Ltd
Printed in Great Britain by The Cromwell Press

The other morning, deploying all my athleticism and muscle power, I sat up in bed. My wife observed this. "You looked," she said, "like an old seal clambering onto a rock." Since for forty years Elizabeth has shared the rock with me, it is from that vantage point that I dedicate this book to her.

Contents

Preface

In early January, when Kenneth Roy asked me if I'd ever considered writing an autobiography, I laughed. When, in his nonchalant way, he said I'd have to finish it by September, I realised laughter wasn't going to work; Hogmanay was over. By the time he'd outlined details and dates, I was hooked into the view that doing it would be less trouble than arguing. That turned out to be true only in the sense that Kenneth then left me alone. I suppose I should thank him.

I certainly have to thank my son Stephen. Many evenings, and most weekends, after hard outdoor work with the Scottish Wildlife Trust, he would debrief me after my time-machine travels in the armchair and word-processor and sub-edit papyruses I brought back from distant haunts.

A different kind of gratitude wells up inside me when I reflect on the great favour done to me by Alice, my daughter, and by Elizabeth. Their parade of total disinterest in what I was writing relieved me of any need to consult, explain, apologise or argue.

I owe Kenneth's skilled colleagues at the Institute of Contemporary Scotland for their warm support.

And I bow respectfully to the many versions of myself that I met on my travels. Without them this book would have been impossible.

The distinguished agnostic journalist Robert Kee once said to me that when he came to die he would feel overwhelming gratitude. "Life's been a party and I was invited." I have borrowed that thought, which I share, to kick-start this book.

Ian Mackenzie
Helensburgh
October 2003

Prologue

Not the spark of life, but sparkle. That is a fundamental memory of childhood in blizzard-blown Fraserburgh. Even the dark sparkles. The world is not only white, it is smashingly white. The wind is howling, screaming. White stuff is cascading into white cliffs marbling the garden, the gate, the gables, the whole manse. Then a sudden gap as whirlwind clouds part from each other, and there, impenetrably deep in the chaos of the sky, stars, far, strong, sharp, bright, the sparkling of the universe. The clouds coalesce again, the raw wind bites, life is a siege, but those stars did sparkle, there is a trap-door into infinity. Light exists.

Summer. Strawberries, raspberries, loganberries, gooseberries, the huge garden, my father mowing one lawn, my mother mowing the other, both with burning cigarettes between their lips. The manse is vast. For example, we have two lavatories, what bliss. Dad uses the downstairs one; pipe smoke mingling with maleness. His study, next to that toilet, smells of pipe smoke, books and cat. As he writes, the cat sits on the big desk. When he is reading a Greek or Hebrew text he walks up and down holding in one hand the book, in the other a black thread attached at the other end to a pipe cleaner which twists and flies like a bird while the cat stalks and pirouettes. I've no doubt my father was an honorary cat, whereas my mother was an honorary dog; curiously my wife and I have played equivalent roles in our animal-rich lives; I can't imagine existence without other species: they seem to carry a summer sparkle at all times except illness and death.

Christmas: everyone wild with happiness. Every huge room sparkling with coloured paper, lanterns, streamers, a world gone dippy with delight. A child is born? Something is crawling from Bethlehem to our house.

March. Storms. What devil drives the steam drifters over the walls and towers of water? Up, down, further up, further down.

Topsy-Tipsy-Turvy boats cascading towards the herring, safe under the heaving water. So they think. Many fish will die. Some men may die.

Summer again. The creamy beach, curving into the two-mile bay. Breakers, sparkling as they play with people's legs. Dunes, warm ovens of sand. My older brother and sisters, companions to the sun, running, leaping, lounging upside down, sand enfolding limbs with gold dust encrusted by salt.

Autumn. The horizon becomes dark. We are alone again in a universe. The wind moans.

War! Sunday 3rd September, 1939. My sisters sunbathing, upside down as usual, their bums burning. My father and grandfather, both ministers, pacing the lawn, talking. Their world upside down. What is God's will? My elder brother goes to the army, the Cameron Highlanders in East Africa, and to be wounded in Burma. My eldest sister goes to nurse troops. My seventeen-year- old sister, captain of the Fraserburgh Academy hockey team, joins the WAAF, first to lead a mutiny in a London barracks over a rat found in a pie; then to Bletchley to decode Enigma.

And I'm banished to the balm of my Auntie Etta in Ardersier on the Moray Firth. Fraserburgh is unsafe, liable to be bombed from Norway. At the age of nine, I am at a stroke away from home, siblings and parents. First home-sickness of my life, but, and it is a huge but, my aunt is very, very funny. I return home a year later, to be bombed and machine-gunned by black swastikad aeroplanes rattling and whistling death. I carry my gas mask in its cardboard box to school and I run when the siren goes and I wake up most nights when the siren goes and I am bundled into the gas meter cupboard under the stairs where I wonder whether the next bomb is aimed at me. In 1945 the war ends and almost simultaneously my father dies of a heart attack.

At that, there is silence in heaven and in me for a half hour which goes on across the desert of that long summer where nothing moves. Life is so empty that my mind dulls to the point of extinction. My heart, like the world which once sparkled, is, it seems, dead. What reactivates it is an unimaginable experience about to engulf me. But now, back to the beginning.

1

A Vulnerable Boy

I can't identify the moment, or even the period, when I began to be aware of a carapace which was introducing itself to me as my body, and a self which had to negotiate a life within that body. It would be too strong to describe the relationship as dysfunctional, but I began gradually to register areas of discomfort. They included ridiculous activities with other boys like "Cowboys and Indians"—what?—football—why?—or accepting the challenge to walk along a high wall, falling off, and having one's elbow banged up in a sling. What was almost worse than any of that was being taught to swim by Dr Slessor, our charismatic family doctor.

He was a rowing blue which he seemed to think entitled him to push my head repeatedly under the North Sea as an incentive to the flailing of my legs and the filling of my lungs with salt water. The predictable result was that I have not only failed ever to swim, but for a long time had grave reservations about water as a medium for any activity undertaken by forms of life other than aquatic.

I felt inadequate in comparison with my brother and sisters. Not only did they have bodies bigger than mine, being respectively ten, eight and seven years my senior, but they appeared to inhabit those bodies with ease, swimming, doing athletics, playing tennis, all as to the manner born. In the case of Etta, my tomboy sister, she scored prolific hits against the ankles of other school hockey teams with every sign of complete satisfaction. The scale of my bewilderment at siblings with such fully operational physiques leaked into the public domain on my first day at Fraserburgh infant school.

I didn't mind the first hour and a half in the classroom—a box of chocolates was handed round by a kindly woman whose wittering seemed harmless; but then, without warning, we were thrown out onto a wasteland of tarmac upon which all my new peers ran around screaming. I sat alone on a distant patch of grass and observed this madness. Another kindly woman appeared and leaned. (An additional allergy I had by now acquired was to tall thin female adults who leaned.) On this first day of being washed up on the foreshore of school the woman now addressing me was the headmistress.

"Ian," she said, "would you like to go and play with the other children?"

I suppose, five years old, this is when I did my first growing up.

"No," I shuddered, and adhered to the grass.

It wasn't that my body was abnormally abnormal. It was normally abnormal, that is to say it was different. I wasn't a clone, a film star, a model, or a cosmetically adjusted humanoid. I was—I gradually realised—me. My various bits worked. There were parts that were below par; my arms, for example, were weak, as I was to discover when by exponential stages P.E. teachers required them to be more powerful than was possible on the horse or the wallbars. My legs, on the other hand, were kiltworthily robust, not that I wore a kilt beyond the age of five. I'd seen Alan, my elder brother, in one, and immediately took the view, pace my Highland ancestry and George the Fourth, or because of my Highland ancestry and George the Fourth, that he looked silly beyond belief.

For this reason, I still find Scottish weddings resistible; increasingly even those whose receptions are not in castles or castellated hotels proliferate in clusters of male posteriors aiming at the mass simulation of the tail-ends of peacocks but achieving mainly the effect of turkeys stuffed for Christmas. I exempt from this stricture those faded kilts surmounting knobbly knees which have clearly just walked off the hill.

I did not walk off hills. Fraserburgh had no hills. It had lots and lots of water which as I've already explained I had developed a keen interest in avoiding. Fraserburgh didn't even have trees, if you except those protecting our garden; but I was under instruction not to climb these as they overhung tarmacadam roads and pavements. So my natural habitat was terra firma, and in the case of Buchan, the north-eastern knuckle of which Fraserburgh was the extremity, the terra was of a distinct bareness. I suppose that is why in my thirst for colour and drama I turned to the theatre of natural events: the sparkle of snow and frost, the melodrama of thunder (soon to be echoed by German bombs), the screaming of gales, the crashing of breakers over harbour walls, the glare of summer, and towards nightfall torrid sunsets, which I would later discover to have been choreographed by Walt Disney, or later still, Richard Wagner.

My body did have four outstanding features, but two of them cancelled out the other two. The two giggled at by girls were blue eyes and long eyelashes, the latter, it was said by aunts, "wasted on a boy". This I didn't begin to understand. The other two were freely commented on by sniggering boys: feet which stuck out like stabilisers and jug ears. While my feet were solidly on the ground, my ears gave the impression I was a pair of radio telescope dishes listening to the stars. I was not impressed, but my parents were, by a famous Czechoslovakian footballer who, studying my feet, said I was destined to become a famous Scottish footballer. Never in the history of prophecy was a misreading of the future more pronounced; though as I was only three at the time, the evidence available to him was limited.

This misprognosis was delivered during my year in Prague. Prague? Some mistake surely. That is what my mother and father wondered when in the autumn of 1933 they found themselves plus a toddler stranded for a weekend in Dresden. The cross-channel ferry had been so delayed by fog that all the train connections across Europe were missed, and the substitute arrangements ran out at Dresden. There survives a small black and white snap of a demure two-year-old Scot in the street of a city which was one of the glories of our civilisation. Naturally, therefore, just over a decade later it was to be turned into a charnel house by one nation of the Christian west attacking another nation of the Christian west.

Prague was my first adventure. The Presbyterian Church of Scotland had wide historical links with the Reformed churches of the Continent and maintained a number of English-speaking churches in capital cities. Partly because of my father's language skills, and having studied theology in Marburg, he was sent by the Kirk to minister to such a church in Prague. My older sisters were happily farmed out in Fraserburgh.

My brother was less fortunate. While I cavorted for a year in distant parts, he stayed alone with a solemn and unintentionally repressive lady in a dark house. Alan was already an introverted twelve-year-old. By the next year he was a sad thirteen-year-old. After he died forty five years later, I discovered diaries in a battered tin trunk he had carried round the world. In painfully candid self-examinations conducted throughout his life, this gentlest and most imaginative of men judged that his subsequent depressions and alcoholism had their roots in that year when he felt rejected by his parents and cut off from his sisters. He thus presumed himself less valued than his siblings and particularly less loved than his little brother who had been chosen to go with mum and dad. Poor Alan! In later life, any time I have had any success d'estime, I've been unable to shake off a sense of guilt about my rejected brother.

It was, they said, the happiest year of my parents' lives. They went to the opera and they enjoyed automatic kitchen waste disposal systems half a century in advance of Scotland's. I was, they said, happy too. I had, after all, their exclusive attention. I was looked after, when they were busy, by a young nanny. I confirmed her existence when I grew up by finding another small black and white snap of her wheeling me in a pram in Prague. She was an elegant Russian girl who had fled from St Petersburg after the Revolution; her father, as city architect of St Petersburg, being of the elite. That winter, as I turned into a three-year-old, I was taught the beginnings of English by this Russian beauty. After the Germans took over Prague we never heard of her again. But when I returned to Prague in later life, I scanned Prague's streets, slushy in winter, golden in autumn, looking keenly at every elderly woman.

In the summer of 1934, my father shuddering at the thought of fog in the channel, we flew to Croydon via Rotterdam, an unusual move by a poor, rather shy Scottish minister in the early thirties. But then, in the 1920s, as a poor shy minister in his first parish of Cranshaws, he had driven rapidly over the Border hills on his motorbike with my mother in the the sidecar, once almost killing both of them after an over-enthusiastic approach to a corner. And this painfully shy man who had taken four years to propose to her—"Oh John, just do it!" all my aunts had shouted at him—had spent the 1914-1918 war working his way from Seaforth Highlander private to captain, in the attrition of the trenches. Shy, but determined, was John Kennedy Mackenzie of Gairloch. As a growing boy I was to see in home life his shyness, modesty, tenderness, but hardly ever the inner steel which astonished adversaries. We understand our parents as little as they understand us.

In view of later incidents in the skies, it is worth recording that despite being sick into a paper bag, an incident of which I have a clear mental snapshot, I loved the single-engined Prague aircraft with little portholes. On returning to Fraserburgh as a toddler with several hundred flying miles, I burbled incessantly about the "sky puff-puff". The adults loved it.

I am a vulnerable boy. I don't feel my body is something joining me to people but something dividing me from them. This is not because I am physically gauche. I can be surefooted leaping from rock to rock between the beach and the harbour. I can run and walk as if flying. At the age of four I ride my cousin Jim's tricycle up and down the pavement of Edinburgh's Manor Place. The tricycle is all but airborne as I growl like the aeroplane engine from Prague.

But these are all solo activities. Something inhibits me from social exercise. Exercise needs commitment, the pitting of body against the world, and I am afraid of exposing my commitment in case I am laughed at by my peers, small boys and girls who don't speak my language; though I'm dimly aware that the fracturing of potential bonding is due more obviously to the fact that I don't speak their language. They speak the hard Doric. I speak a soft gentrified English, because my parents are Highland. Worse, I am literally walled off from them because I live behind the walls of a huge garden and inside the walls of an enormous house. Worse even than that, it is a house called a manse, and that really cordons me off because children who live in manses are thought to be holy, which by definition means they are hardly human. Far from giving me a sense of privilege or power, this makes me feel socially excluded, low in communal self-esteem, psychologically abnormal. All that on top of sticking-out feet and ears.

But that is on the outside. Away deep down it's a different story. Not only can I fly on my feet but I can fly in my imagination. The fact that this does not lead me into a divided self is due to my gradual discovery of real power. Power that exists in the objective world. Power that I can relate to. Power that unites my individual soul and body to the world of substance. The vulnerable carapace of my body is harnessed to the magical powers of physical phenomena beyond my dreams: the magic of pedal power, not on the bike only but the pipe organ; engineering power—the steam locomotive; religious power—direct line to the master of the universe; cosmic power—that very universe; and the power of nature, that universe transmitted to my senses. All these are mixed up in one existential thrill. I am, after all, one being, whole and efficient; mind, body and soul fused together. I'm not powerless. It is the opposite: I can do anything. Open, Sesame, I am invited to something remarkable. Amen, extraordinary world, let it be so.

There always was an Edinburgh connection, but shadowy. It lurked on the margins. Despite which, it commanded our lives. Deference isn't the word; my parents, though quiet, were firmly rooted, and never bowed the knee to Baal, let alone to my Auntie Jean and Uncle George, even though they were Edinburgh as to the Manor Place born.

From this distance I can't decide whether in our minds Edinburgh derived its patina of authority from the personal authority of these two of its citizens, or whether it was the capital city which carried the clout in which they basked. Also much discussed between us louche Mackenzie children was whether the steely control my aunt and uncle wielded within the velvet glove of Edinburgh manners came from Jean Cameron, younger sister of my mother, or from George Alexander, highly respected Edinburgh doctor who had played rugger for George Watson's.

Auntie Jean was for long the chief suspect When she was stern, flies would jump to attention and mice scuttle back into their holes—a complete calumny as no such creatures would be tolerated in her house. Uncle George tended to be exonerated from tightness of control because when young he was jolly. As a young country doctor in Duns, he would take my brother Alan from nearby Cranshaws, my father's first parish, on his daily rounds before a carefully planned (everything in the Alexander family was carefully planned) diversion to see the Flying Scotsman crossing the Royal Border Bridge. Alan remembered those days as liberating, speeding round empty Border roads, astounding cows in the fields and fish in the Tweed with comic ballads delivered as raucous uncle and nephew duets.

I'm lying flat on my back looking at a white ceiling with a dim light in its centre. I'm supposed to be asleep but there is no way my command and control system is going to allow me to let go of consciousness. If I go through the door into unconsciousness, can anyone or anything guarantee I will return? I'm not being melodramatic. It's not death as a sinister personalised figure I'm thinking of. I'm simply aware of being absolutely alone in a totally alien environment, with unknown risks on all sides; the least my brain can do to limit the risks is to stay awake.

I'm six years old and spending my first night in Edinburgh Royal Infirmary. It's been months of long nights, misery for me, and, possibly more so, for my mother. Earache has been the problem, night after night of it. I'm not a cry-baby, so my mother knew my shouts of agony were for real. As a highly trained nurse she was not only losing her own sleep, but was utterly frustrated. Dr Slessor was a charismatic holistic practitioner of the old school. His surgery, complete with leather couch, had all the right smells, and his shelves were laden with jars of powders and lotions worthy of a mediaeval alchemist. His science, however, my mother had come to think, might not have kept up with the times. He was confident this was a cold in my ear which would sort itself out. My mother was edgy about hurting his feelings: he was my father's senior elder; displacement of professional credibility would involve loss of face. But increasing alarm gave her the nerve to ask for a second opinion. "Of course, of course," this clone of James Robertson–Justice roared, clapping me on the back. "Should have thought of it myself. I'll arrange it right away."

In a couple of days I was in the Aberdeen Kepplestone Nursing Home. After I'd been given a going over, the consultant spoke in grave tones to my mother. I could see she was not happy. A lot happened fast, though not as fast as the consultant wanted. I had a mastoid behind the ear. Before penicillin, the only treatment was surgery to remove infected bone. It must be done urgently, before poison burst through to infect the brain. He'd like to operate that evening. As a last resort, pressed by my mother, he'd fix it up to be done in the Edinburgh Royal the next evening. Her reasons for preferring Edinburgh were that she had trained in the Royal with a friend who was now the sister in charge of the ear, nose and throat department there; and she could stay with the Alexanders in Manor Place, where I could convalesce afterwards.

All this I am revolving in my mind as I lie sedated after surgery. I am alive, that seems to be the main thing, and there is a teddy bear whose eyes light up beside my bed. But head and shoulders above all the other images crowding in from the previous forty-eight hours, stands one visual experience. Dr Slessor had driven us to Aberdeen in the least debilitated of his fleet of antique automobiles. As my mother settled in the carriage of the Edinburgh express, the good doctor—that is, the good man who happened, more or less, to be a doctor—took me round the curve of the long platform to see the engine. I goggled. I'd never been in the presence of any artifact so massive. It was one of Sir Nigel Gresley's Pacifics, which regularly hauled the Flying Scotsman on to London. It wasn't streamlined, like the record-breaking Mallard, but that only made this all-green beast more masculine, more proud, more godlike, king of the jungle. It hissed quietly, gently pawing the ground.

All the way to Edinburgh I watched the front of the train, visible round curves. That sublime engine made me feel safe, even crossing the Tay and Forth Bridges. We drew into Waverley station as dusk fell, and there was Uncle George, masterfully welcoming. He drove fast to the infirmary, wished me good luck, and drove my mother away. Her white-uniformed friend, the sister, in whose busy hands I now was, settled me in, there was coming and going, a mask covered my face, gas took over, the teddy bear whirled round faster and faster...

Now here I am. I won't go back into that whirling dark cavern. But what is this? It is Aslan, the great green engine. I am safe. I sleep.

The post-operative therapy, digging the pus out from behind my ear, was exquisitely painful. Then they took out my tonsils, because in my first six years I'd caught every infection there was. So Edinburgh, even more than Prague, came to represent breaking through to a southern world beyond the mundane. Pain was exploring.

2
Clank...Puff

In 1939, that silken southern world came to cotton-socked old Fraserburgh. On the outbreak of war, evacuation was à la mode, it being assumed that all cities were vulnerable. We were pincered from two flanks. From Edinburgh came my Alexander cousins Jim, Katherine and Margaret with their nanny, Kathleen. Though I came to know and love them as individuals, as a group they initially smothered us in the smoothness of Edinburgh manners which made us feel like peasants.

From the opposite flank came a blast of the direct opposite: two evacuees from the east end of Glasgow. With the benefit of compassionate hindsight I can see how awful it must have been for them. Brought up in teeming Glasgow tenements they were unceremoniously dumped at the edge of the known world, sans trams, sans streetlights, sans mates, sans family, sans their kind of fish and chips—the Fraserburgh fish, being fresh, lacked "taste"— incarcerated in a house the size of a castle, eating meals round a long table preceded by my father saying grace, and confronted on a bathroom-sharing basis with a family from the west end of Edinburgh. No wonder John, the younger brother, erupted into fisticuffs at the drop of a raised eyebrow, and scored a black eye the first time he was referred to as "that loon", misconstrued by him as "loonie"; and no wonder his shy elder brother Frank was constantly caught stealing desirable possessions from the wealthier Edinburgh family.

I was also rather sorry for myself. I envied my cousin Jim's battery car with long-distance control and his elegant wrist-watch and I was also jealous of the table manners which elicited my parents' approval—to the extent of waking up one morning and throwing my slipper at his sleeping face. I also threw my father's Bible at him, crying, "You love them more than me".

There was no excuse other than overcrowding. But after six months, all the southerners folded their tents and melted away back to their cities.

Pssssss... —CLANK... PUFF...Puff-pf-pf-pf-pf
"Ian, are you being a train?"
The trouble was that I was. Not any old train. I didn't do any old train. I wasn't into trains as an abstract concept. Trains were a startling actuality, the word made fire, smoke, and gleaming rails snaking over a horizon; though in this case, sitting at a front row desk, there was no horizon. The train I was being was a tank engine straining to shunt a heavy load of freight wagons within Fraserburgh station; and any potential horizon was blocked by the stout lady with spectacles and hair in a bun who was my not-to-be-trifled with teacher throughout the year 1940–41 at Ardersier Village School. It hadn't occurred to me that my secret obsession was detectable.

From then on I was more discreet in public. I could usually get away with being not an engine but the interior of a passenger coach. By very gently clicking one's teeth and whispering ums and ahs one could do a creditable impression of the clicking rhythms made by a passenger train over jointed tracks. As in "ta-ta-ta-tum... ta-ta-ta-tum..." I could do whole journeys this way, making allowance for differing rails such as "ta-ta-ta-ta-ta-ta-ta...". The visuals—white smoke down the hill, black smoke up it—had to be silent. On one further occasion a "toot" escaped my lips but I instantly bent my head over my book and though I heard an intake of breath from the teacher, she made nothing of it. Which was just as well; the black leather strap suggestively peeping out of her desk drawer was in her hands by no means a soft option.

That strap is not a whimsical detail, it segues into the main subject: power. In those days democracy had not reared its head in the classroom. The teacher was all powerful, the pupil all powerless, and that equipoise was maintained by martial law represented by the strap. As most teachers were reasonable one tried to forget one's helplessness; and one of my strategies was to be in charge of a bucking steam engine battling up a one in sixty gradient to the summit and rattling down the other side to deliver passengers, of whom I was powerfully in charge, to their destination. The route varied, as did the engine and even the weather. On days of classroom tension I would be a big Stanier Black Five hauling a double headed thirteen-coach express from Inverness up to the 1,500-foot summit of the Drumochter Pass, hoping we could squeeze through to Perth before snowdrifts finally blocked the line. On days of halcyon calm in class, I would be on the swaying footplate of a summer's day excursion from Fraserburgh into Aberdeen. Whatever.

But by now, in Ardersier, I was nine years into my planetary journey. It had been in earlier years and in another place that a core discovery had begun to open up before me: that one could be carried beyond the limits of one's fragile frame by engaging with larger forces.

I rush headlong out the Fraserburgh front door. Walt Whitman cried, "The sea, the sea", but my soul is shouting, "The train, the train". Down the drive between the lawns, unlatch the big iron gate, stop on the pavement, run across the crossroads past the War Memorial, hammer my feet along the Beach Road, run the quarter mile between the two parts of the links. The sea glitters, the beach bay curves to the south, but I'm not interested. Within seconds I'll be on the bridge. I'm racing the Aberdeen passenger train due in at 10.18, a remarkable train because the only one of the day which doesn't stop at Rathen and therefore hits seventy mph on the downhill home stretch past the little halt where Lord Saltoun may demand even the 10.18 to stop, a condition of the Great North of Scotland Railway's access to his land. The train is passing the golf course (I can hear the engine and the carriages clattering now), passing the cemetery (where my father, mother, brother, and sister will one day lie), past the toolworks which the swastikad bombers will one day attack. The engine is shrieking its whistle, it's nearer and nearer, I jump on to the wooden fence at the side of the bridge, the train is slowing but still seems fast, the engine pounds past the signal box, the leather token slams into the metal arm by the track to unlock the section of line it has just vacated, from under the bridge the smoke rises to cover me as I dash to the other side, I smell for a moment the steaming iron, see for a moment the crew on the still rocking footplate and the roaring furnace like the sun come down to earth. The train clitter-clatters across the points, beside the goods yard lines leading to the harbour, the boats back from the North Sea, the circling seagulls. The guard's van at the rear of the train slides into platform 2 of the roofed Victorian terminus, and squeals to a stop opposite the 10.25 train to the fishing villages of Inverallochy, Cairnbulg, and St Combs. At the head of that non-corridor train the small tank engine exhales contentedly before pulling out to puff behind its North American-style cowcatcher which will gather up any stray sheep it hits on the unfenced golf course it will cross between the cemetery and the sand dunes.

I sigh with satisfaction. This is only the beginning. It's Saturday, so I can be here till lunchtime. Or I could dare go somewhere else: the holy of holies, where the Holy Grail is.

The holy of holies is approached by a path between the links above and the station below where there stands another wooden fence. Standing on this, I am backstage among the props, or in the dressing-room as King Lear takes off his make-up. These are retrospectively conceived metaphors, but I don't think it would be too recondite to suggest that the holy of holies I am hugging to myself could be represented as priests preparing for their mysteries. Here behind the veil is the engine shed, the turntable, the all-important water and coal. The engines stay here and every day have to be cleaned, polished, oiled, fired up, turned from dead sculptures into living dragons, kings of the road, masters of time and space. Cape Canaveral, when it comes, will be nothing to this. Then Bob Rae looks up and grins.

"Hello, Ian. Come on down."

My heart stops. The high priest has spoken. His acolyte, I fly down to him.

During these growing years, Bob Rae made my life feel increasingly whole because in himself and his work he united opposites. He was calm yet his work brought me to a fever pitch of excitement. He was down to earth, yet unleashed magic. He was modest, yet controlled the sort of power I yearned for. He was always available, but never possessive.

He offered knowledge of exotic complexity. Over countless hours in his small council house, while his wife plied me with the cholesterol of which we then knew nothing, he instructed me in the minutest theoretical and practical detail about the engineering of the steam locomotive; yet before I developed intellectual indigestion, he took me one day, then another, then another, onto the footplate. First, in the engine-shed, shunting. Finally the whole sixteen miles to Strichen, where I went to school after my year in Ardersier. That half hour of fully fledged swaying on the footplate took me wholly beyond myself. I was in heaven, and I can tell you: angels are men with dirty hands and grimy faces.

Bob Rae was kind. But he was more. He was the only communist on the Town Council. He wanted to improve the world. My father, the minister, the mystic, the speaker of many languages, told me that Bob the atheist was the best Christian in town. Bob had a dream: that his town, society, the world, would work together as harmoniously as all the parts of his engine. Dr Beeching took away his railway. But Bob stayed. In his eighties he was still swimming, probably against the tide. I hope his secular dream will one day come true.

Even if I were to lock you in a dark room to watch reels of grainy black and white archive film I would fail to do what I now want to do; with words it is simply impossible. So why try? Because I was there. I saw it. I am goaded into pummelling words to get you to see what I see. I want to drag you back through seventy years, widen your eyes, and bruise your brains to jolt you into a perception of how it was in Fraserburgh harbour in the 1930s.

Try being there. What about a bird's eye view? Be a screeching, greedy, fat, brutal, baleful, barbaric bird, hovering, howling, soaring, pouncing, scrapping, wheeling, in aeronautical dogfights with a brouhaha of other white-winged, power-diving North Sea seagulls. From whatever angle, what's below you is a sea-city of a thousand spires, a thicket of funnels, a forest of masts, hundreds upon hundreds of low-slung steam drifters jammed together so that in the maze of the several harbours fanning out from the one perilous gap in the harbour wall, no water can be seen. It is a boat-park where boats are meant to scrape each other. Parking, however, implies being static. Here, the energy surge has fish slithering, overalled men bending and heaving, carts and lorries fighting for space, shunting locomotives grinding freight wagons in and out of sidings. Only a remote eagle eye would see the pattern, the rhythm, the industrial logic running through the pandemonium. This is the fishing industry at its zenith and it is awesome.

Even my grandfather, a broad-shouldered professor and Moderator of the Free Kirk in his seventies, on a holiday visit from his widower flat in Edinburgh, would spend hours in the harbour. He didn't bother to conceal his fascination, picking his dignified way through the salt watery chaos and talking to the men at great length. He would have taken off his dog-collar of course: it was a given that ministers and fishermen were as lucky together as *Macbeth* and actors.

The whole seething mass of movement, like a military battle at its height, distributes itself by stages towards the end product: hundreds of fishergirls from the west coast, the islands and round the east coast, gut the fish; men pack it; and long double-headed express freight trains equipped with the LNER's latest container vans speed south, cheered on by one exultant boy vigilant on the wooden fence by the bridge. By the next morning those fish will be on the breakfast tables of the great London hotels, and, the day after, distributed throughout Europe.

That Europe on the altar of whose landlocked bureaucracy Fraserburgh's fishing industry lies is, as I write, near its death throes. Not much may be left other than a palimpsest of memories.

❖

Over sixty years ago, a seagull poised on the spire of Fraserburgh's High Kirk would have on one side looked down on the town square, a plateau raised above the harbour, roads leading off in every direction. The gull, being unversed in ecclesiastical history, wouldn't know it was surmounting the senior of the many Fraserburgh churches, though it might have a sense that it was the largest, and that its position enabled it to dominate the harbour. Even so, the gull's herring eyes would probably miss the movement of a ten-year-old boy skulking down the length of the church, turning towards a basement underneath the east end, opening a door with an iron key, and passing through to be swallowed up by shadows.

I shut the door behind me and pause to adjust to the light. Outside it is a brisk-bright Saturday afternoon. Here all is gloom. Silence rules, except for the moaning of wind in distant eaves. I know that now being down the sloping road under the main building, I have to climb a steep spiral staircase, as my father, despite his heart condition, does every Sunday from the vestry before entering the church, and only then embarking on the steeper ascent of the High Kirk's high pulpit.

I hope nobody saw my furtive approach. Normal healthy boys don't spend spring Saturday afternoons indulging lonely addictions in sepulchres. I need like a hole in the head my strange image as a manse child to be coloured in even more lurid tones. But beyond that, what I am about to experience is nameless, unshareable, soul-shafting. For a couple of hours the earth must leave me alone so that powers from outer space can transport me out of the body. I grope up the stairs, a couple of feet along the mat, take a door handle, hesitate for a second, throw the door open, step across the threshold.

A sledge-hammer hits my heart. My eyes bulge. My ears sing with a silence which is no longer restrictive. I'm inhabiting a space flooded by sunlight pouring in the south windows. I drink in a cocktail of smells. The flowers, arranged only this morning for tomorrow's services, the polished pews, the smoky currents of air from the radiators in the floor already warming the building from furnaces in the basement. Before I play a note on the pipe organ beckoning from the far end, I am on stage. This, though I don't yet know it, is feeding my first intimations that life here on earth has operatic potential.

I walk along one of the two aisles. The church seats twelve hundred, so by the time I reach the choir room within the organ case, the door I entered by seems distant. I grasp a solid iron wheel emerging from the floor. A few hard turns, and a stomach-churning sound begins to perturbate the wood. The organ is stirring into life. This is a formidable instrument, formidably powered. As befits a sea-facing church, the organ is hydraulic, driven by water. H2O which brings in the fish brings on the Bach. I'm at home here. Day by day I'm taking on board the powers of the universe surging through the smoke and fire of railway engines, boat engines, and now this organ engine, to visit me with the rhythm of the spheres. The stars are in their courses, and their physical energy is coursing through me.

I take from my bag a pair of shoes with wooden blocks fitted underneath. These enable my feet to touch the pedals of the organ as they empower me also to activate the pedals of my bike. In the next two hours the organ and I make sounds. The deep burbling pedal notes shoogle the pews. The trumpet and piccolo notes rattle the rafters. I'm learning to blend them like a chef. At a quarter to five I go home for tea.

My father asks, "A good practice?"

Practice? Practice? I hadn't been preparing for a performance; it had been the performance—God and me doing a gig.

Then my father says, casually, "Muir and Jim came to ask if you would go to the beach with them."

" So what did you say?"

"I told them you were in the church playing the organ."

"Oh DAD!!"

3
Ardersier Dream

According to a number of my female Highland relatives, I was born under a curse. It was one of these wise and wonderful women, cousin Katy, who, after eyeing me speculatively, first drew attention to my basic plight. "What wicked fairy," she asked, "made you be born and brought up in the east?" Her mien left no doubt that in her opinion dark forces had been at work, but a glint in the eye seemed to suggest I was open to the suspicion of having in some way connived at this malediction.

Even Highlanders less enmeshed in the unseen world expressed unease. On occasional visits, or in flights of fancy fed by vivid imaginations as they brooded in distant glens, they would be incredulous. No mountains? No lochs? No glens? No Gaelic? No Gulf Stream? Just flat brown fields, freezing winds, and rough people who call a spade a spade? Poor Ian! It has to be explained that in their mouths the word "poor" acquired connotations not so much of pity as of doom. It should also perhaps be added that to a Highlander of that era, a spade was never a spade. It might be a blessed manifestation of divine grace, or a beautiful implement. Then again, if you had just tripped over it and twisted your ankle, it would be a device of the devil.

I suppose I exaggerate, but as I do not myself speak the Gaelic I had to go by impressions, and plain speaking never struck me as top of the Highlander's agenda. In truth their innate kindliness gave them a horror of hurting your feelings. Aberdeenshire folk sometimes interpreted this to mean that a Celt would manufacture any lie to please you, whereas the Highlander tended to suspect an Aberdeenshire man as willing to utter any honest opinion, no matter how much it would wound you. I know there is some truth in all this, because my Highland parents and my siblings had been wonderfully happy in gentle Stornoway, where my father ministered before he was called to preach in Fraserburgh, where my mother was called to give birth to me. Just as they never became completely acclimatised to the bitter North Sea weather, they had difficulty adjusting to the relish with which Christian Aberdonians freely spoke home truths in love. On top of these contrasts in style, Buchan people thought of west coast people as lazy, while Highlanders saw the Doric-speaking Brocher (a citizen of Fraserburgh) as preoccupied with work and money. At which point the old story of Martha and Mary occurs. When in later life I returned to live and work in Peterhead I found these stereotypes to be seriously flawed, but as a child, they affected me. Increasingly absorbed into my imaginative hinterland was the myth that the Highlands and islands constituted a forgotten past, a lost inheritance; and for a while at least, that myth had the power to outshine reality. Any visit to the west, therefore was, even on a bus, more exciting than any other available experience.

My first trip west was to be by bus, but it was a bus journey with a difference. First of all, it was to be a journey of almost a hundred miles. That was relatively rare in the Scotland of those days, where rail travel was the norm except for local journeys. And those colourful buses were run by a local business. The service to Inverness was on a higher plane. It was provided by no less a status of bus than one of the Bluebirds which radiated from Falkirk, a far off southern metropolis of which I knew little. The Bluebirds' deep blue lent them dignity, while the matching uniforms of the conductors and conductresses suggested a sophistication appropriate to a voyage of romance. When I learned years later of the way America's Greyhound buses ran through whole states like butter, it began to dawn on me that a sense of distance and discovery is all in the mind. Going seriously west at last, I was now in my mind reaching out to a world of untold vastness. Nor was I to be disappointed.

We foregather at the bus-stop at 8:20 am. Two of us are

travelling: myself and my sister Etta. I've noted her already as swinging a mean hockey stick and in the war as a decoder of Enigma. As the sister nearest my age, when it was announced that Bounce, our collie, had found me under a bush, she had taken command immediately and from then until now had regarded herself as my executive parent, the honorary mother who had birthed me being allocated a walk-on part now and then, and my father allowed to be an elderly friend.

Because she never lost this motherly concern, we were always close, but for that very reason less matey than I was with my even older sister Catherine who bonded with me through a shared disability: a failure to control giggles. If one of us started, the other couldn't stop. However it is Etta, the sturdy sixteen-year-old who now stands beside me, a praetorian guard ready to do battle with all that the omnibus world can throw at us. She has done this run before, being a favourite guest at my Auntie Etta's, after whom she is aptly named; aptly, because she has inherited not the name only, but the nature. What I don't know is that this short holiday is a try-out for a dastardly scheme to evacuate me by myself to Auntie Etta's in time for the autumn term. Blissfully ignorant of this treachery—it has never entered my head that my saintly parents are capable of such wiles—I step onto the bus with a singing heart. This is a road movie and I am in it.

Given such nomadic buoyancy, I'm prepared to overlook the utilitarian character of the bus handed down today for the first leg of the journey to Macduff; it has the air of having carried supplies in the Boer War. It's grey rather than blue, the interior is minimalist, lacking even luggage racks, and on encountering the mildest adverse gradient, the engine whines; skirting Mormond Hill it develops asthma. After Strichen we strike—well, crawl—inland up onto the dreich moorland before reaching cliffs where gravity takes over and propels the bus, with coughing fits, steeply down into Macduff, about thirty miles from home, though a seagull navigating the rocky coast would knock ten miles off.

It doesn't feel like a different country yet. The bus station is on the harbour which also serves Banff, the Georgian country town separated only by the river Deveron. Sea and fish smells accompany us into the waiting room where we avoid drizzle. But the arrival of the posh Bluebird marks the beginning of serious travel. For one thing the destination board carries the name Inverness, for me the gateway to the promised land. Then the seats are sinkintoable. There is a diamond shaped clock which is working. And when we draw speedily away, the engine carries an iron fist in its velvet sound. Am I betraying my beloved trains? Only a little. I'm allowed a little fun, aren't I?

We scoot along the coast, scurrying in and out of fishing villages. From the curving cliff escarpments above them I can look down the chimneys of the painted houses. And driving down Cullen's raked main street, an Aberdeen–Inverness coast train trundles over the viaduct straddling the shops. Bit of a thrill, this, not least because the teak carriages (same colour as ours at home, but more handsome) are drawn by a bigger locomotive than Bob Rae can boast. This one, with six large driving wheels, not four, was designed for East Anglia's Great Eastern lines, but, with others of its class, has been sent to the north-east of Scotland to haul heavy trains, up gradients of one in sixty (you see, I do know my stuff). And the sun is coming out. I will remember that, because it synchronises with an effusion of magic. Everything is about to turn upside down. Not so much a new country as a new world.

I notice it after Buckie, the last fishing port we dive off the A96 to visit. Buckie is no picturesque village, it's a serious town like so many seatowns from Berwick to Lerwick, grey business-like commercial buildings punctuated by severe Presbyterian spires. Its no-nonsense plainness serves to dramatise the epiphany waiting round the corner.

I'm looking casually seawards, because I'm on that side of the bus and there is the sea—technically the Moray Firth, but not a Firth as in Solway, Clyde or Forth: this is a wetness stretching to the horizon. Except. What in the wide world is that? I nudge Etta. "Look!" I command. "At what?" Her calmness baffles me. On the far horizon, out of nowhere, an entire continent has arisen like Atlantis, and she asks at what! I've done geography, I've seen maps, I know that between Fraserburgh and the North Pole there's not a lot other than sea and ice. Orkney has to fit in somewhere, but it has no mountains. And that's what I'm looking at, from left to right on the far-off horizon, a panorama of floating blue mountains. To Etta the matter is rudimentary. "Sutherland hills", she announces. Oh, how worldly-wise she is, but her flat statement makes no contact with my excitement. Wherever Sutherland is, if it's got anything to do with this mirage shimmering at the edge of the world, then I must get there some day.

As we travel west, fast now on the main road, between the small and stately towns—Elgin, Fochabers, Forres and finally Nairn, those ephemeral mountains float above the horizon, gradually changing their shapes and their relationships to each other like a mobile hung from heaven caught in air currents. I can't take my eyes off them for long: only to observe how the town architecture we're passing through is changing from challenging grey to soft sandstone and from useful buildings to elegant ones. The voices coming on to the bus are softer, too. And through the open windows are coming new smells, not of salt, sea, seaweed, upturned brown earth, manure, sharp tangs on a snell wind, but warm perfumed air from trees, flowers, rivers and something indefinable. Could it be the hills beginning to rise in front of us, forest-clad, mellowing in patterns of green and gold, a deepening palette of nature bathing my eyes in a soothing mixture of sensations? Of course I'm not thinking in such language, I am adrift in a land-ocean of beauty for which I'm in no way prepared. There's a straightforward word for it: spellbound.

Auntie Etta, my mother's middle sister, drives us from Nairn by the back road to her house a mile up from Ardersier. We lunch, I guess, but I'm hardly noticing; I'm as high as a cat on cat-nip. I can't believe any of this, the balm, the lushness, the sense of fairy-land. I roam the garden. It is on the wild side, with grass, trees, bushes, undergrowth, and in the back a yard for timber, a small car, and a large Red Cross ambulance in which my aunt drives ill or injured soldiers from nearby Fort George to hospitals in the south. The house is called "The Cottage" which to me is a joke. It isn't austerely huge like the Fraserburgh manse, but its two storeys plus basement make up a long and graceful building in light stone. As well as back doors it has two front doors, leading to elegant rooms transparent with light from casement windows. There are multiple stairs, quaint hidey-holes, cosy snuggeries, and everywhere eccentric objects, many from China where Uncle Freddy served as a medical officer. And, nearly everywhere, the heads and horns of beasts he shot on several continents.

In the meantime, overhead, like the summer buzzing of bees, aeroplanes are circling, Beaufighter fighters stalking Lysander daddy-longlegs aircraft which languorously pull white targets. This RAF training activity is unceasing in daylight through the week, and as it is based on Dalcross aerodrome a few miles along the bay of the Beauly Firth, I have a grandstand view of the airshow. My cup is now near running over, trembling at the brim, when from a window I catch my first glimpse of the Fort George Flyer (I forget its actual nickname).

The Fort is a couple of miles from Ardersier, on the point of the peninsula which faces the Black Isle across the entrance to the Beauly Firth, but the station in the middle of Ardersier is called Fort George as most of its passengers come from the garrison, where Uncle Freddy earns his penny as medical officer. I watch this Titfield Thunderbolt chug sedately across the bridge over the road along the embankment to reach Gollanfield Junction on the main line after which it will return. My cup of satisfaction spills over when from the higher bedroom window I see the connecting main line train, the size of a caterpillar, its red-liveried LMS carriages crawling to a standstill at the junction.

I have two more discoveries to make on this epoch-making day. The first is that I have a Highland relative whose every day is not edged in black. She has painful arthritis, but you'd never know; she treats me as if I'm a fully paid up member of the human race; and she doesn't just snigger a lot, she has a dirty chuckle. Etta and I stand in the basement kitchen as she makes a supper of poached eggs and proper coffee. The two pans heat together on the first electric oven I can remember seeing. "You know," she tells Etta, "they say that if you drop an egg in the coffee pan it does wonders for the taste." Saying which and not looking what she's doing, she plops the three eggs for poaching into the coffee. Etta is aghast, but that's an inappropriate reaction, for Auntie Etta is giggling. We have eggy coffee. Within forty-eight hours I've learned to relax among a new species of adult. Spill jam, soup, gravy, at meal times (which are formal in the dining room) and Uncle Freddy laughs louder than Auntie Etta. Break a plate and joy is unconfined.

When I go to bed, the bubble of happiness is collapsing. A quietness descends. I stand at the back window and look north-west. I'm homesick. I'd like to share the day's magic with mum and dad. Do I sense that they are for ever shut out of this, their kind of world? Do I intuit that I shall soon spend a year here? I feel drawn out of the fairyland bubble, out into a realm whose manifest beauty doesn't exclude darkness. Across the firth, the Black Isle grows shadowy. To the west, though I can't see Inverness tucked into its corner at the head of the firth, I can see the smoke rising from its chimneys drifting up towards the sunset; and beyond that the sentry-like mountains I shall get to know as the Affric Hills. I tuck myself up and take comfort from the snorting of a late train working hard on the climb over Culloden Moor. Its passengers are heading south, and to an even wider world beyond that, a world I dimly know from adult conversation is disintegrating into horror.

Sure enough, as the Battle of Britain summer turned the corner into autumn, I found myself making the bus journey back to Ardersier, but this time with a knot in my stomach, for my father was accompanying me. That could mean only one thing, that he regarded this occasion as seriously as I did; I was leaving home for the first time, at a moment when a German invasion was expected. Throughout the coming months I would have to stand on my own sticking-out feet, without parents as emotional stabilisers, but also without my other props, the trains, Bob Rae, the boys I went about with at school, not great friends, but the devils I knew. And without the pipe organ to make solitary love to. In compensation, I had a new bicycle, solemnly purchased by my father and myself. The palaver of getting it delivered by freight train to Ardersier had already been seen to. It was to be my closest friend. Dad understood that. Before he left to return home to a children-free house—Alan, Catherine and Etta now all away at the war—he showed me how attaching an empty cigarette packet to vibrate against the spokes of the back wheel would make the sound of a motor. "I know you'd rather be a train," he said, "but in wartime we all have to make do." I made do, all right. It was a year in which I learned to be resourceful. With the cigarette packet I was a Bluebird bus. With no cigarette packet I was a Highland train supplying my own noises. And going very fast down a steep hill with two cigarette packets, I was a Spitfire winning the Battle of Britain. If the folks at home had known what I eventually got up to, no hands, on the bike, they would have rushed across to take me back to the relative safety of the Luftwaffe.

This is the dream that actually happens. Now it's a dream. Then, I actually lived it.

Monday to Friday, after porridge and an egg, I walk the mile and a half down to Ardersier Village School, passed by the Nairn bus which I disdain. I like walking, I'm good at it. But I also like the cows in the field I talk to, and the plethora of diverse grasses and wild flowers which I address, though on windy days when they nod and bob I let them do the talking. The wind is seldom cold but it can blow off the firth with prejudice, and when the 4,000-foot plateau of Ben Wyvis is white, a north-westerly carries a sting.

The school has no sting. Mr Macdonald, the headmaster, is a brisk scholarly man who wouldn't hurt a fly, as he beetles about with a display of purpose which fools nobody. And my class teacher, the very one who caught me being a train, is anyone's granny; it's only the big boys she attacks with the strap. I walk home for a snack lunch of soup or meat, but take the bus back, to catch the bell. And when afternoon school ends, I walk back again up to the delicately crumbling house standing out against the sky flaunting its high trees.

It may not sound a dramatic dream, but all the time my eyes, nose, and ears are absorbing drama: the wide stage of mountain and sea presenting phenomena ranging from the technical marvels of planes charging round the sky to the minutiae of plant and insect life unknown in rockbound Fraserburgh. Army lorries, even tanks, roar along roads and in the distance, trains hoot and whistle as they carry their human cargoes along the horizon.

After a tea of scones and marrow jam made by my aunt for the war effort, my bike takes me flying around lanes and roads. Supper is called dinner, my hosts being regimentally trained. Uncle Freddy usually presides, back from a day at the Fort, or back out of bed after another of his turns; his heart is so dicky that I keep looking at his chest as if expecting it to jump out like a clock cuckoo. He is a doll in nearly every sense, small, polished, trim, impeccably turned out, with a bristling moustache and a voice which has found no way of expressing itself other than the bark. The final *coup de theatre* is, I kid you not, a monocle. Meet son of Colonel Blimp.

Where on earth did my mother's sister, brought up in a Free Church manse, first in Brodick, then in Edinburgh, bump into, let alone pick up, least of all actually marry, this animated piece of military porcelain? Like my sister Etta, she excused herself from school, but, there being no WAAF in 1914, she went hotfoot to France to drive an ambulance. There she met Freddy Graham–Bissel, a dashing army doctor. They flirted theatrically, I've no doubt, and that was it. The only snag: he'd no money, other than his pay. He hadn't expected money from his father who was poor landed gentry and was pushed to put him through Harrow, where a certain Winston Churchill was his fag ("A bounder," said Freddy, "but right for Hitler"). He had, however, expected to inherit a packet from a batty great-aunt. Unfortunately she was so batty she kept posting cheques into the wireless for Henry Hall who was a famous bandleader of the time, and failed to arrange anything for her great-nephew. No matter, he and his Etta whirled around regimental balls. The thirty-year age difference between them might not have mattered then, but now it shows. She is his carer. Within a year his bark will no longer be heard in the land.

After dinner, Auntie Etta and I stroll up the back lane in the gloaming with Bruce and Sammy. Sammy is a white Persian cat with a crosspatch face; Bruce the most melancholy of spaniels, a venerable old and smelly gentleman whose ears trail the ground in despair. Not the cheeriest of company, and I'm beginning to notice how arthritis is bending my aunt's spine and stiffening her knees.

But she bounces into every weekend deploying her scalpel brain to entertain me. Saturday is always a trip. At the very least we embark on the train for a day in Inverness. The morning begins with coffee and cream cakes in the enormous Station Hotel lounge (later imitated in the Titanic), with Highlanders and islanders in tweeds and tartan skirts in deep armchairs from within which they greet islanders and Highlanders yawning their way off early trains from the north and the west. On everyone's tongue is the Gaelic or lilting English punctured by the braying of Sassenachs in yet more tweeds and tartan skirts. This entertainment can only be capped by a shopping expedition sweeping lunch in on the way before we settle in the picture-house's perfumed grandeur to watch a movie; after which we stagger home in a rather riotous state for an aunt and nephew who haven't touched a drop.

Or she may take me on the Red Cross ambulance for a jaunt to Perth or Forres, picnics on the way, including three flasks for coffee, tea, and tomato soup shared with the horizontal soldier or airman installed in the back to provide authenticity. Then my favourite supper, macaroni cheese.

But now the summit of the week: Sunday. Sunday has highlights: bacon and egg breakfast; the walk to and from church; a Sunday lunch to kill for; and my 3.15pm date at Gollanfield. The bacon and egg goes with fried bread and strong coffee. The church service at noon goes with the Rev Willie Graham, padre at the Fort and before long to be my Uncle Willie. (His wife and Uncle Freddy will die congruently, creating a mutually convenient and brilliantly amusing vacancy.) The Sunday roast goes with roast potatoes so perfect I will look for their equal until I die—meltingly soft inside, coruscatingly crunchy outside. As for Gollanfield at 3.15... Words cannot convey this; however, one can but try.

Some background material is required if you are to touch the hem of the garment of this experience. On Sundays at 3pm, a gigantic train of up to sixteen coaches heaves out of Inverness station. It is packed with servicemen and women of every arm of the crown from anywhere north and west up to Scapa Flow— virtually the whole of the Highlands is a reserved military zone. But instead of turning sharply south to surmount Culloden and the Slochd summit, as weekday London sleepers do, this monster, gathering speed on the flat, begins charging eastwards, its two engines stunning the air with funnel blasts of escalating fury. It will stop at Nairn and Forres, then turn south for the long climb over Dava moor before descending to Aviemore where it will join the more direct Slochd route.

At about quarter of an hour out of Inverness, this Boadicea of a train will hit Gollanfield junction, thundering under the road bridge where I, God willing, will be. No, whether God wills or not, I shall be. But I have to earn it. At 3pm, turbocharged with roast potatoes, I ease onto my bicycle saddle and ride off. It's a race, and a serious one, for I shall have to pedal with commitment to cover the two-plus miles and get into a viewing position in time. Even in howling wind and rain I don't ever miss it. I'm there, leaning over the wall, my heart beating like a swain on a first date. All is silence. It is, after all, the Sabbath. The people on farms and in scattered domains have been churched and lunched into comas. No wind today. The air doesn't move. Suspense rules. As before a storm, birds go quiet, wary, tense. The grass stops growing. The silent crowd of nature waits.

WHOA! There is never a warning, because it roars round the corner from behind a high bank. At this distance I look into the eyes of the two Stanier black fives, among the most beautiful locos ever made. Not only are they spitting with rage but they're careering headlong towards me. The way their boilers taper down to the funnel, they seem to have their heads down for the charge. It only takes a few seconds. Pistons pounding, smoke, steam and fire exploding, they're under, the bridge shaking, and the swaying tails of coaches whooshing and clattering beneath me as I run to the other side. Suddenly, it's over. I watch the rear coach diminishing down the straight towards the curve a mile away. I would reach for a cigarette if I smoked. I pedal thoughtfully home.

During the evening I periodically opt out of whatever I'm doing to mentally plot where are those thousand people whom I had barely discerned within their blacked-out windows. Depending on where German bombs are landing in England tonight to cause railway disruption, those officers and other ranks might still only be passing the smoking furnaces of Midlands steel mills long after dawn, arriving in London after twenty-four hours in the compartments that had cascaded under my feet. Or maybe everything is going smoothly. If so, that would be a bonus, but not a paradigm of their future. For they are on their way to theatres of war, in the air, on land, or at sea. Some will never return. My learning curve is steep enough for me to know that my magic train is taking men and women to the gates of hell.

I cannot dig geologically through the many emotional layers of those months to identify any one condition of mind. To change the metaphor, there was, there had to be, a ground-bass of feeling lost. Losing bits of me was beginning to be a pattern. After my few days with Etta and Auntie Etta in early summer, I'd spent some weeks with Auntie Jean, Uncle George, and my cousins in a summer holiday house in Biggar. My Aunt Jean, the youngest but most earnest of the three sisters, had shown that she understood I was acquiring the properties of a redirected parcel; she would see me to bed at Biggar and talk to me in a kind way about my family. But beyond my increasing mobility I was becoming aware of family life receding to the margins. As an afterthought baby (brought on by the shock of the east coast climate, my mother would say) I was almost a lone child, but had basked throughout childhood in the rackety boisterousness of the older children. Now they'd gone, as had the Glasgow evacuees and the Edinburgh cousins.

The manse was to fill up again soon, indeed to overflowing, which may be why I was taken home earlier than I expected; though also it may have weighed heavily with my father that on one of his visits to Ardersier I had spoken of homesickness. I don't think I whined. He knew that I loved my aunt and was much amused by her; and I would have spoken about how much I enjoyed cycle runs in this friendly countryside. He, born near Gairloch, had gone to school in Inverness Academy, so he would perhaps assume that I carried in my bones a sense of this land as home. But after we'd gone to the Inverness cinema to see the documentary film *Target for Tonight*, and before he caught the bus back to Fraserburgh, I said, "I'd like to come home." "So you will," he said, and a month later I was. He must have known he wasn't well. He wanted me back. That was all I needed to know.

4
Nights Under the Stairs

My leaving Ardersier was the end of childhood. And the end of that dream in which I had been floating somewhere above events in the world and in the family. Despite periodic gulps of homesickness, it had been tranquil and I had been free of stress. Now the idyll was over, the struggles of Fraserburgh life and adolescence began to pile on top of each other and I was going to have to handle them. The town wasn't the one I left, nor was the manse, nor was the school. Nor, for that matter, was the war the one I'd left. Hitler had missed his window of opportunity to invade Britain in the summer of 1940. Apart from fronts opening up in North Africa, the Mediterranean, Russia, what was developing was a grim process of attrition in the air and in the North Atlantic; a sort of equivalent of the locking of horns in the trench warfare of twenty-five years earlier, but this was nearer home.

So whereas I'd been sent west to be less vulnerable to invasion and to escape school disruption due to troops being billeted in school premises, the threats I now returned to were more immediate. Enemy planes had begun hit and run raids on Fraserburgh, flying in low over the sea under the radar, dropping bombs, sometimes machine-gunning, and getting away back to Norway before the Bofors anti-aircraft guns near the beach could target them. Which also meant that the air-raid sirens were often too late.

At night the tactics were different; the bombing was high level, and the sirens gave the town time to prepare; my mother to the first aid post, where she was not only second in command, but as the senior fully trained nurse, actually running it. Somehow characteristically of my parents, when the Duke of Kent, not long before his fatal plane crash in Caithness, came to inspect the first aid post—actually a highly effective field hospital—it was the county lady nominally in charge who received the honour. My father, once I was dragged out of bed and put on my mattress under the stairs, was usually on a fire warden rota, if there were other adults in the manse.

This was a wearisome way to live. It didn't compare in horror to the murderous blitzes on London and other cities but something like two years were spent with days and nights interrupted on what seemed to be a regular but random basis. After the war it was said that outside London Fraserburgh was the most attacked town in the UK per head of population. The main target was "the toolie", a pneumatic tool factory, which, we were told (we were told many things by the various people billeted in the manse), was making one tiny but vital component for Rolls-Royce aircraft engines. I certainly saw one German air photo of the town with the toolworks ringed in white. It was a good clear photo. Our manse, just up the road, stood out nicely. We weren't ringed but that wasn't inordinately comforting as the hit and run bombers seemed better at running than hitting; and after a night raid, it could be any house which revealed a gaping hole the next morning; a boy who had sat next to me at the infant school met a nasty end in one of these holes. I stood looking at the space and absorbed the fact that the next whistling bomb might do that for me.

These events were so dramatic as to create a sense of threat powerful enough in my theatre of memory to provide to this day regular material for unhappy dreams. One Saturday forenoon, going to the shops, I was machine gunned from behind by a Heinkel which had flown in over the bay at house height and without warning found me, a little running creature, in its sights. I dived into a close, saving my life by seconds.

In contrast, one night, Fraserburgh's biggest store went on fire. It was a night to remember; the light in the sky was said to have been visible in Stonehaven. That can't have been true, but it was indeed a notable combustion. Soon half of the town, some wheeling prams, gathered in the town square to enjoy the blaze. It just so happened that this was the first night of the Clydebank blitz. Earlier, we'd been on alert as the German squadrons droned over on their way from Norway to the Clyde. The police, realising these angels of death had to return, eventually managed to persuade most of the crowd to go home. But the pub next to my father's church was still packed when a bomb from a returning Dornier, drawn by the conflagration and seizing the chance to dispose of unused ordnance, scored a direct hit on the pub, killing over thirty and wounding scores. That summer, as a variation on the theme, came a noise like an earthquake. An unexploded landmine had to be exploded near the manse. That was the evening the kirk session was meeting at home and, in response to the bang shaking the house, went on their knees under the dining-room table as my mother was bringing in tea and sandwiches. I don't recall what happened to the sandwiches but some knees sustained collateral damage; as Presbyterians, the elders were unfamiliar with the process of bending the knee.

So once again my parents decided to pack me off; but this time only to school. From Monday to Friday I would take the 9.10 Aberdeen train as far as Strichen, a big village with a secondary school serving a wide agricultural area. My father knew the dominie (headmaster), a mild man with a classics background, and arranged that I would be permitted to arrive three-quarters of an hour late, a concession that did me no favours with Baldie Watt, the far from mild science and R.E. teacher. I would lunch in solitary state in the Station Hotel, to which I would also repair to do homework after school, before catching the 5.30 train home.

The hotel arrangement was temporary; after two weeks I was taken into the embrace of two redoubtable ladies, Mrs Adams and Miss Adams. Their house faced the school playground, a piece of geography which had given them the entrepreneurial urge to cram as much food as they could into as many children as they could fit round a table the size of a mill-wheel. They must have built the table in the room or built the house round the table. The banqueting circle, mostly from outlying farms, included all ages and shapes, turnip-bright farm loons (lads), apple-cheeked quines (girls), a handicapped boy with family in the Far East, and a senior girl of whom we were in some awe, unnecessarily; she was just a clever farm girl.

It is only now, as I write, that I realise this little group was my first community outside the family. Released from my manse branding, here I was one of them; a country boy with a stomach. We ate, chattered and laughed with gusto, and grew together into our teens. Despite strict supervision of our table manners the two women were kind. On a few occasions, like the school concert and village ceilidh, I stayed overnight and was treated as family. Straightforward goodness is what they exuded and an unspoiled human environment to nurse us along. On that basis, I opened up naturally to the whole school community in which the farming stock mixed with people in trade to create a culture of hard work. The "scholars", as we were all known, were expected to apply the same diligence to learning as the grown-ups did to crops, livestock, and business. This was the famous "Scottish education" which no longer exists.

The best, indeed outstanding, thing about Strichen Secondary was its English teacher. Mr Shanks stood tall. A craggy face, torso like a Scots pine, legs like two Nelson columns and to crown the edifice in the open air a soft hat set at an angle. Inside the classroom he towered over us in every sense. The gravelly voice gave everything he said an edge, so his discipline was effortless. He radiated force without intimidation. He was the Scottish dominie incarnate, inculcating standards of clarity, logic, sharp analysis, and systematic hard work, while investing every task with calm bonhomie. This was local education straight from the Enlightenment, and that isn't a conceit.

Thirty years later, retired on Islay, he wrote to me after hearing me on the radio. In meticulous longhand he brought me up to date on some ex-pupils. I replied to thank him and paid tribute to his teaching, specially its quality of logic. That set him off! He was thrilled that the logic had shone through, for at Glasgow University he'd majored in logic and metaphysics; logic at the philsophical level was the love of his life. In fact, he went on writing about it—to me. I now bitterly regret that my replies, both in number and length, were hopelessly inadequate, BBC work taking up all my hours by then. Even more, I regret that when I was free to visit him on Islay, it was too late; he'd died. Alistair

Shanks, just a village schoolmaster, was the only person, apart from my father, who actually taught me how to learn. I still treasure and use the collected works of Shakespeare he gave me the day I walked away from Strichen for the last time.

We are a queue. But not an ordinary queue. What we are is a quaking queue. As in a queue that quakes. As in a quaking that is queue-like. As in a crocodile of boys and girls descending the stairs in knee-knocking formation; and at a speed so spectacularly slow as to be almost going back up the stairs, which is exactly what our sense of self-preservation is pleading with us to do. We are with caterpilliary velocity approaching the science laboratory; we are Mr Watt's next class. And like all science lessons, it is to be a double period.

Mr Watt is a multi-gifted schoolmaster who happens to have an ungovernable temper: that's the long and short of it. Yet there is so much more to it than that. His gifts are so outstanding and his rages so dangerous that no simple prosecution or defence will meet the case. It is said that he has twice been in court for assault; but we know no details. He does however, confirm to us, in one of his confiding moments, that he has been "betrayed" by Judas Iscariots who claim to be Christians, so he is aware of flaws with consequences.

His gifts? He is as infinitely patient in expounding the science as he can be volcanically impatient with the dullness of our brains. He imparts the glory of a sprouting bean in a jar with an eloquence to match his astonishment at the wonder of the galaxies. His teaching of R.E. is of a depth few clergy match; he stands there, old family Bible in hand, venturing into soliloquies of an almost Shakespearean pungency, ventilating wounds in his soul which we are too young to understand, let alone heal. The Shakespearean reference is not misplaced; he is the unchallenged star of the local drama society. I never see him do it, but I gather he gives cathartic performances, and I can well imagine his frustrations being partly unleashed, though bridled by his intellectual respect for structure and perspective in the objective world which he tries to convey to us.

Yet the flaws are serious. When he rages, he completely loses the plot. He can howl, scream, roar. With impeccable aim from across the room he can hit me on the head with a wooden blackboard duster, and it is nothing to have one's head cuffed in his passing. His strap is an evil-looking reptile and the scowl with which he administers it robs the victim of any hope of mercy. Worst of all is his sarcasm. The voice which can thunder can also whisper in tones of velvet. His tongue then lashes with a personalised wit carrying a payload of venom. I cannot say he is mad, because some lessons pass in serenity as he talks to us about his life and what he hopes for our lives. I cannot say he is bad because at the end of term he throws each of us a generous carefully parcelled gift. What he actually is is a lonely farmer's son, living, I believe, somewhere in the bleak country outside Strichen.

Every now and then, after school, he passes on his bike. I always greet him and he always returns the greeting with a wave and a gentle smile. If I have any limited understanding of cruelty; if I am prepared to credit tyranny, torture, violence, brutality, sadness, madness, badness, as ingredients in that mixture we call human; if I feel compelled to call Pilate, Stalin, Hitler, Pol Pot, Saddam Hussein, my brothers, it is because I lived through four years of dread in the power of Mr Watt. He was a Christian gentleman, albeit with problems. I never had even to think of forgiving him, for I never began to think of him as other than intrinsically good.

That's my elevated emotional or spiritual position. But in terms of justice, as a civilised society attempts to arrest the pull of the negative demiurge back into the jungle, I finally have to say: no human being should have this power over any other human being. That battle has a long way to be fought before it is won.

Through the gauze of time, events and places defocus to the point where one's perceptions of them create their own stereotypes. If I don't think hard, then my Ardersier year, which was mainly spent in winter, presents itself to me as a perpetual summer, bathed in impressionist light, with sensuous Delius conducted by Beecham on the soundtrack. Whereas Fraserburgh is in straight lines of black and white, structured like Dutch kitchen tiles, resounding to bold Berlioz lines of brass.

My life in the Broch from 1941 to 1945 was, despite all the wartime intrusions, a structured existence, and even the intrusions seem to resolve into black and white. For my first two weeks at Strichen school I was, like McCavity, not there. The great 1941 Spring snowstorm had blocked the railway line. A company of Norwegian soldiers, stationed, like apparently half of the world's armies in or around Fraserburgh, set to with a will and a shovel. Even they, who, unlike the British, regard snow and ice as a pattern, not a freak of nature, were impressed by the height of the drifts in railway cuttings. After two weeks they reached Strichen. Thereafter I joined them, settling into my new school routines while the Norwegians continued to dig on to Maud junction. My first visual impression of the Buchan landscape after Ardersier was indeed white with black lines of rail, fences, telephones wires.

The seascape too. Black rocks and white spray. Swooping in from the sea black German bombers, white swastikas.

And lines of war. Black-out. Nights under the stairs. If I don't include rationing, that is because my mother was a brilliant improviser in the kitchen, and fish, game and eggs were left at our back door by well-wishers. But we were a town turned into a barracks. Not a splendiferously stylised Georgian garrison like Fort George, but a sprawling town stiffened by lines of smartly defined uniforms marching everywhere, so that sometimes we civilians looked like guests in our own streets.

And in our own homes. The manse having sixteen rooms, we were one of the first ports of call for officers, chaplains, ladies and assorted intellectuals. We became a sort of college; at times it was quite jolly. The intellectuals came first. These were not the boys in blue fighting the Battle of Britain over the south coast, but the men in brown fighting the battle of the beach on our northern coast.

This was the Pioneer Corps. It brought together mature males unfit for combat because their wits were too dim or their bodies too feeble. It was the second category that fell into our clutches. Their job was to build pill-boxes and concrete blocks all along our beaches, for a purpose never disclosed but presumed to be an extra five minutes delay in any German invasion across the North Sea. Our intellectuals would return home, after a day toiling in the wind and rain on the shore, fit for nothing but hot baths and dry clothes. We became a communal launderette and bath house for a sizeable group who coalesced round the couple of professors for whom we were actually responsible. After tea and food, this flock of brains would resume its alternative role of common room analysis of the war.

By the time I returned from my Ardersier year the Pioneer Corps had vanished... I was about to write without trace but that would be to underestimate the effect of the concrete sculpture in which the beach was now swathed. In place of the Pioneers' agreeable congruity of minds the manse was populated with a medley of military and civilian prowess. The military strand consisted at first of a well-known minister of a distinguished ecclesiastical pile whose name the horses of the Apocalypse wouldn't drag out of me. He was probably not the outstanding chaplain of his era.

His distinguished ex-cathedra place—yes, he was a High Church wallah—was taken by his constitutional opposite. Whereas he-who-shall-not-be-named had been a tall willowy monument to ascetic living and much prayer, the Reverend Vipont, an RAF chaplain, was short and tubular. He did, however, have a pointed wit which he much enjoyed deploying in teasing my sister Etta into a rage when she was home on leave. I now think he fancied her, but then I thought he was just a tease. In either case he spoiled the effect by riding on a motor-bike encased in a helmet worthy of Wotan. Alongside Mr Vipont were Edna and Dick, two high-powered civilians. Their role in overcoming Hitler was "hush-hush". They were distinctly London, Edna only a couple of tones short of brassy, which is a Scottish way of saying she was ebullient; the tall bearded Dick twinkling through donnish spectacles. My parents liked them and they corresponded long after they had gone.

To complete the ranks of the civilians we featured a weekend speciality: the missionaries. They weren't actually all missionaries, they just seemed to be.

During my childhood there was a tendency, if one answered the front door bell on a Saturday afternoon, to find on the doorstep a man in a loose suit with a tight smile. When I was older I recognised the smile as that evangelical variety which forgives one for existing, but in those days I didn't even know that a poor suit meant that this was no Mormon; it was, of course, the weekend missionary. They always seemed gloomy, an indication, perhaps, that paddling up the Zambesi wasn't always a bed of roses; but did they have to patronise so? One gave me as a farewell present a rather expensive book, the life of Birdie Bowers. "You're too young to understand it now," he forgivingly smiled, "but later in life you may." I read it through that night and thought I understood it very well. The best missionary was a Salvation Army captain with a totally unforgiving squint which fascinated me. At breakfast, offering him the *Press and Journal*, I asked, "Would you like a squint at the paper?"

The manse contained so many architectural interstices that assorted members of the armed forces could nestle within them for weeks, popping up every now and then without much impact. Bert, an RAF flight sergeant, was not one of those. His was an impact of continuous sight and sound, especially sound. He was large of girth, charismatic of manner, handsome of face, Yorkshire of origin, and overwhelming of voice. To say that he was of the singing tendency is putting it mildly. Song burst from him like a canary mutated from a bull. Actually, it was a beautiful voice, and my father soon pressed him into solo work in worship. In our domestic circle he didn't have to be pressed. It was understood all round that in the pause between high tea and supper, if Winston Churchill was not speaking on the wireless, what would be more natural than that I should be wheeled onto the drawing room piano stool and Bert would clasp his hands to starboard.

We would be thrilled to bits by the subsequent vibrations.

Floorboards would shudder, gaslight chandeliers tinkle, and Roy, our new collie, moan with what we took to be satisfaction, as the great voice soared over the war in *The Holy City*, *The Lost Chord*, *Land of Hope and Glory*, the twenty-third psalm, and *Bless this House*. It was difficult to resist tears during this last, as Bert sang it *sotto voce*, as a benediction. Those were days in which one felt blessed just to be alive, free, and together. In no ordinary way we shared a sense of need for a hand to rest on our uncertain lives.

5
Icon

A beautiful Saturday in late May was ending. The manse was happy. By chance, both Catherine and Etta were home, Catherine from saving the lives of wounded servicemen at the Astley Ainslie hospital in Edinburgh, Etta from the bunker in Bletchley where she was saving the lives of seamen in the waters of North Atlantic convoys by wrestling with the Enigma code. There was much merriment. Despite the telegram telling us that Alan had been wounded leading a platoon of East Africans across a Burma river, we assumed the war was all but over—as the European war almost was.

At last, I went to bed. My father, as always, came upstairs to kneel by my bed and pray. But whereas the normal sequence of events was that he would tell me to share anything that was worrying me with God (God was that real to him) and leave the room, on this occasion he walked to the window and looked at the setting sun irradiating the sky. There was in the silence an atmosphere. It was his sunset call.

Around midnight, commotion. Running feet, crying, shouting. Dressing gown on, I ran downstairs to monitor events. Catherine in her nightie fleeing out the back door, jumping on mum's ancient bike, careering out the back gate, nightie billowing behind. We had no phone. Ten minutes later, two bikes hurtling in the back gate, first Catherine's nightie, then old Dr Slessor, stately in pyjamas, crowned with smoking cap, old leather case on handlebars. There was nothing to be done. It was over. We talked for hours, laughing hysterically at the pyjamad procession through the town.

Later, as I lay in bed numbed by the incomprehension of the

calamity of death, something happened which was so startling and so intimate that I doubt if I have ever fully understood it until now as for the first time in my life I'm looking at it fully fair and square and putting it down on paper. Reactivating the moment unlocks certain perceptions which belong to the story I'm telling.

My mother slipped into my room and hurled herself at me. The embrace was more than a loving gesture, more than a bear hug. Her heart was breaking and she enveloped me in its shrapnel. It lasted a long time. She released me, looked into my eyes in a way I couldn't begin to fathom, hissed, "It's up to you now", and ran from the room. Nothing like that had ever happened between us or happened again. In the remaining forty years before she died in her nineties we evolved a close friendship in many ways, but that moment when she gave herself to me and took what she could from me might have happened in a previous life or another dimension; as in a way it did.

My parents were warm and loving, but not tactilely demonstrative. She was a tall, elegant woman, had been a beauty when young, as one can see in photographs. No wonder my father had trembled for four tongue-tied years before proposing to her. But both of them had Highland dignity and reticence, treating emotion as too precious a coinage to throw around.

After that night she withdrew into herself. She walked through her remaining years incognito. She constructed a new persona, strong, witty, lively, unsentimental. Only once did the mask slip. In her late eighties, in hospital for the umpteenth time with a broken hip she wondered if life was worth the effort of yet another course of physiotherapy. For the first time since he died, John had spoken to her and cheered her up. When, later on, George MacLeod told me of a similar manifestation of his dead Lorna, I recognised the healing power of such experiences, however you explain them.

The perception unlocked by reliving my experience is that what must have propelled her towards me at her moment of supreme crisis was a recognition that the nearest she could get to her partner was now the person he had invested most in, namely me. And that explains a lot.

A psychologist might say I had, still have, an immature relationship with my father, almost an arrested development towards him. Psychologists say that kind of thing. And why shouldn't they? Theologians say all manner of things which throw a professional shroud over normal life. Anyway it's obviously true, though I doubt if the word immature suggests a particularly mature way of looking at it. In no way can I have a rounded, still less objective, picture of my father as a human being. If he'd lived another few years, I would have begun to view him more dispassionately, even critically. Now there you go. I found myself shrinking from the very notion of criticising him. So yes, I idealise him. He's an icon. But he is an icon that lived and moved and filled my being.

I can, however, perhaps catch some unexpected views of him, as in a mirror angled towards others. My elder brother Alan told me that he once gave his dad an essay he'd written at Edinburgh University. He was quite proud of it, and was crushed when eventually the father he respected and loved handed it back without comment. When Alan told me this awful story I was plunged into an almost catatonic conflict. I knew that Alan never lied. But it could not be true. The father I knew was incapable of behaving in that way. The father I knew. So that was not the father Alan knew. Alan also told me once that he thought our father (John) treated our mother (Murilla) with a certain detachment which detracted from her warmth. This didn't bother me, because it wasn't a factual conflict of evidence, but a matter of judgment which could rest on misunderstanding, or be skewed by a sense of distance Alan himself felt.

It is true that my father put my mother on a pedestal. Possibly till the end he couldn't believe his luck. There are other explanations. He was a mystic. Everyone (older than I) who heard him preach said so. For much of the time he was elsewhere; most people, listening to thunder, do not say, as I once heard him say, "I love listening to God's artillery". But this did not remove him from practicalities, as when in the 1930s he organised work and food for the unemployed in Fraserburgh, and during the 1939-45 war he set up an ecumenical canteen for the forces which was open seven days a week.

But, to dig deeper into matters of the psyche, it may be that his emotions ran so deep that he put a lock and key on them. Three clues suggest this. First, I suspect I have to some extent inherited this dilemma. I don't resort to lock and key; I run in and out, lurching, as you will see in this book, from emotional indulgence to defensive flippancy. The second clue is a telling fact my mother told me in old age. John's father (also a minister) had a terrible temper. His son, my father, inherited it. Once when young my father lost his temper. He was so appalled by his own rage that he resolved never again in his life to lose his self-control. In all the thirteen years I was with him I never once saw him angry or even raise his voice. Third clue: his mother died early. His father remarried a wealthy woman. They had children. That whole second family, including my grandfather, cut off all contact with us. The hurt this caused was never mentioned but my mother said it never healed.

I think that's enough exhumation of the man I loved. He was, apparently, human after all. And he had a dark streak, no doubt. He'd survived the trenches in France, but never spoke of it. And he was a Highlander. If you take the road from Gairloch in Wester Ross, where he was born and grew up, and travel down the long shore of Loch Maree to Achnasheen, where my mother was born, you see the light and shadow in constant play. Loch Maree is the most magical loch in all the Highlands. But there towers over its eastern shore the giant wall of the mountain Slioch. At certain times of day and in certain conditions of weather, that implacable slab of rock casts shadows on the water and these shadows will envelop any man or woman travelling south into time and history.

It was now Sunday. More cycling to convey the news. The gathering congregation was sent back home, bewildered, lost. "Like sheep without a shepherd," said Hector, session clerk. Curtains were drawn all over a shadowy manse. On Monday, aunts and uncles arrived. Friends in and out. Letters started pouring in, black-edged envelopes and paper. Boxes of them, extravagant in praise of their dead minister. My mother read a few, then said coldly, "It would have been more useful if they'd said those things when he was alive." She left most unread, and retreated to a dark place in her mind. I caught her constantly gazing into space.

It was a great funeral. The tributes amazed me. I didn't recognise this man. He had just been my friend.

I am not sympathetic to criticisms of parish ministers (as distinct from mobiley upward political ministers), because I know how hard their job is, and because so many of them have been friends to me. Norman Robinson was a true friend. He'd come from Orkney a few years before to be minister of the Fraserburgh South Church. I knew he was a friend because of three indicators: he was small but had a large and hilarious Irish wife; he made droll jokes and looked ironic even when being serious; and, above all, the pair of them, who lived along the lane, were the only people who could make my serious parents laugh helplessly late into the night when they slipped in the back door for an evening of playing rummy.

They made no drama out of my father's death. But they suggested that I might stay with them for a couple of weeks while my mother and aunts set about the heroic task of cleaning and closing down the manse and my father's enormous library.

There was, however, one drama which for a couple of days eclipsed my upheavals. At breakfast the maid brought in Dr Robinson's newspaper—his doctorate prefigured the eventual professorship of divinity at St. Andrews. The maid was agitated. She burbled about a bomb that could destroy everything on earth. Dr Norman assured her that this could not be so. She pointed to the headline: Hiroshima.

After breakfast I shot down to the town parliament, which met on an ad hoc basis in the barber's shop. My hair didn't need cutting, but I needed the widest available exchange of intelligence. The debate was confused. Repairing back to base, I interrogated my *in loco parentis*. Norman Robinson sucked his pipe. He understood that I seriously wanted to know how a loving God could make universal destruction possible. His answer, more or less, was this: he'd been wrong, at breakfast, to say that we couldn't destroy human civilisation. Clearly now we could. And because God gives us free will, He couldn't stop the Hiroshima bomb being dropped. But God also had free will, and given all the contingent possibilities of human history, God, in co-operation with free human beings, might arrange matters so the world did not end prematurely. It was an important moment for me. In the throes of my personal disaster, the possibility of human rationality and love surviving in some sort of process of hope, so calmly expressed on that first day of nuclear judgment, steadied my wallowing mind.

I am sitting on the front doorstep waiting for the car that will take me, my mother, Roy the collie, and some luggage to the station to catch the train which will take me away from here. I am old now—fourteen in a month.

I am sitting on the stone step which is my stone step. Right above is my room, the room above the front door which has always been mine.

I sit on the step and press my bottom against the stone. It presses back. I didn't know that stone could press back.

I'm sitting on the step. It presses back. It's my stone. My front door. My house. I was born in this house. The step is mine, the door mine, the garden mine, the trees mine. That bit of sky is mine. The sound of the breakers on the beach is mine. My bottom hugs the stone.

I cannot get round this pain. I have a pain of loss which is so sore that I don't know where to put it.

The car is here. This is it.

I stand up.

The only person seeing us off at the station is Mr Rothney, the saddler, the elder who is driving the car. My mother hands over the big front door manse key and tells him to go. We get into the train.

I am not off to Strichen School and coming back home tonight. There is no more home tonight. There is no home.

We're off to Edinburgh, into rented accommodation.

I have Roy on the lead.

My mother has me.

She also has an envelope with £30 in it. This is a gift from the Woman's Guild; quite a lot of money in those days, but one envelope doesn't seem much to take away from all those years. She laughs without humour and reminds me of the Christmas she had to step in at an hour's notice and be Herod in the nativity play, because the woman playing Herod had a mood.

At 12.35, the guard waves his flag, blows his whistle. This really is it.

Pssss…Puff—pf–pf–pf–pf. Clank.

I am no longer being a train. I've no idea what I'm being.

6
Stupid or Lazy

I haven't had the experience of entering Alcatraz. But on a September afternoon in 1945, bereft of father and home, I entered Fettes. There were, I suppose, differences. Even when Alcatraz was a working prison inmates did not approach it in an uncle's car driving up a broad avenue from Edinburgh's Comely Bank. I was unmanacled and theoretically acting of my own volition when I allowed my legs to carry me through the door beyond which five years were to swallow me up. If you would like to venture on a comparable experience, try taking the old drover road across the mountain pass to Applecross on a day when, halfway up, the mist enveloping you suddenly parts to reveal far below a gaping gash in the mountain ready to devour you if you steer one inch the wrong way.

In case you think I'm painting too rosy a picture here, let me not beat about the bush. The next two years of my life were to contain elements of hell. But I'm going to cheat you of sadistic frisson. My three last years at Fettes were in the main to be heavenly. And even from the beginning there were moments when the clouds lifted to reveal sunlit uplands. Fettes was a roller-coaster. Once that door banged shut behind me I was on a roll.

I can be succinct about the realities. Hitherto an intensely private person, I was in a matter of seconds sucked into a world where I was but one atom of consciousness being smashed against hundreds of other atoms in a boyhood bomb which at any moment threatened to explode me to bits. That was the relaxing part. The uncomfortable elements extended from compulsory communal cold showers at dawn through "school runs" on afternoons when the rain was too heavy for rugby, to lying after lights out in a Florence Nightingale-type dormitory amid surreal communal conversations in a time warp (three weeks) beyond which, if I survived, there would be a Sunday leave allowing me a few hours with my mother.

Those were among the dodgy moments. But I've yet to mention the really bad bit: games. Games? As a misnomer that takes some beating. I liked actual games. Chess, draughts, snakes and ladders, rummy, Monopoly, model trains, table tennis, even tiddly-winks; in all these, if not always a champion, I was up there fighting my corner in the melee.

But second row forward in the scrum? (For the uninitiated this is a technical term for being squashed into a mudbath in a cheek by jowl situation with boys stronger than you.) Lacking elementary skills like catching a slippery ovoid and running with it in the right direction, I was indeed for a couple of years firmly incarcerated in the second head-bashing row of the scrum. This activity wasn't optional. A large segment of Fettes life in those days revolved remorselessly around it. Being a disaster area in this respect was not the most obvious entrée to popular acclaim. In fact, as a physical wimp who regarded competitive sport as the height of corporate insanity, I was a prime candidate for the category of Fettes misfit of the year.

Yet, oddly enough, I failed to carry off that prize. Not only did I fit in surprisingly well; apart from the aforesaid hellish bits, even in my first year I began to enjoy life. Indeed, enjoy it hugely. How could this be? The first answer is people, the second music, the third words, and the fourth excitement.

Taking the last first, Fettes was not dull. In Fraserburgh I'd responded to the drama of the weather, trains, pipe organs and bombs. Fettes, from its exotic chateau superstructure down to its cavernous basements wriggling with cockroaches, was a fairly epic stage on which to audition for one's life. It wasn't a choice. You just had to step on stage and do your damnedest. The Fettes stage was a whirligig of people, music and words, more colourful than a play, faster than opera, tantamount, as one experienced it, to a gigantic musical going at an inexorable place from morning till night, sweeping cast and audience—I was both—from one situation to another with never a break except an occasional Sunday off and the holidays.

The holidays seemed impossibly short, just time to breathe, nod to relatives, have clothes cleaned, then the bell, back on stage, run, jump, sing, hurl repartee around, eat, go to classes, sleep, the horrors of rugger, the pace ever more furious, the whole carousel a blend of dream, nightmare, and joke. It was wild, yet you had to learn the discipline, the basic skill of coping. If you didn't create order out of this chaos you would go under and be trampled on. You had to go with it, love it, hate it, ride it, sing to it, cry and laugh with it, dance to its rhythms, expand the lungs of your courage till they might crack open and spill blood, but no, jump higher, higher, sing louder. This was life. Or if not itself the whole of life, it was an amazingly complete preparation for adult life, that still-to-come voyage in every kind of weather.

I said that, apart from the adrenaline-busting nerve-dance of the basic setting, the essential ingredients in my recipe for survival were music, words and people. It was the music that catapulted me out of the chorus into the role of soloist. The chapel had a swanky organ but not a swanky organist. Tommy Evans, the music director, was not yet demobbed from the Second World War, and the trouser bottoms that had skidded up and down the organ stool had been worn by masters whose grasp of three manuals and pedals was equal to my grasp of rugger ball and cricket bat. But here was I, already a competent organist.

Whee! In the twinkling of an eye I was pushed front of stage, throwing the organ around morning and night while the earth's supreme panjandra—school prefects, with supporting cast of headmaster and masters—had to stand and jump to my cues and four hundred boys, impressed by the decibels at my command, forebore to jeer. What a turn-up for the book. All those lonely hours in Fraserburgh, an outcast from my peers spending solitary Saturdays in my father's church, the oddest of the odd, now transformed into a role not only decibelic but heroic. Out of the blue, raw power. The very stuff of a musical storyline. The pipe organ rules, OK?

But not much of the day was spent at the chapel organ. It gave me an opening, but I had to exploit the opening. So I opened another salient: my mouth. This was an eye-opener. I hadn't until now had the slightest notion of being an effective speaker. I had considered myself among my Buchan peers to be an etioliated murmurer of an effete English surrounded by virtuoso exponents of the true Doric. Now I was one of four hundred young men from all over the world enjoying surfing the expressive possibilities of English vocabulary. Suddenly one could offer an ironic flippancy and people would laugh. And someone in the group would return the serve with a volley. This was social table tennis. What a discovery: I not only had the gift of the gab, now I needn't apologise for it. I was now a fish swimming in a warm sea of wit. It was like coming home to a foreign land where I should have been born.

Which brings us to the people.

Nothing I can write could convey the full flavour of the adults I found myself surrounded with. Fettes has recently published my slim volume of cameos of some of them. The devil, or in this case, the delight, is in the detail. I won't reprise all that here, except for one brief snapshot of a remarkable reforming headmaster, himself a comic creation.

There were a very few dull masters. "Consty" (constipated), a slow-moving monolith, and "Fudge", a wooden-headed maths teacher, were, despite their competence, two of the few crippled by a failure to entertain us. Happily, our rampant craving to be entertained was satisfied by a wholehearted willingness and ability on the part of most of the staff to keep us agog in the wake of their manifold and majestic eccentricities.

Some of them surrounded their capacity to amuse with an aurora of inspiration, notably my first form-master Daniel Vawdrey, a Gandalf-like figure who ran his class like a cosmic circus, conjuring intellectual order out of apparent chaos. Some were deeply cultured men, one of whom, the music master Tommy Evans, led the four of us in the musical sixth into endless musical adventures.

And there were two actual geniuses. George Booth, the histrionic English master, infected the whole school with words, ideas, theatre, and God. He refused to mark my essays. "Never trample on flowers," he said. Bill Minay was an organ genius. In a few revelatory years he took me to the summit of organ playing. Without him I wouldn't later have found my musical home in St Giles.

In the blizzard of inter-personal and institutional communication that Fettes turned out to be, and in the context of a burning light of culture, in art, music, literature, and theatre, it became natural for me to figure out that all that was missing was a subversive magazine edited by me. I called it *The Wart* and it built up a circulation of two hundred. When a senior housemaster threatened to resign unless the headmaster banned it, Donald Crichton-Miller, himself an individualist, defended me and the mag.

Before sharing a pivotal encounter with Donald Crichton-Millar, it may be historically appropriate to place it on record that to me Fettes had nothing to do with elitism. The fact that I was there and that I became happy there owed nothing to money, social class, or influence. My mother and I were penniless and homeless. I passed a scholarship exam on the strength of what I learned in Scottish village schools. Because of my straitened circumstances the Fettes governers upgraded my scholarship to cover all fees including full board. Like many such schools founded to support children in need of educational support, Fettes was a charitable foundation. Many of the friends I made there were in one form or another similarly in need of help. Fraserburgh, Ardersier, and Strichen schools on the one hand, and Fettes on the other, were equally the educational rocks on which I built my life. Questions about education should not be overly embroiled in political ideology. It's still a good idea not to mend what works.

"Sir, I want to go into the church."

I was bearding the headmaster in his lair. I had had a religious experience during the Edinburgh Festival, meeting God on Blackford Hill after a performance of Verdi's *Requiem* by the La Scala Milan orchestra and choir. Now I wanted the school's top person to know about this other top person. And practically, should it affect my immediate career choices?

Donald Crichton-Miller, sitting vastly behind his desk, contemplated me. He had a predatory air as if considering me for lunch, but baked or sautéed?

"The church?" he said softly to himself, and continued to rake me with silent appraisal.

"Mmm. Pipe. Out. Tobacco." It was a transparent playing for time, but it served to get him out of the room. I pondered the mystery of power. The headmaster was a human being. He'd been spawned by other human beings. He would get old and ill and he would die. How could someone who from time to time had a twinkle in both eyes elicit such a sense of awe? When he re-entered I was reminded. Not a twinkle in sight. Sternness was all. The pipe, relit, was now adding philosophic tone to the act.

He thrust his chin forward.

"So you're not content to believe," he grated nastily. "You want to be paid for believing. There are two reasons why anyone becomes a clergyman: stupidity or laziness. Which is it with you?" I was floored. I'd come for reassurance. I'd come as high as one could in a school hierarchy. If one couldn't expect seriousness, let alone civility, from the top, where was one to look?

He was by no means finished with me.

"Highland, aren't you?"

"Yes, both parents Wester Ross."

"Apart from your father, any other minister relatives?"

"Several."

"I presume you've considered that your 'call' may be programmed by your history."

Actually, odd though it seems now, I hadn't.

"So it would be the Kirk. The highest you could go would be Moderator. For a year. Allowed to dress up like Dick Turpin for twelve months."

His manner was elusive. Was I being played with? The eyes were steely. "When you began here, you had one distinction: you had the flattest feet of any boy in the school. I remember writing that in your first school report. It was the only thing I could think of. Of course, I was new then too. Since then you've done rather well. I gather, for example, you're rather good at amusing notices." (As deputy head of house, I was allowed to pin up official notices and I reckoned it was my duty to make them funny.)

This threw me. My housemaster must have told him. It never occurs to boys who gossip about masters that masters gossip about boys.

"Therefore," D.C.-M. said, becoming weary, "you might be good at children's addresses."

He rallied, rose suddenly to his feet, and barked,

"Go. Go away. Go away and think. Not feel. Think. T. H. I. N. K. That's what you're here for. That's what I'm here for. D'you think I run this school by feeling things?"

With as much confused dignity as I could muster, I withdrew.

He was right. I hadn't thought. But after this, the most searching interview of my career, I did think—for six years. For that I'm grateful.

7

Pipe Tunes

Losing my home five years before, Fettes had become my home. I now needed to discover a new family and at first Edinburgh seemed unlikely to deliver it. My sense of deprivation was natural. As well as the substitute home I'd lost, I was registering specific blows. Nearly all my close friends had gone south, either into National Service, or to university. And of those, nearly all had gone to Oxford or Cambridge and had become members of college communities, the very experience I had craved as the natural extension to school community life. Even those being hurtled headlong into National Service would be discovering a new experience of human sharing (I had failed the National Service medical because of my ear problem).

It was simple: I felt lonely. The confusion that was to characterise the decade I was entering into subdivided into two areas. I was to be searching for relationships with individuals or groups which would compensate me for being uprooted from family, and that would only be resolved when at the age of thirty-two I found a partner with whom to build a future.

The other area of confusion was intellectual. I really didn't have the faintest idea of what I wanted to do with my life; or rather, I had too many ideas, and like a centipede playing Hamlet, couldn't choose between them. The fact that I was now to study music wasn't due to my having chosen a music career. It was due to my having failed to choose. It was due to having failed to win a scholarship to Oxbridge, but having succeeded in winning a scholarship to the music faculty in Edinburgh. And by an appropriate irony, it was the verdict of my school tutors that this denouement was due to my own dithering: I had tried for several English and music scholarships in both the ancient universities, the resultant division of effort yielding neither.

The sharpest academic comments had come from Christchurch, Oxford, and King's, Cambridge. J.I.M. Stewart at Christchurch (Michael Innes was his novelist pseudonym) wrote to Fettes to say that in his opinion I was the best candidate, but the external examiner thought I was the worst. Faced with such a deadlock, all the college could offer was a place without a scholarship. The only consolation he could hold out was that mine was too individual a style to survive reading English in as stuffy an English school as the one in Oxford. He added that he was sorry I had also not succeeded in becoming the next Christchurch organ scholar but though he was not a music expert, he thought it possible that I might benefit from making good my escape from that fate as well. I read all that man's books and found them as amusing as their author.

From the opposite side of the universe came a letter acidly penned by a Cambridge don I had crossed pens with at King's. Despite having recoiled from my prose, his languor at the interview was impeccable, extending to extending himself horizontally on a divan, in the course of probing my career motivation. "Of course, you will want to write," he essayed with a flourish of the hand, "they all do. Every one of your competitors is going to be a great novelist, dramatist, poet, critic, or writer for the radio." The curl of the lip on "radio" was too convoluted to describe.

"So what," he swivelled his swan-like neck to enquire, "is your ambition?" I'll never know why, but what I said was, "to write pamphlets." He sat up slowly to digest both me and my answer. Not much speech followed. His subsequent letter to the school lacked even a whiff of cordiality. "In view of Mr Mackenzie's lack of literary taste, his talents may lie more in the field of music; perhaps not, however, in Cambridge."

I now have to say that my plight turned out to be not so bad after all. Living in Edinburgh admittedly did not in itself set the pulse racing; I knew it too well. Having been looking at its skyline through school windows for five years, getting out there had all the thrill of lifting a stone at the bottom of the garden and joining the insects underneath. After a few weeks one acquired an insect's perspective. In close-up, it transpired, there were more interesting things going on than I had given Scotland's shortbread capital credit for.

As the Fraserburgh seagulls saw the eleven-year-old boy steal into his father's kirk to play Bach solitaire on the organ, I now look down the decades at the twenty-year-old boy stealing in through the north door of St Giles. I see that the hinge of these years was indeed music, and the gold out of which that hinge was fashioned was the organ. If I was made by nature for anything, it was to be an organist. If there is anywhere I'd like to be at this moment, it is sitting on an organ stool co-operating with the physical universe to make well-judged sounds. Thanks first to the Fettes chapel, and then to St Giles I attained in those years many moments of happiness. A Christchurch organ scholarship? Goodbye! Its organ was horrible. No, really; its tracker action was so rough, it was best played by the elbows.

During my first year at university, I didn't have an organ job. My time was divided between helping out at St John's Episcopal Church at the west end (now conspicuous for the social conscience of its crypt) and St Cuthbert's presbyterian mausoleum, right next door, where my organ guru Bill Minay reigned. Bill didn't only reign at St Cuthbert's, he reigned over me, so I faced a thoroughly unpalatable moral crisis when my professor of music hatched the idea with Herrick Bunney, the dynamic new master of music at St Giles Cathedral, that I should move up to St Giles and have a proper job as his assistant. I don't know which of these two men initiated the move, but it was presented to me as a *fait accompli*; not in the sense of *force majeure*, but as a self-evidently benign arrangement which would benefit everybody and enhance my career.

I wrestled with it. I needed to wrestle because there was a sting in the tail: it was built into the package that I would switch my organ tuition from Minay to Bunney. Sidney Newman, the professor, and Herrick seemed unaware that they were tempting me into an act of betrayal. Neither knew how much Bill Minay meant to me; but I knew. And yet in the end, I bowed to the inevitable. The professor was, after all, the boss, responsible for my practical as well as academic progress.

When Bill Minay, Herrick Bunney, and Sidney Newman all said my going to St Giles was the right thing, they were, as it turned out, right. In the matter of St Giles I'd put in my thumb and pulled out a plum. The levels of luck I found myself vibrating on radiated outwards from one thing: I fell in love with St Giles. I adored the building, instantly, wholly. And I adored the organ. You can't separate them. An organ without a building to resonate in is metal, wood, wiring and cables. A building without soundwaves massaging it into life is asleep.

There's an even bigger mystery, though. Even the building plus the organ isn't the glory; it is the conduit to the glory. The true glory is that other thing which becomes transparent. The human artifact is the way through, the access to the glory, or if you're tired of the word glory, what a literary essayist in my youth called the overplus. What you call it doesn't matter, but it is the extra, the alternative universe, the beyond bending backward to penetrate your heart. It is what religious people limit by calling God.

In those days I could not walk into St Giles without all that happening. Many of this generation will, I'm sure, find their own spiritual Odyssey in the gleaming liturgical spaceship that has superseded that old tall ship of the soul with its fading colours, tattered flags, and ageing Willis organ.

Herrick Bunney was elusive. You thought you'd grasped him, and then, without any discernible movement, there he was, over there on the opposite side of the room, smiling enigmatically. This seemed so ingrained a feature of his magical character that it was shocking when in the last two years of his life we met to eat and converse on a number of occasions and he whipped off his mask.

By "mask" I don't imply anything false. The way he had dealt with his deepest feelings, indeed, I suspect, his torrential, perhaps torrid feelings, was to discipline his interface with the world so as to ease the way for others as well as for himself. In our last conversation before he died he spoke even more nakedly than before. "Ian," he said, gaunt eyes harpooning me from a suffering distance, "I have not been a good man."

That one statement would be enough to suggest the reverse. But over a lifetime of vaulting achievement, and specially over the decade we worked almost daily together, I seldom found the coinage of his friendship to falter; he was kind to me beyond the call of duty, indeed beyond the requirements of friendship.

As a musician he was not in the top rank; or so he periodically informed me. I put this ritual confession down to insecurity, an inferiority complex, or the fact that professionally he was marooned on a presbyterian peninsula rather than swimming in the sea of English cathedral music. I sensed him retreat psychically when he didn't make the final leap from the short list for Westminster Abbey to its master of music.

As regards his self-assessment I was in two minds. Although as his pupil I faithfully tried to do what he asked, namely to develop a flowing legato style, I did it without conviction. In the case of Bach, Bill Minay had exposed the innards of contrapuntal phrasing on the basis of Albert Schweitzer's forensic analysis. Herrick, by comparison, did not aim to build up the edifice of a fugue by exposing the inner parts; he aimed for the broad architectural design as a whole tonal experience. In Minay's Bach, the inside, as with the Lloyd's building, was on the outside. In Bunney's Bach, as with a classical frontage, the engineering, though all there, was concealed.

I have no wish to be technical so let me visualise it in terms of two pairs of hands. Herrick's hands were graceful, almost feminine in their plasticity, as they floated effortlessly over the keys. Bill Minay's hands were on first observation like ancient crustaceans, his gnarled knuckles knotted as an athlete's legs. When he played, the effect was of a mobile holograph. Each finger operated independently of every other finger as if every finger was operating under the instructions of its own particular brain. No wonder all the independent parts sprang into life.

That, however, is not the whole story. When Herrick played nineteenth century and twentieth century French and English music, his sense of theatre rose like Neptune from the deep. He had musical courage. He didn't flinch from seizing the organ with both arms and chucking it round St Giles till the organ burst into flames of sounds and the foundations seemed to heave. That was the force which empowered him in his early days to galvanise the sturdy Edinburgh Royal Choral Union into performances of oratorios and motivated him to detonate many national occasions in St Giles into Handelian or Wagnerian grandeur. Even a modest procession of Edinburgh toon cooncillors became royal barges lit up by fireworks; and aged knights of the thistle, dragging their feet up the aisle like crippled grasshoppers became gods tottering towards their twilight while Herrick set the organ on fire with fanfares from Valhalla.

Above all, Herrick's evangelical soul sensed the surge of a liturgy. More than any organist I've known, he knew how to turn a congregational hymn into a symphonic event, grasping the import of word and tune, harnessing the tonal capacity of the organ, and matching it to the eccentric resonances of the St Giles acoustic so as to rocket a bourgeois Sunday morning congregation into orbit.

The gods were kind, to allow me to savour the complementary musical visions of a Minay and a Bunney, the outside and the inside of the musical cosmos. To cap it, Herrick, exhausted by a hyperactive schedule, contracted jaundice and was made to rest for several months. In his absence I was in charge of the organ, and choir, and to tell the truth, was not so sorry about his jaundice as I was happy to be throwing the organ around à la Herrick and winkling out the inner parts à la Minay. All of which was so diverting that I had to keep reminding myself I was actually supposed to be studying how to analyse music to destruction at the university faculty of music.

Before turning to that mordant scene, I'll recount two incidents which illustrate a trait in Herrick Bunney (as well as a string of people who were to influence my life): a preparedness to take risks. After her coronation in Westminster Abbey, the young Queen came north to be Scotticised in St Giles. We Scots, being a pernickety lot, still grumble about the ridiculous advice she was given to wear a skirt and carry a handbag—when she now regularly appears at St Giles to initiate a new Knight of the Thistle, she, Philip and the knights are all swathed in gorgeous gowns. However, then she was young and beautiful, and everything else was glorious, every feudal honour, garment and colour from all the airts crammed into St Giles.

Herrick's preparation was relentless, every fanfare oiled for blast off, every voluntary timed to the second, and Richard Dimbleby ensconced in a lofty nook to ennoble the occasion with gravitas. There was, however, a little ripple on the surface of my equanimity. At the climax of the service, following on the Queen taking the Honours of Scotland into her hands, Herrick had decided to throw me over the parapet. I was to improvise a very loud noise to take the Queen from that point down the nave and out of the west door. I had been dumbfounded when he told me of my assignment; but not so dumbfounded that I didn't immediately suggest that I would improvise on the prairie song *She'll be coming round the mountain when she comes*. Herrick, never highly coloured, went paler than usual. "If you do, sonny boy, it won't just be you that's unemployed, or me, it will be the Dean of the Thistle."

A week later I went to the old News Cinema in Princes Street and saw the hour-long film of the event. At the end, as I listened to my organ thrashings from the comfort of a cinema seat, I thought, hey, that's not bad. But I can't prove it. That was before videotapes and compact discs.

What was bad, though—oh, God, it was bad—was the most terrifying musical experience of my life. I sometimes deputised for the accompanist to the Royal Choral Union. In the summer in question, this (in girth) redoubtable choir was featured in the Edinburgh Festival programme, singing *L'Enfant du Christ* by Berlioz, and Delius's *Appalachia*. On the eve of the last pre-orchestra rehearsal, the accompanist went ill, and Herrick asked me to step in. I reminded Herrick that I didn't know the music and the rehearsal was the next day. Herrick had a way of dismissing such problems airily. "Don't worry old boy. I'll play most of the time, I might just ask you to fill in for a few bars while I go to the back of the hall to listen to the balance."

Yes? Oh well, all right. But not really. I don't do all right when I'm sight-reading Delius in front of two hundred witnesses, under the baton of Sir Thomas Beecham. See that last name spelt in tracer bullets and lit up like Las Vegas? I had the sinking feeling that I was going to go public as a busted flush. The conductors I have worshipped in my life included John Barbirolli, Adrian Boult, Georg Solti, Paul Kletzki, and Tommy Beecham, but Beecham was paramount. The others were magical but he was the Great Wizard. Whatever he touched alchemised.

Moreover, I adored his wit, his sarcasm, his evilness. But what if I were to be the butt of the razor tongue? I managed the Berlioz, fairly simple stuff. Then Beecham swept us into *Appalachia* and Herrick disappeared to the back of the hall and stayed there. The score was splashy; so I splashed. I was back to having my head thrust under the North Sea by our charismatic Fraserburgh doctor. Where the hell was Herrick? I didn't even attempt the notes. I had a vague idea of how it might sound, so I did a sort of pub impression of how it might have first emerged at the back of the composer's mind one drunk night before he got round to composing it.

After fifteen minutes of splashing, Beecham put down his baton. "Mr Mackenzie," he purred, his face registering the mild surprise of David Attenborough on finding a sick catfish defecating on the top of Mount Aarafat. "Have you ever seen this music before?"

The floor declining to sink below me, I swallowed and said, "Well, actually, no, not."

Herrick was already running down the hall. Leaping onto the platform he gallantly yelped, "Our usual pianist was taken ill."

Beecham pondered this, then silkily asked, "Well, Doctor Bunney, could you possibly be so good as to make yourself available at the pianoforte?" It was no comfort to me that at the final afternoon Usher Hall rehearsal when the orchestra joined in,

Beecham exercised his tongue on the chorus. Disappointed by the lacklustre tone of the sopranos on high notes, he addressed them solicitously, "Poor dears, you sound like a Scotch mist. What did you have for lunch, ladies? Haggis?"

At their next annual general meeting, members of the Royal Choral Union defended their honour. They passed a motion that Sir Thomas Beecham never again be invited to conduct them. Thus was born the Edinburgh Festival Chorus. And I thought life in Edinburgh might be dull?

I would like to be able to say I loved every moment of my time in the faculty of music, But I have a problem: I didn't. After three years I failed my MusB degree and then I failed the resit. But from a position of Olympian detachment I'm delighted to award students and staff of that faculty full marks—for trying. In my case they were on a hiding to nothing. An excess of academic treatment of music bored me. Every afternoon at 2pm when Dr Hans Gal walked in, clasped his hands, and embarked on a sixty-minute musical history lecture, I felt the skin round my cranium tighten like an elastic band about to snap.

Or when Dr Mary Grierson gathered a group of us around in the small music room in George Square, to guide us though the intricacies of sonata form in the string quintets we were supposed to be "composing"—oh, the spontaneity!—why did I not jump on the grand piano, dance a rumba and rattle my castanets? Only because I had no castanets and couldn't dance. And when Dr John Fairbairn sucked his pipe supervising our attempts to transcribe an orchestral score on to a piano keyboard, why did I feel a compulsion to crawl away through the city sewers to St Giles, let myself into the organ loft with my key, and let rip?

It wasn't their fault. Jock Fairbairn was a practical musical journeyman. Mary Grierson was a distinguished pianist. Hans Gal was an eminent Viennese musicologist and respected composer. It was I who was the dud. Nor was my dullness due to my fellow students. They were warmly sociable people of all ages. The fact that most of them were bent on securing qualifications which would buttress careers as music teachers was no reflection on their talents. Some became performers, conductors, composers; one a concert pianist, another a fine singer who became head of music at Winchester. But, unlike me, they were prepared to undertake any amount of academic drudgery that would ensure them a secure career. To me, music was only a part of life.

You could say I was a careless daydreamer, an idle fantasist, a dilettante. And you could be right. Half-way through one three-hour music degree exam, Mary Grierson, invigilating, came alongside my desk. "But Ian," she said gently, "you haven't written anything. Where are you?" Her troubled eyes searched my face. She was spot on. I was far away. And I couldn't explain it, even to myself.

What about the dog that so far hasn't barked? At choir rehearsals, where I had to make a piano sound like an accompanying orchestra, Professor Newman barked at me all the time, even when I did intuit which bar we were going back to; his articulation on such matters having the reliability of a rogue cruise missile. His language in such situations was robust, but even though it was at this time I was first aware of a stomach ulcer, I enjoyed his tantrums. They emanated from a passion for the music.

He never looked nervous, but he suffered from nerves. When he was conducting the Reid symphony orchestra in the Usher Hall, he was known to vomit before walking on to the platform; and throughout my second year as a music student, he had a nervous breakdown. That year he didn't miss a day at work, though his secretary frequently wished he had. I perceive that the picture I'm drawing is not flattering. So why do you think we put up with Professor Sidney Newman? Because he was a lovely person, a warm-blooded musician, and the most inspiring choral conductor I ever sang under. More than that he saw music as only one expression of the cosmos. One of his colleagues complained to him that instead of swotting for the music degree exams, I was spending long hours in the gallery of the Kirk's Assembly Hall (half a century later to be the first venue of the Scottish

Parliament) listening to debates on ethical, political and theological issues.

The professor retorted that I would be the better musician for having a rounded interest in life. I know this because he told me himself, adding, "But you know, you might just be a little more tactful talking to people here for whom music is the be all and end all".

He was a mystic; thus the way his face shone when he was conducting music with a spiritual reach—Vaughan Williams' Whitmanesque *Sea Symphony* just as much as Bach's *St John Passion*. And his vocational perspective was holistic; in one lecture he summarised a musician's calling as follows: "You will spend 99% of your time moving music stands". This fine man had been schooled in those wide-ranging values that should animate a university, yet time after time I heard him dismissed by members of the Edinburgh musical establishment. I was becoming attuned to the Edinburgh syndrome.

8

Damascus Road

As she bustled around talking, and cooking a classic English breakfast, Mrs Harris said, "It's a pity you've no universities in Scotland."

This was Teddington, London, in the home of Arthur plus his three brothers and Mr Harris. Arthur was about to marry my giggly sister Catherine and as the baby brother I was made welcome to stop over on my way from Fettes to Oxford and Cambridge to sit scholarships. I had come on the night bus from Edinburgh, cash being short for the train. I'd been met, all the men in the house had gone off for the day and through a sleepless haze I heard this nice intelligent woman being sorry for me because a poor Scots boy had to take a bus to England to go to university.

Returning to Mrs Harris's excellent bacon, egg and fried bread, I realised ruefully that I had rather asked for it. I attended what most Scots would think of as an English public school, sat Oxford and Cambridge school and higher certificate exams, and was now whoring after two English universities when we had four perfectly good ancient ones of our own.

Well, poetic justice was to deliver me at the gates of one of these four, of which Edinburgh was the least ancient. It had also struck me as being by far the least charismatic. Consider the competition. Aberdeen boasted Marischal College, glittering like a mad Bavarian castle, and down the road in the leafy enclave of Old Aberdeen the King's campus with its gem of a chapel, and its mediaevally glorious St Machars Cathedral. St Andrews, also mediaeval, clung romantically to a history as rugged as its coast and its weather, and blended grey town and red gown into one historic mosaic. As for Glasgow, aside from the sheer excitement of the city Roy Jenkins was to fall in love with as the British Chicago, the pile on Gilmorehill was, from any point of view, an architectural tour de force making Marischal College look sober. As against all those, what did Edinburgh have to offer? Grim, dark, sullen Colditz, a.k.a. the Old Quad.

If I am to be beaten round the head for the *lese-majesty* of dismissing the work of Robert Adam let me defend my expression of the impression it made on me. As a great cathedral and a great pipe organ liberate each other, so a great secular building needs, if not a great, then an adequate environment. In the dismal context of mean, narrow, messily commercialised South Bridge, the Old Quad looked like a mangy elephant crouching in a cage, looking gloomily for a means of escape.

Seen from Chambers Street, the dignity of the north wall was allowed to breathe, though the pastiche of Adam House, opposite, was no help, and the combination of traffic and car-parking denied the Adam design any full perspective. But the frontage onto South Bridge was simply invisible. On a wet winter morning you just dived from bus or pavement under the bulky arch to find the lecture room or library. Some of the interiors were resplendent, and if you were one of the tiny minority who was staying for an evening meeting of a society or club, you would hurry from a deserted Old Quad to dive for the comfort of the cafe across the road which served a robust mealy pudding and fried egg.

But I do not know about such things, being schooled neither in architecture nor town planning. All I know is that as I was trying to have a university experience of the lightness of being, the Old Quad frowned at me. No wonder my elder brother Alan had suffered depression at Edinburgh. This heavy environment from nine to five, then back to lonely digs and his homework.

So I rebelled.

My campaign, though that erroneously suggests a plan, turned out to have two phases. In the music faculty, based for three years in the more salubrious environment of Teviot Place, I made sporadic undercover forays into what I regarded as the university proper. The two obvious targets for infiltration were the union, called the union, and the student magazine, imaginatively named *Student*.

I was in two minds about the union. I didn't drink and didn't dance. I didn't even do sex. That left two union functions which did appeal to me: eating and speaking.

I knew I could speak. Not only had I spent five years gabbling away at Fettes, but I had won a school debate leading for the Tories. Wassat? You might well ask; indeed a traumatised school musical sixth passed a motion of no confidence in me for such an offence against nature. I had been coached by my other brother-in-law Charlie Terry, the swashbuckling Portobello confirmed bachelor who married Etta and, so far as I know, has read every copy of the *Daily Mail* produced in the last half century from cover to cover.

To the union debating hall, therefore, I gravitated, first to observe, then to rise from the floor, and finally to pontificate from the front bench, as chancellor of the duchy of Corstorphine in James Weatherhead's famous reforming Liberal administration which in truth had little aim other than to entertain, an aim which like a lantern in a storm has guided the aforesaid Weatherhead throughout his abundant life up to, including, and since being Moderator of the General Assembly of the Church of Scotland.

That was the light relief. Getting on board the magazine *Student* was more serious. My strange ambition "to write pamphlets" was coming home to roost. At first I wrote letters to the editor, then I visited the editorial den up a cobwebbed stair in the slums of Potterow behind the Old Quad. The editor, a domed intellectual with the unusual gift for a student editor of being able to write, commissioned me to turn out regular music reviews. With one bound I was free: combining my two warring sides, music and words. I even got readers' reactions. Well, I did when I wrote a destructive review of my own organ recital in the McEwan Hall. "Shame on you," the readers cried, "it wasn't that bad." Finally the editor annointed me his successor before proceeding to the greater depths of a career in journalism. It was beginning to feel more like a university.

Somewhat to my surprise, I found myself representing the university union at a riotous inter-university debate in Belfast, and a month's exchange visit in Helsinki, never to be forgotten because of my arrival and departure. The arrival was as in a vision, gliding across the Baltic at dawn as against the rising sun a thin silver horizon gradually revealed a sparkling city of domes and spires, capital of one of the most brave and cultured people in all Europe. The departure followed a rowdy farewell student crayfish party which proved an unsuitable basis for a Baltic crossing in a storm.

In Phase two, I left the music faculty to mount a frontal attack on the Old Quad and all its works. It is that expedition to which I now turn, because at last I was to discover what really made a traditional Scottish university tick, namely brains of considerable size casting pearls before hundreds of notebooks open and ready for active service.

The Scottish humanities tradition, harmonising, as I understood it, with the European tradition, was the broad "ordinary" course covering a wide horizon. I now have to resile from any idle cynicism: I found this purview inspirational. I know I was lucky to sit under three intellectual giants who also commanded powers of oratory, and I resent the fact that when my son Stephen, encouraged by my memories, did his MA at Edinburgh, he did not have such luck.

On the first Monday morning of my non-musical embarkation on the good ship philosophy and history, I joined a swarm of up to two hundred students, mostly three years younger than I, pouring into an Old Quad lecture hall. I see it still, and capture the awe with which we beheld John Macmurray enter, white beard and all. There was a hush at these lectures. I think we all felt that either Socrates was among us, or Christ, or both. In fact, it was Macmurray who was in our midst and that was more than enough.

An awed hush was not the mood in the Pollock Hall, where Sir Alexander Gray reigned. His subject was political economy. I attended the first Gray lecture without optimism, economics not being on my agenda. But I was confounded; he was a spellbinder. I guess he did teach us the subject, but that was the least of it. He was, of course, an outstanding Scots poet. And he was a wit. And he was a hoot. The overall word has to be pawky, but cross-fertilise that with Spencer Tracy being formidably funny in a court scene and then suddenly plunging the knife into an argument.

When Alexander Gray plunged his knife into the plight of the poor, the thunder of laughter collapsed in a mortified gasp. He was the most formidable all-round Scottish orator I ever heard.

As if that wasn't enough, enter stage left, also in the Pollock Hall, the tragic figure of Richard Pares, professor of history. He'd come to Edinburgh from Oxford where he was considered the most brilliant young historian of his time. He was still young, but a university servitor had to wheel him in on a wheelchair. Some paralytic disease had him in its grip. It was inexorable. It was a matter of time, and not too much.

How awful, I mean aweful, of fate. Here was a great man struck down without rhyme or reason. And particularly cruel the absence of reason. For reason was his *raison d'être*. If Macmurray gave us wisdom, and Gray the brilliance of social insight, Pares dispensed rationality. He was paralysed from the waist down. He turned his few notes with a finger, not a hand. But the brain lit up like Bach's B Minor Mass, every motif in tune with the whole structure. He talked for an hour, and it was exactly timed. To the second, his span of thought described a perfect rainbow. Then he bowed his head. We applauded like mad. And the servitor wheeled him out.

I knew colleagues of his. When he resigned to return to Oxford and die, they said there were no redeeming features. He was desolate, bitter, angry, at the waste. It was meaningless. For him, yes, for us, no.

These three great professorial bearers of light expanded and annihilated me. I felt ashamed of my shallowness and despised myself for having thought Edinburgh a poor substitute for Oxbridge. And then, just when I thought I might gracefully settle into this academic framework, the universe (I wouldn't say God) played its next trick; and it was a stoater. It was in the December of my second year in the arts faculty that the people who ran my digs packed it in, and I had to find a new pillow to support my head. For a year I had been conducting the New College (divinity faculty) student choir. They told me there were a couple of spare beds in the New College residence, which one didn't have to be a divinity student to occupy. In January I moved in. And that, once and for all, changed everything.

Just off Princes Street if you stand beside the art galleries and look up, you will see, if not the pillows I laid my head on for the next four years, the window within which those pillows lay. Up there on the skyline are the twin towers of the Assembly Hall. Move your eyes fractionally to the right and you're looking at a five-storey residential building attached to the New College structure. This was the New College residence.

I wasn't wildly enthusiastic about entering an enclave of budding ministers. I had resisted joining any of the university's Christian societies; they appeared to present a patina of intellectual bias and moral prejudice. Now was I to be trapped in a ghetto of the terminally biased? For heaven's sake, I'd have to crackle-pop my cornflakes with them! All for the sake of a bed?

Yes, alas, that was the sole reason. I'd been given a few weeks' notice to locate a new lodging, and those jolly theological students who formed the New College choir that I conducted had found a convenient solution for me. Needs must, and why should I look a gift horse in the mouth?

Looking back over decades I do now wonder if the smiling open faces of those demure students who nudged me in that direction actually concealed a nasty streak of low cunning; perhaps they knew me better than I knew myself. Anyway, confident that I could outwit any theologising or proletysing at breakfast, I walked in the door, an innocent Daniel into a den of lions.

And lions is what I found: some of the sharpest brains I've met in my life. Not a pride of lions, though. The pride was in myself; and it was about to fall, with all the elegance of the Humpty Dumpty I hadn't realised I was turning into.

Yet simultaneously the same period was to raise me to the kind of heightened bird's eye view of the seagull over Fraserburgh, of my year at Ardersier, and any of my latter period at Fettes. It is the simultaneity that is the point. My experience is that the rising is not after the falling, nor is it before it. They are enfolded in the one reality. In the same way, this next period was to be both a period of deepening emotional confusion and clarifying focus. Again, simultaneously. That is the problem with words, or at least words that are slave to logic: they're trapped in sequential order. Drama, film, poetry and fiction aren't so trapped, nor, supremely, are music and visual art. They all depend on structure, but retain a freedom to marry events in paradoxical ambiguities which reflect real life, for example, in bridging the hairline cracks between human love and hate. I'm not consciously trying to sketch a case in defence of the ambiguities of my music and writing and life choices, but near the end of my journey I think I can see how, using George Matheson's words, I was simultaneously not only trying to trace the rainbow through the rain, but create rain into a rainbow. The muddle is not a negative, it is the swamp out of which life grows.

And one analogy to that might be that a most tremendous muddle is the *bene esse* of God; and that when modern New Testament scholarship exposes the contradictions endemic in the Gospel narratives of the crucifixion and resurrection of Christ, it misses the point. Of course the writers and collaters of these manuscripts were in a muddle. They were in the most tremendous muddle, for simultaneously their lives and their minds were crashing around their heads and lifting their heads skywards. The reduction of paradox to black and white choices has been my lifelong enemy. It baffles me that brilliant minds can fail to grasp that if there is a contradiction, for example, in saying that we are free, yet subject to intervention, the contradiction may only be in our minds. During my philosophy studies in the period leading up to walking into my new home at the top of the Mound, I had written in my diary: "Logic is a very bizarre form of poetry". I still think so. Not that logic is a poor tool. Like science in general, it is a necessary, indeed a brilliant tool. But a troublesome master.

There were, I think, about forty in the community I was joining. I was adamantly resolved to remain detached from a tribe of Gadarene swine rushing to the cliff-edge of a life in dog-collars. I was only a bed and breakfast seeker. And dinner; yes, I was happy to eat dinner. And chat. And share a room, because that was the deal. As the latest entrant, and in mid-year, I had no choice. But with whom? Quite so. It is on such arbitrary details that any kingdom hangs. Meet first the room where I was to hit the Damascus Road.

Here it is, then, my room of destiny, though I did not yet know this. The interior aspect did not lift my spirits, highlighting as it did three beds and lockers, to tether three caged people. The exterior aspect, on the other hand, was exalting. Looking through the windows one was poised on an escarpment overlooking everything down to the Forth estuary and beyond. Even on a January day, I would discover that when the east coast haar lifted, or a gale scudded clouds across to Fife or on to the Ochil Hills, one might catch through a corridor of landscape the snowy top of Ben Lomond fifty miles to the west. And on a Spring morning, waking intoxicated on a unexpected tide of perfume, one would stick one's head out of the window to gasp at the Princes Street Gardens below; for there the blossom was rampant in an explosion of self-expression, as if in that one dawn the whole of nature was reborn. But back in the moment of this discovery I knew human beings still had to be confronted. Were my spiritual fists up? Hardly. But perhaps I had a raised eyebrow. And in walked Dave Harned.

As if that was dramatic! It was, after all, his room, and the entrance, I would guess, was polite and dull. I say "guess" because I'd be kidding if I pretended to remember the conversation, let alone many of the conversations of the next few months. In fact I doubt if conversations is the right word, for that implies discrete events with beginnings and endings. My memory is of slipping naturally into a continuous dialogue in which our two brains exchanged their contents in the language currency of each of our backgrounds. Don't get excited, I wasn't going to fall in love with him; but I was going to fall under his influence, because his brain seemed huge, his character strong, and his life position highly focussed as a result of a big decision he was wrestling with but in principle had taken: that being the catalyst for his sudden journey over the Atlantic.

He had just finished at Yale, literature being a core subject, and he'd edited the literary magazine. I gathered a wealthy background and a lifestyle of socialising. At a convivial farewell party of peers, someone had asked what he planned to do. He heard himself say, "become a preacher". The room fell about at the joke; one was given to understand that his caustic tongue, cynicism, lifestyle and irreligious attitude made the notion absurd.

He didn't know why he'd said it, but the fact that he'd said it haunted him, to the extent that he contacted the Edinburgh divinity faculty. He had an urge to test his strange utterance to destruction as far from home as possible. In this web of unforeseen consequences where human freedom and outside intervention inextricably link up, the New College principal, John Baillie, replied at once: just come, think afterwards. That act of direction untied his knot. He came. Whereupon, as I was to find, he began to be tied in another knot. He attended the Christology lectures of Professor Tom Torrance and was overwhelmed by them. A Torrance lecture was indeed overwhelming, a massive structure sucked out of the core of the earth and disappearing beyond the solar system. There are many paths to the divine summit, but the Torrance route was not for the faint-hearted. It required strong climbing boots and a plentiful supply of critical crampons. The climb inspired you, gripped you by the throat, or went for your stomach.

In Dave's case it was the stomach. The Torrance take on truth was so total you felt you had to take or leave it. Dave's problem was that he swallowed the aesthetic beauty of Torrance's interlocking constructions, and rejected their truthfulness. How could he do that without being schizoid? Three or four days a week he believed everything, for the other four or three days he believed nothing. When he believed he was happy as the day was long. He was saved. Edinburgh was magic. Christ was a friend of infinite grace. On these days he laughed a lot, he was witty, he ate the dreadful college lunches and decent residence suppers as if they were edible, his eyes shone, he noisily typed long incomprehensible essays during the night a couple of feet from my ears and eyes, and pulling the bedclothes over my head I cursed him.

On the other days, he had dinner out alone and after a couple of hours brooding over a solitary meal and wine, he would arrive back late, a thundercloud on legs. Edinburgh was the pits. Why didn't it have proper restaurants? (It was the mid-fifties.) He wanted to go home, to civilised living, to a bright social life. All the Torrance stuff was rubbish. Jesus was dead. He stared ahead looking suicidal, or he read a novel with such palpable gloom that I pulled the bedclothes over my head and cursed him.

But if he was a man riven by indecision, how on earth could I be led under his influence to make my own big decision? Because of his indecision. Precisely because of that. Because it mattered. Because it mattered to him not theoretically but existentially. Which was true? What is the case? Is Jesus alive or not? Was he, Dave, a Christian or not? This was no joke. One or the other was true, the other was false, and his life depended on the answer.

During the next few months I saw the balance of his belief tipping over into acceptance. It was partly an intellectual process: he was thinking further into theological problems and finding language to handle dilemmas. It was partly the pastoral care of Tom Torrance, who came to admire Dave; Torrance once said to me, "David has one of the strongest senses of sin I've ever known."

Maybe it was partly the ebbing away of a Scottish winter and the anticipation of going home. Or, simply, and Dave could sometimes be simple, God reached him. Whatever the reason, he reached a relatively serene state of mind. But too late for me. He'd done the damage. The missile of his anguish had hit me amidships. It had never mattered to me whether Jesus was dead or not. I'd inherited the whole God package from my father and his forefathers. I believed without thinking. I knew about God. I knew God. He was just there. He was life, He was love, He was nature. What was all this other stuff? Does it matter?

Well, it mattered enough to move Dave daily between despair and joy. And I could see that it wasn't just a question of individual salvation. The world was a suffering place where, at best, ignorant armies clash by night and, at worst evil dislocates and destroys. The Christian centre of faith does at least have a narrative which faces that. Suppose the cross really was crucial. How could I have been so shallow? Was I still playing with my life? Answer: yes. So what would I do about it?

A chasm opened before me. The question was: would I leap?

The problem with hindsight is that it is totally irrelevant: you leap or you don't leap, that's all. What you or anyone else says about it years later is academic. And as I've indicated, I didn't do academic; I tried a bit, but I kept being diverted by an instinct towards action. A leap of faith would be an action.

I can rationalise it now as well as the next person. I was in a long-standing muddle as regards devoting myself to words or music. I was in a muddle about career. I was in a muddle about spending an increasing number of years in what could be represented as eternal studenthood rather than doing some decent work. I was in a muddle about helping myself or helping the world. And now I was in a muddle as to what my religious faith, which I had never seriously questioned, was actually about. If— if—I were to do the one thing I had so recently shuddered at the very thought of, on entering this residence for budding ministers, and decide—my brain crunched itself into bits at the thought—to go for it, give into my genes, leap for clarity and focus and a purpose—at a stroke the muddle would be over.

On top of all that pressure, there was the psychological pressure to join in the adventure being embarked on by this new friend.

And there was the pressure of sheer curiosity; I now wanted to find out if there were truly compelling reasons for making the figure of Jesus central in human history and in personal life.

I was aware of a change in me, almost a metamorphosis. Some kind of new focus was rearranging the atoms in my brain. There was a new fork in the road. Martin Luther, I would learn, said that apprehending the Gospel is like a cow looking at a new gate. And Harry Whitley—we haven't come to him yet, but we will, oh we will—once said simply at a St Giles communion, "When the Gospel faces you, you either go back or you go forward. You can't stay where you are."

I guess that was it. I couldn't stay speculating about everything. I must commit now for life. Either music. Or the church. I chose the church.

Dave Harned was aghast. He'd perceived that he was making an impression on me, but he hadn't anticipated this move. He beseeched me not to throw away my music without giving the matter much more rigorous thought. Then he threw a hand grenade which exploded in my head and left its mark to scar me as often as I remembered it. "Ian," he said, "if you do this you won't know for the rest of your life if your real motive was to avoid the risk of failing in a music career." It was his equivalent of Crichton-Miller's asking if I was motivated towards the church by stupidity or laziness.

But I was older now and stronger, and anyway a child could see Dave was, as my headmaster had, using it as a tactic to shock me into thinking again. Exactly the same argument could be used against himself. And I'm a Highlander. I may dream and dither for a while, but once I commit I'm difficult to shift. They say the Buchan folk are stubborn; well, I was brought up there, wasn't I? My only concession was to attend some of Torrance's lectures with Dave, to test the ground. I did and found them engrossing. Tentatively, I asked to have a private interview with Torrance. He could be very persuasive pastorally, if he sensed that the enquirer was serious. I explained all my muddles. He waved them away. He said—it may sound corny, but it worked for me at that moment— "When you come to study Christology, you will learn that all that has to be done in your life has been done already by Christ. You are free now to enter into your inheritance."

Those were perfectly chosen words. He had said "when" not "if". And by the word "inheritance" at one stroke he evaporated my long-held determination not to yield to my clerical genes. Luther's new gate had opened. I was coming home.

At the beginning of summer I saw Dave off at Glasgow Airport.

For a moment I faltered. I felt alone and frightened. What had I done?

We wrote for a year or two, then silence. About twenty years later we met in the university staff club, when he was a visiting theological professor and author of important books on theology and art. We didn't find much to say to each other.

The finger moves on.

9

Band of Brothers

ar from housing a dull tribe of the conventionally pious, New College turned out to seethe with red-blooded individuality. As divinity was then a post-graduate degree, nobody was young and some were more mature than others.

Several, mainly from abroad, were studying for doctorates, others had done National Service in the armed forces. Yes, while I had been knocking around Edinburgh knocking corners off myself, they had been knocking around the world; Tom Scott, for instance, amply fulfilling his hospitable talents by running an officers' mess in the Korea war, James Weatherhead fulfilling his lifemanship talents by proving he could rule the waves without too obviously waiving the rules. Not to mention Bill Shaw whom we all finished up rather revering; he'd been an international squash champion. Then there was Alec Cheyne: he was distinctly adult. He became warden of the residence before becoming a superb professor of church history, a post virtually guaranteed for him by being tall, willowy and epigrammatic in so dry a style you needed a humidifier to flush out the jokes. His predecessor in that chair, Principal Burleigh, had been tall, willowy, and of such a dry wit it could have been marketed as a sherry for dons who find Tio Pepe too sweet.

When I joined this band of brothers (then almost no sisters) it was impossible to tell where they'd end up. Weatherhead as Moderator? No way, lack of gravitas. Bill Shaw as professor of divinity? Probably not dry enough, very clubbable bloke. Jim Harkness as the first non-Anglican chaplain-general of the armed forces, and then Moderator? Hardly: he was a nice quiet boy from Dumfries who wouldn't say boo to a goose—and there were plenty of us geese around.

But I was even luckier. I found, all ready for action, a shining new model of my Fettes musical sixth. Not that they were musical, well, not excessively. Brian Casebow was a musician; he could make a piano go, and he sported a light tenor perfectly suited to 1930 musicals. Colin Morton can't possibly have been as tone deaf as his father, deputy leader of the Iona Community, or I'd have noticed, though both father and son had brains which were never flat, and usually dangerously sharp. And Tom Scott? Definitely a lead in any rugby club madrigal, given a pint of beer to conduct with. So what bonded us? Brian, of course, would say the Holy Spirit: he was an enthusiast who would attribute pneumatic inspiration to an apple falling from a tree. Whatever began the association—apart from all being in the residence— what gave us a common purpose was a small cafe in the High Street. We were the Pop-In people.

We worked tirelessly for that wee cafe. We made it look perpetually full just by sitting there. We tried to avoid overworking the staff by making one coffee go a long way. We didn't tell too many people about it in case it got crowded.

Much though we yearned to sit at ease in Zion, sprawling lazily in comfortable warm lecture rooms basking in the reflected glory of devoted professors unveiling the complexities of Hebrew, Greek, the Dead Sea Scrolls, the forensic correspondence of St Paul or the ins and outs of jolly old Calvin, we knew our duty; we were at our post in the Pop-In, exchanging the gossip of the day, laughing merrily, and setting the world to rights.

I must be exaggerating? Of course; but not entirely. We attended most lectures, not because we had to, though obviously if we avoided many it would be noticed and we might miss rather valuable information as to how to pass an exam or two. But we attended mainly because we wanted to. The subjects interested us; and we recognised that even the subjects that were less interesting than railway timetables were necessary tools for us to unlock the secrets of questions exercising our minds and lives. And truthfully, often stimulated by lectures, we conducted thoughtful tutorials among ourselves, in the cafe or in our rooms, without interruptions from a podium. Which is how it should be at a university. And that is why the work at New College and the exploration of ideas in the residence made me merry. I was enjoying this. And the staff? They were, or became, friends.

One has to begin with Norman Porteous, professor of Old Testament Studies. I can't call him godfather of the college: he was too small and too rapid. I can't call him the regimental mascot: that would diminish his role. I can only describe him as I saw him. Despite the fact that the gown flying behind him was black, he was without question the White Rabbit, maniacally hurrying everywhere. Whichever corridor I was in he would hurtle round the corner, feet hardly touching the ground. "Can't stop, late, important meeting, how are you, did you read that Tubingen paper on Deuteronomy…?" And he was off. In the classroom his enthusiasm for his subject was so contagious it was self-defeating.

The events of the pre-Christian age were so real to him, he enacted them in front of our eyes. He was particularly splendid on battles. An innocent inquiry about the battle tactics of Goliath would lure him into a hyperspasm of pyrotechnics. He would rush to one corner of the room. "Here are the Philistines," he would cry. His lively sense of geospaciality then obliged him to rush to the opposite corner. "And here is David." He was an endearing man, but not only that. His abiding love was the college, and he was, behind the scenes, its master planner. Over decades he had plotted to assemble an outstanding faculty of teachers; and he had triumphantly succeeded. It was due to the international reputation of the teaching faculty that Edinburgh was attracting a huge number of post-graduate students from all over the globe.

Among the outstanding teachers was not Willie Tindall. But he excelled in one department: he was even more endearing than "Mickey" Porteous. Willie was the professor of practical theology. He was responsible for initiating us in the mysteries of liturgy, that is, the conduct of worship. The college had a small chapel where in turn each of us preached and prayed. I thought he was rather good at this; he was a sensitive, civilised man with a good ear and a good heart. He gave us space and was never judgmental. I admired him, despite, or more likely because, he didn't take himself or his job very seriously. He knew, and it was a knowledge no doubt enhanced by his war experience, that pastoral care can't be taught any more than life can. I'm thankful I was under his stewardship rather than the socio-politico-economico-managerialo-psychobabbilo-jargon that now rules.

But I can't leave it entirely there. About that time I was in the St Giles organ loft playing the organ for one of those special services which tended to take over Sunday afternoons. My all-time favourite was the dedication of the International Poultry Congress, but the one which Professor Tindall found himself in charge of was the National Girl Guide something or other. It was certainly national in its reach; the St Giles walls threatened to bulge outwards as girls of all ages from every part of Scotland pullulated in a multi-dimensional ectoplasm of ennui. Towards the end of the service, the "offering" was taken up. (I've never understood why the optimistic word "offering" was substituted for the realistic word "collection".) The cathedral vibrated as every girl deposited in one of the collection bags her large, heavy, copper penny. The collectors (offering receivers) at last fell in and en masse processed up the nave, into the chancel, finally halting in front of the east end communion table.

Professor Tindall had been briefed about the drill. He lifted the huge brass offering plate and positioned himself in front of the table. Gosh, it was heavy. There in front of him were the girls. Gently he inclined his spine. With an avuncular smile he lowered the plate to their height. One by one they plumped on it their bags weighty with copper coins. On and on it went. Did the world contain so much copper? The professor's arms became vertically challenged. The plate began to tilt forwards. He tightened every sinew. The plate began to tremble. Every sinew began to loosen. The plate tilted further. One bag fell off. Then another. Out of the bags fell pennies. The plate was tipped beyond the point of no return. Pennies in their thousands cascaded down, clanging, clinking, joyfully resounding across the stone aisles. In the organ loft mirror, I could see Professor Tindall's shoulders. They were heaving. He was fighting a desire to giggle. Do you see why I liked him? He had no illusions about himself. Also he had a large number of attractive daughters: one of them, Tessa, had an occasional meal with me. The last time I saw her she was a senior don at King's College, Cambridge. Well, there you go.

So far, you may think I'm teasing. Not so: I'm honouring human qualities which ultimately not only out-reach brain-power but in their loving qualities can redeem lives. But if you insist on brainpower let me advance the cause of New College as a then turbocharged engine of theological power. Step forward, John Macintyre. Why he? Why not the internationally renowned and unquestioningly powerful Tom Torrance? Oh, we'll come to him; in fact we've already come to him, via Dave Harned. But think. If you were a citizen of Fort William and woke one Monday morning to discover that during the night Lochnagar had moved from Deeside and was now standing beside Bonnie Prince Charlie's monument, would it be Ben Nevis you were talking about over your porridge? John Macintyre had moved from further than Deeside: Australia, where he'd famously reformed a theological faculty. Nobody was quite sure how he'd done it, but the rumoured advice was to watch him like a hawk. He would appear to be doing nothing for a long time, but he'd be observing, thinking, getting settled in. Then in his own time he would move. The prince from over the water would begin to move levers. Mysterious figures would rally to his support, and one day, maybe years hence, the old world would have passed away and reform would be on the agenda.

Anyway, much of the advance publicity about John Macintyre turned out to be justified. At least in style, it was chalk and cheese as between him and Torrance. Macintyre was like a cool breeze after an intensely hot day. Not that he was as energetic as to breeze into a lecture; he sort of strolled. And not that he lectured; he sort of just was there. Up till now, the lecture rooms had been irony-free zones. Now, given Macintyre's oblique questions and deadpan supplementaries, the problem wasn't to guess if one was being led up the garden path, but which garden?

His method was Socratic; but which Socrates? He was leading us to doubt everything we took for granted, including glib uses of language. And his jokes were worth waiting for as the penny dropped. His face was inscrutable, specially when for long periods he gazed silently out the window.

You can tell a lot from how a man gazes out a window. The great J.S. Stewart, famous preacher and at this time our professor of New Testament, would stop after a paragraph of heavenly discourse and, lost in wonder, love and praise, look out the window with a rapt expression. The wives of American students who came to the Stewart lectures to be enthralled were sure he was seeing angels. We cynical Scots conceded the point of substance but added the codicil that the angels he was seeing were scrabbling at the glass desperate to get in and hear Jamie Stewart's honeyed voice. This was not the way John Macintyre looked out the window. He looked reflective. Was he thinking of lunch? Pondering the latest Test Match score? Working out the next question to trip us up with? Or working on the 47 chess moves ahead to take over the faculty?

He was conning us, naturally. His apparently infinite openness could spring shut like a vice. Underneath the teaching method, designed to activate our sluggish brains, he had as firm beliefs as J.S. Stewart. He just held the view that such beliefs should not be bought cheaply.

If any of my old New College teachers were to read what I've been writing—there are one or two about—they might be hurt, or their relatives or successors might feel hurt on their behalf, if it appeared that I was being disrespectful. That would sadden me because the opposite is the case. I'm just trying to be truthful, and the truth is that these were exhilarating years for me. So how does one express exhilaration? Not in sober prose. Well, I can't. But then, isn't that the problem I've always had in presenting the turbulence in my mind? One tries to balance the turbulence, but if the spinning top is not spinning in the first place there won't be anything to balance, just a dead brain lying on its side. The world spins round, catching sunlight and darkness in a day. Life spins round reflecting one moment comedy, the next tragedy. Spring blossoms, then autumn leaves carpet the road. Birth. Death. It's quite a mix to incorporate in a narrative, let alone in living a life.

Is that why the Christchurch external examiner and the Kings' don were allergic to my verbal mix? And why I couldn't compose according to the rules? Obeying rules is drawing fossils. Jesus broke the rules in a big way. No wonder the scribes were confused.

All this is why the lectures that mattered most to me were those of Tom Torrance and Robin Barbour. I admired the pellucid and challenging Old Testament exegesis of the radical James Barr, who explained both the book of Genesis and the role of angels so memorably that I still find both explanations real as well as making sense in a scientific context; and I admired John Macintyre. I can't remember a single word from his dialogues, but it was a helpful process: I enjoyed the ride.

Torrance and Barbour were exponentially different from the others: they were nakedly struggling. They weren't merely wrestling, like Epstein's Jacob with the angel. They weren't just as in Michelangelo's *Creation*, exposing themselves to a new world by letting a creative God touch them; they weren't as in *Piero della Francesco*, waiting for the spirit to descend; they weren't, as in *Gerontius*, daring to see God and on seeing holy reality, shrivelling into nothing. At different times they may have touched the hems of all these garments. But the feeling in those lectures was both more subtle and more direct. Each of these men was wrestling with himself. I don't mean that their personalities were split, though Robin's beautiful face, often tortured, sometimes grew dark, and Tom could switch from Dr Jekyll to Mr Hyde if challenged. In one class when a German PhD student merely spoke up for the (relatively) radical German theologian Bultmann, Tom spat at him, "You speak as the anti-Christ. Please leave the room". In the break, Tom Torrance, urinating beside me, asked serenely, "I was right, wasn't I?"

What connected me to these two was that it so clearly mattered to them. It mattered so much that they were "bending backwards" (a favourite Torrance phrase) their considerable brains to make sense of it. Torrance was in theology no legalist. He broke the rules of language. Considered a traditionalist he was really a post-modernist. In the end, he convinced me that being a Christian was about being free.

By a liberating serendipity, Robin Barbour's wrestling with Pauline texts led to the same conclusion. All Paul's tortured arguments with himself about law and Gospel, rules and freedom, found their resolution when the world's rules, even religious rules, crashed into the miracle of love. Result: crucifixion. And the freedom of enduring that.

The Pop-In people were elated by this fabulous congruity. We were like a tinder-dry forest. With appropriate irony it was the laconic John Macintyre who dropped the lighted match. In a lunch-time conversation he said he had no objections to cheating in an exam. An exam was a device to put the examinee under pressure and catch him out. A well-organised cheating system was a device to break free from an unethical pressure to catch out the examinee. The positions were morally equal. We were happy to hear this. Here was a guy who really did believe in freedom. We decided to put this to the test. We invited Macintyre, Barbour and Barr to have wine and cheese with us in one of our rooms, I think Colin's. We included James Barr because exams were approaching, and we were least confident about the Old Testament. Our intention: to explain that, having learned from our mentors about the radical nature of Christian freedom, we felt free to excuse ourselves from taking up our time preparing for exams based on rules, preferring to spend the time more creatively exploring the theological ideas which had so recently excited us.

We got our come-uppance. At breakfast on the day of the supper, Colin took a call. He came back to the table crestfallen; it had been Professor Macintyre. All things considered, why didn't we go round to his house where Mrs Macintyre would be delighted to serve dinner to such distinguished guests. It was a question, but no question. How were we to retaliate? Not turning up wasn't an option. But we must do something to maintain our dignity (what?) and exemplify our freedom. We decided to arrive in a taxi, all wearing pyjamas. Moreover, instead of the classy wine we had purchased, Colin would present the prof with a bottle of cheap acidy wine he'd recently brought back from Israel.

We clambered, Casebow, Morton, Scott, and Mackenzie, out of

the taxi and rang the Macintyre bell. The prof and wife opened the door together to behold a pyjama'd quartet. Neither of them twitched an eyelash. *Au contraire*, they greeted us with a kindly warmth which persisted unabated until three hours later they closed the door on us. Our dress sense having appeared to have aroused neither surprise nor interest, Mrs Macintyre served a superb banquet and the wine flowed. Ah, well, that wasn't so good. John accepted Colin's cheap Israel plonk with aplomb. He took a bottle of red wine standing invitingly beside glasses and said, "I was going to offer you some probably very ordinary claret, but now that Colin has brought this very interesting Israeli wine, let's enjoy that right away." Its bouquet, taste and after-taste reflected poorly on the bladders of Israel's cats.

Guess who won that round on the playing-fields of freedom.

Youth, however, is resilient. We arranged a return match. It must be on neutral territory. And we must be as generous as Mrs Macintyre. We booked a table at a Greek restaurant in Rose Street. On this occasion it was Macintyre who gracefully declined, but Messrs Barr and Barbour accepted. We were determined to stint nothing. Wine would flow freely. And in a spirit of lofty truth-seeking we would gently probe the parameters of our guests' understanding of the ethical dimension of freedom.

One thing only did we forget—or it happened too late to do anything about. Greece and Turkey suddenly explored their ethical freedom to go to war over Cyprus. This had two consequences. First, the restaurant, apart from us, was empty. Greeks were glued to radio and TV. Secondly, the proprietor, an alarmingly big and combustible Greek with a voice that was certainly a loss to opera, spent the evening orating at us on the subject of the Turks. On the odd occasions that he retired to the kitchen one of us would draw breath to expatiate on the ethics of freedom, only to be cut down by the Greek rushing back to our table to launch another patriotic fusillade. Our guests ate a hearty meal, punctuated only by giving understanding nods to the Mediterranean. With warm expressions of thanks they clambered, fully clothed, into their taxi.

We gave up. But I've sometimes wondered: did they bribe the Greek to give the performance of a lifetime. Robin, did you?

Talking of Greek strikes a jarring note. Greek and Hebrew were then obligatory. I understood why. My father, a linguistic scholar, had begun his career lecturing at the Old Testament department at St Andrews before deciding that the parish was more important. But the languages remained relevant to him. He wrote his sermon notes in Hebrew, and at bedtime he read me Hebrew children's stories, translating as he went along.

His belief was that the nearer you get to the original language, the more you are led through its nuances to the core of what is going on. I completely understood that and would have loved to carry that torch. But I'm now sure that something in the wiring of my brain precluded it. I did try, honest, but as my problems with Hebrew were to delay my exit from New College, my difficulties with Greek were to threaten my entrance. There was a hurdle known as the Greek entrance exam. That was surely dotty. Someone with a "call" to the ministry was to learn Greek before he or she could enter the college where there were Greek language lessons? I suppose it was understood to be quixotic, because the reality was that you were allowed to resit your Greek entrance exam any time up to your last year—even Christian freedom would be pushed to allow you to leave without obtaining entrance.

Eventually, I passed, thanks to two theologs whom I still regard as special friends, even though we now see each other every other decade, if that. Neither was a New College product. Ian Strachan was Aberdeen, William Johnstone Glasgow. I met Ian on Iona. That is what Iona is for. Meeting. New friends? God? Yourself? Whatever, it was one of the two summers in the fifties I was in charge of the Iona music, and Ian was one of George MacLeod's new Community members spending the summer on the island rebuilding the abbey and studying the Bible under Ralph Morton. I took to Ian at once. His brain power was not in doubt; his wit was so caustic that only humour and natural grace made it palatable; and I liked the way (Oh God, this is going to embarrass him) that at the Saturday night concerts in the Iona refectory, when someone sang a sentimental ballad, he turned and faced north-east, as a Muslim might turn to Mecca. He came from Peterhead, and his fiancée Moyra was thereabouts, waiting. Ian's father was classics master at Peterhead Academy and Ian had inherited that skill. So nightly he tutored me.

Then, to put the icing on the cake, there was William. In the fortnight between Iona and my last chance to pass the Greek entrance exam, William invited me down to his parents' holiday house in New Galloway and drilled me with compassionate ferocity to the point where I was able, just before my departure, to enter New College.

But the way I met William is historically interesting in illustrating how, long before the obvious threat to a national church ministry, the tectonic plates of traditional Scottish preaching were scratching, scraping, getting ready to collide and perhaps finally to disintegrate.

New College and Trinity College, Glasgow, had theological societies which arranged inter-debates. At one of these, in Edinburgh, one of the Glasgow speakers was a certain William Johnstone. I still have no hesitation in saying that it was the most sophisticated piece of student oratory that I ever heard and by a wide margin. The logic was relentless, the style classical, the voice powerful and finessed, the imagery precise, and the flamboyance disciplined.

The only problem was that it missed its audience by a mile. Some yawned, others sniggered. I was mortified. I could see it through Edinburgh eyes: here was a pompous fellow from the west indulging in old-fashioned oratory rather than making sharp debating points. But why could my colleagues not see it through my eyes? Here was an Icarus aiming for the sun, and nearly getting there before being scorched. He risked all, and lost. Uhuh? He may have lost the audience, or some of them. But he won me. I wrote to him, apologising for the negative response, and stating unambiguously that it had been mind-blowingly good. He wrote back, we met, we became friends, and he invited me to Trinity College lectures. I got to know his fiancée Elizabeth, and when, years later, my wife Elizabeth and I lived in Peterhead, we regularly met up with William and his Elizabeth in Aberdeen.

By the time that he retired as professor of Old Testament at Aberdeen, he had become an illustrious Old Testament scholar, respected across the world. On the evidence of that one speech, he could have become one of Scotland's greatest preachers. Or could he? Have we become so mundane, so bland, in our expectations of pulpit speech; have we so bowed to management-speak, sociological jargon, political sloganising and evangelical soundbiting, that the poetry, the music, the glory of high language is beyond us? Two hundred, even one hundred years ago, even sixty years ago when my father preached his guts out to plain Buchan folk, there was a listening in the air because people were tuned into the sonorites of fine language honed by some of the most truthful brains in Scotland. Now we have TV quiz-shows, hand-clapping *Songs of Praise*, and celebrities massacring language in tabloids.

I chose to repeat a year at New College. I decided to exercise my freedom not to cheat at the Hebrew exam (there were well-known systems). I worked at it, and was licensed to preach in St Giles in the summer of 1960.

10
Loving

Being twenty-nine is, among other things, being stuffed with hormones increasingly anxious to graduate into purposeful activity. My body was not different from that of any other male of the species homo sapiens in the last few hundred thousand years in that it included a part with more sap than sapiens. Keeping it in its place, though I was sometimes confused as to where its place should be, had involved the usual strategies; I was uninterestingly normal. Uninteresting, and not unduly interested. It was like having a multi-channel cable, satellite and digital TV remote control; one could in theory switch over at any moment to sport or porn, but hardly ever did, because where would it get one?

A Fettes acquaintance who became a distinguished writer used a letter to have my writing analysed, and reported that I had a strongly repressed sensuality. Now I understood why on walks along the Granton foreshore I made overtures to a tree. And to think I had just thought I liked its leaves! Although deeved by normal physical feelings, in my teens I'd found sex to be simultaneously comic, tragic, sad and elevating. Well, dammit, the thing kept elevating, not least on the top deck of buses, which required getting off a couple of bus stops later than planned. Having endured that process I retain to this day a sympathetic identification with all men, even those whose sex drive leads them into deviant activities. When all is said and done, we didn't ask for this problem.

Intellectually, I divide the problem into three.

First, the curse of testosterone. During the Cuban missile crisis I stopped outside a toy shop near Edinburgh King's Theatre. There were elevated rocket launchers in the window ready to launch their rockets. "Does it all boil down to this?" I thought. "The world could be ended because of the male sex drive." Pass.

Second, how could I reconcile this inbred drive with divine freedom offered by a loving creator? Pass, other than a nod in the direction of evolution.

Third, how can one sort all this out in relation to the soul?

Pass. Pass. Pass.

But in real life one can't pass by any of these questions. Oh really? I made a pretty effective job of passing by all of them—till I was twenty-nine. I'm not saying I had absolutely failed to sort it out before I was twenty-nine. I'm not sure I've got it sorted out even now that I am—er—over twenty-nine. But I don't want to sound too humble, too unclear. For insofar as I've had any control over my life, I've run it on one principle: love.

Why? Because love has run my life. My father adored my mother, put her till his last night on a pedestal. She loved him so badly that after his death she retreated into a dark cave for twenty years. He loved me so entirely that after his death, the waves of love in his wake swamped me. He loved, also, his parishioners, which is why they were desolated by his death. Yet none of this love was facile sentiment. I recall almost nothing of his preaching, but what I am about to describe is seared on my memory.

During the Hitler war, owing to the impossibility of blacking out the large church windows, evening services were held in the church hall, situated at the fishing end of the town. My dad loved the atmosphere, in every sense warm. People who never felt well-dressed enough to worship in the church crowded in. The singing was wonderful, borne aloft by the pains of lives costly in wartime suffering and bereavement. My dad preached, as he so often did, about love. He just stood, Bible in hand, talking from the heart. Then he announced the last hymn. By this time he and I were close; it wasn't long before his heart gave out. During the lilting, rising waves of the congregation's last singing, my father knelt by the table on the platform. His hands were clasped in an iron grip. I knew, I just knew, what he was thinking. He was thinking: I have failed. I've talked about love, but they haven't understood. All my life I've tried to talk about love, to live by love. It has meant nothing. I've failed. God forgive me.

No, dad, you didn't fail.

What that gave me was the rock on which I have stood. On that basis the vagaries of human feelings have been waves lapping at the feet.

I'm not saying there weren't moments of doubt, when the wavelets became breakers threatening to dislodge one's composure. Which is what happened sometimes when I got into deep friendships, like male friendships in the years following Dave Harned. To give a full account of these shining people would be to write a separate book. Let me attempt not even sketches but subliminal impressions.

The year after Dave, Gerhard Koslowsky arrived in the residence. He was from Dusseldorf and, like all Rhine Germans, charming. That wasn't what attracted me. He was slight, swift, earnest. I've no recollection of what brought us together, but my guess is that his intense seriousness compensated for the vacuum left by Dave. His manners were perfect. On his birthday he brought to my room a bottle of Rhine wine and taught me the German way of drinking, eyes meeting in a toast over the rim of the glass. But it was his story which bonded us. He'd been a member of the Nazi Youth.

Evacuated to Poland to escape allied bombing, he and his younger sister had fled from the Russian army in 1945 to walk—to walk—from Poland over the border back to Dusseldorf. It took weeks, but the critical encounter took place in a forest manned by Russians to stop refugees. They suddenly came upon a Russian soldier. They looked at him. He looked at them. Then he expressed sadness (said Gerhard) and waved them on. That was when the idea was born in Gerhard's mind that there was something bigger than nationality: humanity. When he reached home he discovered that his mother had been killed by a British bomb.

In 1946, as Europe desperately crawled out of the pit to attempt reconstruction, Gerhard, still a teenager, responded to an advertisement for young Germans to join a youth camp in the mountains. He went to the relevant building, but knocked on the wrong door. He found himself being invited to join an evangelical camp in Kent, England. He accepted. In this English youth camp, dedicated to European reconciliation in the name of Christ, he found such overwhelming love that he felt he was joining for life the human race and the twelve disciples.

Who could resist such a story? I couldn't. He didn't claim a great brain, though it was, as any German brain is, an efficiently functioning one, but he was burning with an inner glow. He was pious. He understood that I was working though the aftermath of a spiritual crisis. His response wasn't abstract theology. He gave me a beautifully bound copy of *The Imitation of Christ*. His simplicity disarmed me. In hellish weather we cycled together over mountain and flood to Iona. We spent Hogmanay with my aunt and uncle on top of a hill croft overlooking Loch Ness; Uncle Jim spoke one prayer, Gerhard another, and we sang the 121st psalm.

When he left to be a pastor in communist East Germany (he believed he owed that) he presented me with a copy of *Le Petit Prince* by Antoine Saint-Expury. And, at his request, I visited his fiancée Ruth in Zurich. Later I became godfather to his daughter. Later still he became a force in the German ecumenical movement. My faith was deepened by contact with Gerhard. But, and it was an increasingly daunting but, a pattern was developing. After a year of companionship my companion had gone. Everyone I cared for, starting with my father, seemed to go away.

The year of the German was followed by the year of the Frenchman. Gilbert Charbonnier was something else. (Come to think of it, every Frenchman is something else.) He stormed, no glided, no swept, no strode, no waltzed into the residence. Coming from Marseille, he was more Mediterranean than European. Slightly swarthy, with the grin of a shark, he had two modes of communication, the giggle and the shotgun. I'd never encountered anything like it. Equally he found me to be a conundrum he was determined to solve. He never did, but it wasn't for want of trying. He never gave up, though. "Eean," he would say. "You must stop being nice to people. Most people are pigs. Don't waste time with them. Stop smiling. Get serious. Eean, there is a world to be told the serious news of the Gospel. Please stop being charming."

I didn't understand any of this. I had no concept at all of

possessing an iota of charm; I just loved people. Was that wrong?

He worked at it. He had one *idée fixe*: freedom. Ouch! I was vulnerable there. Don't think pyjamas or Greek restaurants. From October to December he was perfectly clear: the Bible was rubbish, Sartre had the truth. Jean-Peal Sartre understood: freedom was all. From January till June his position altered somewhat. "Sartre is rubbish: Paul's letter to the Romans is all we need: freedom is all." Ah, the French. I do love them. I certainly loved Gilbert. Later, at his request, my wife Elizabeth and I visited his fianceé Elizabeth in Italy. I was becoming a carrier pigeon of love. After he left Edinburgh he went straight into the Algerian war of independence as a front-line chaplain. He had said to me, "de Gaulle is the man of destiny. He is a dictator. Good! God uses dictators to bring order. Most people are pigs, you know. It's not their fault, and they will be saved."

I was told some years afterwards by a source in Paris that Gilbert won a military award for exceptional bravery. He didn't expound the Bible back at base. He was always in front-line dug-outs, expounding it as the bullets whistled by. He was one of the coolest intellectuals I ever met, and he didn't give a toss.

His farewell present to me was a large-scale print of Piero della Franscesco's *Baptism*. Despite, or because of, his cut-throat brain, he bought the whole Gospel and was ready to die for it.

Still reeling from all these apostolic friends who kept arriving and abandoning me, I received an air-mail letter from Dave Harned. He said that a certain Douglas Sloan was coming to do a year at New College, and I should "cherish" him. Well, it would round off the collection, American, German, Frenchman, American.

I don't know how to describe Douglas Sloan. I already had a Douglas friend, of whom more later. Could I accommodate a second Douglas? Well, let's call him Sloan. Suffice to say he is still a friend. "Cherish" was *le mot juste* for a singularity. He was that rare commodity, a clever guy who had no concept of his cleverness. He was a country boy growing up in Kansas, still haunted by the distant call of train horns crossing in the night the vast prairies of America. His imagination echoed to the suffering of American sons slain in the American Civil War and the butcher-fields of France in World War I. He was a hopeless romantic pierced by a black humour.

We had a great year, including a weird Christmas journey into Europe. We spent Christmas Eve in a Salvation Army hostel in Frankfurt. Please let me recommend you not to spend any eve, let alone the Christmas one, in a Sally Army hostel in Frankfurt. Suffice to say that one felt relatively safe locked into one's cell, knowing that those adjoining us who were auditioning for Hannibal Lecter were similarly confined. Douglas even refrained from plucking his ubiquitous guitar. The next day—oh, look, it's Christmas—we chugged via a number of unenthusiastic trains to Tubingen, where we were to be received by Walter, a solemn theologian who had just spent a year with us in the Edinburgh residence. Our cashflow being restricted, we spent Christmas day on starvation rations, confident of a prodigious German festive dinner on our evening arrival. Walter smiled at us benevolently. "You will have had your Christmas dinner? Would you accept some cake?"

When Douglas Sloan flew away in the summer, I thought: "Will this end? People leaving me?" And the next question followed naturally. Why am I missing them? Am I homosexual? I knew the answer. But I had to ask the question. The answer was no. Not a nervous no. Not a hypothetical, speculative no. Not a defensive no. Not an over-emphatic no. Just a factual no. Each of those friends had enhanced my life as I could imagine Jesus enhancing the lives of the disciples. There was no doubt that I had loved them. But homosexually? I knew it wasn't so. How did I know? Well, in the first place I rejected the categories. One loves, that's all. You love or you don't love. Drop the analysis. Who needs analysis paralysis? Why not just ride the wave of affection, of caring, of respecting?

In the midst of the Sturm and Drang of all this personal exploration, I was saved from capsizing under the weight of my solemnity not only by Scottish friends who treated me as a human being with whom to exchange the throwing of unwanted currants from rice puddings across the New College residence dining-room, but by one Swiss, who added intellectual glitter to my collection of post-graduate foreigners.

There was no distracting intensity in our relationship, only cordiality, dialectical energy and frequent hilarity. The dialectic was not an added ingredient, it was Christian Zangger's normal form of conversation. He was a German Swiss from Zurich, but his mother, whom I met on a visit there, was classically French, with a sharp irony which he'd inherited. Christian looked like a Zurich gnome, very thin with a large head, and he was deliciously droll. His was the only laughter in which I ever heard actual Ha Ha's, interspersed by the happy gurgles of a baby which can't quite believe its luck at arriving on such an amusing planet. Elizabeth and I have visited Christian and Gabbie in Zurich, and we are happy to pass on the information that the Swiss are not boring.

However, I had in my life intimations of a radical otherness of loving which, blowing in from another planet, plucks the heart out of its socket, and creates a new world.

When I was eleven, my father took me to Kincraig in Speyside to visit his cousins Katy and Dolly. A young cousin was also visiting them, and she was my age. Under a full moon, she and I walked and talked. The next day, ever so insouciantly, I asked my father, "Is it all right to marry at eleven?" He advised a period of reflection. But I never forgot the moment. It had that Speyside magic which happens when in the morning the sun burns the haze away to reveal the rolling grandeur of the Cairngorms.

Eight years later, in my first year at Edinburgh University, I caught sight of a girl's face in the choral society; and my nineteen-year-old heart swung on its hinges. I sought that face. Somehow we met. She introduced me to her parents. Her mother drove a Morris Minor. Day after day, I walked the streets of Edinburgh, hoping for just one glimpse of that Morris Minor. Dr Mary Grierson also drove a Morris Minor and looked startled at the intensity of my stare when she drove past in the university precincts. The girl and I wrote letters to each other. I can still visualise the curls and loops of her handwriting.

And?

One day she kissed me. It was like an earthquake. Unfortunately she was driving along the old A8 at the time and the car was swerving towards the opposite lane. I detached myself; sorry, and all that, but I had not yet abandoned the will to live. More to the point, I had no idea how to respond. Not only was I not ready for a commitment, I wasn't ready for anything. I wasn't sure in what sense as an entity I existed, if I existed at all. I wasn't at all sure what existence consisted of. The nearness of this profound magic was a terror for which I was unprepared. The relationship subsided. I had a long way to travel. I hope she has forgiven me my gaucheries. If we ever bumped into each other in the street I would want to thank her for holding in front of me a pure light to lighten my confusions at that time.

I'll come shortly to the psychodrama of St Giles. But since that must develop into a wider theatre of public conflict, it might be sensible in the context of my emotional development, first to hone into the person who was to awaken, vitalise, anchor and redeem the enigmas of my being: Elizabeth Whitley, my boss's daughter.

Whitley my boss. Who he? Who indeed? We have to retrace a step.

Charles Warr, minister of the High Kirk of St Giles and Dean of the Thistle and Chapel Royal had announced his intention to quit. Well, sort of quit. Let's say half-quit. He instructed the kirk session to appoint a colleague and successor. That was pushing it; lame duck presidents do not instruct Congress to appoint their successors. But Warr thought he knew his session. Emasculated by the long reign of the physically diminutive but royally influential "Boy Dean" Warr, they would surely do exactly what he asked. He went, however, one step too far: he told them who to appoint as his successor. At this some residual blood stirred and a number of spines straightened. "We," they said, "will choose your successor."

They appointed a vacancy committee. One of the committee was my music chief Herrick Bunney. He took his duties seriously. On frequent Sundays at dawn, as was the way with vacancy committees, he and his fellow conspirators set out to penetrate the nooks and crannies of Scotland in search of the right man to take over St Giles. And every other Sunday Herrick crawled into the organ loft in a state of gloom. Nobody was right. It was an exceedingly difficult post to fill. The St Giles finances were in a parlous state. The congregation was, literally, dying. Yet the cathedral remained the church of national ceremony and the historic shrine of world-wide presbyterianism.

One Sunday, Herrick bounced into the organ loft, beaming like a lighthouse. "We've found our man." It was Harry Whitley from Partick. I was still assistant organist. In that capacity I joined Herrick at a meeting chez Whitley in their dark Northumberland Street manse. All I remember is a man sprawling in an armchair as a family of five sprogs and a dog whirled around the room.

Several years later I returned as assistant minister. One afternoon in his study in the new manse in West Castle Road, Tom Scott, senior assistant, and I were discussing with Harry the Sunday services. Harry's wife, Elizabeth, an elegant red-haired woman, was in London serving on the Pilkington committee on the future of broadcasting (in fact a committee to determine whether the BBC should be balanced by a commercial TV channel and if so on what terms). When the study door swung open it was therefore not Mrs Whitley who entered with tea and toast; it was a nineteen-year-old Elizabeth. Her father looked at her. "God," he said, "you're like your mother." I suppose that is when I first took note.

The next time I took more than note. I took flak. The Whitley family had flown to Italy for a post-Easter break, leaving Elizabeth behind to study for Higher exams. Mrs Thom, Mrs Whitley's mother, was through from Glasgow's west end to look after the manse. Tom Scott and I were left to look after St Giles. One of our duties was to check mail and take round to the manse any that Harry Whitley might want to see on his return. One Monday morning it was my turn. Having sorted the mail at the office, I presented myself at the manse and rang the bell. It wasn't, as I expected, Mrs Thom who opened the door. It was an apparition.

Except that there was nothing ethereal about the figure. And do ghosts, even ones as terrifying as this, get the common cold? It may have been merely a common cold, but this girl was having it in an uncommonly big way. The nose was red, the cheeks blotchy, the hair straggling, and moisture streaming from every available orifice of the face. Even so it struck me that the eyes, swollen and hooded as they were, retained enough focus to be regarding me with a concentrated lack of warmth. If I had been a dead bird deposited on the doorstep by the cat, I would have been entitled to more of a welcome. I didn't know that I had come face to face with my nemesis. I just knew I had come face to face with someone who didn't like me at all.

"Good morning," I said. "I'm Ian Mackenzie, from the St Giles office."

"I doh dat," she spluttered.

"I've brought some mail."

She disdained to comment but continued to survey me with silent contumely.

"I duppode you're dadidified."

I was genuinely baffled.

"Dat termon!" she spat out.

I had preached the day before.

Clang, as the penny dropped.

My text had been a particular translation of a passage from St John's Gospel in which Jesus was conducting a debate with the pharisees about their religious legitimacy: "You are all bastards". I had delivered the text with relish, thinking that some of the St Giles oldies were under the impression that they were a cut above the rest. I had reason; on my first day at St Giles as an assistant minister the president of the Woman's Guild had extended a gloved hand and purred: "Congratulations on coming amongst us."

However at this moment what I was amongst was a snarling cat. With much spitting and growling and the impression of an arched back the female standing over me on a higher step than I let go all restraint and laid about me with a torrent of words. How dare I! At those poor defenceless old ladies! Who did I think I was? There was much in this vein. As she stopped for a nanosecond to draw breath, the grandmother appeared to investigate the commotion. I handed her the mail and ran.

At a safe distance, over the next few days I pondered the event. Tom Scott, when told, thought it was hilarious, but I wasn't laughing. Something had got under my skin. I had been rather proud of that sermon, but the more I looked at myself, the less proud I became. There was something else, however, that had got under my skin and I couldn't pinpoint what it was. When my boss returned from Italy I gave him an account of the incident and asked if I could take his daughter out to tea to discuss the sermon at greater length. He was amused and said of course but if she accepted did I have any available body armour?

She was in her final term at St George's School for Girls, so we fixed the rendezvous for something like half-past four, at McVities, the multi-storey coffee, lunch, and tea palace at the west end of Princes Street. As I waited at the front door I was aware of butterflies applying pressure. Then I saw her. Her walk was as elegant as her mother's, but there was an energy about her, almost a bounce, which echoed her father. The wide smile was absolutely lovely.

Once settled with tea and accoutrements, we talked sermon. The bad mood had gone away, as had the cold, but she pinned down my every argument with the firmness of a prosecuting advocate. I had never before been so directly confronted. Why was I not hating it? After a suitable period of time I asked if she would like to join myself and a friend at an orchestral concert in the Usher Hall. The afternoon of the concert she was stung by a bee and by the time we reached the symphony she sported a considerable lump on her head.

Not long afterwards I asked her on a first date: a train ride to North Berwick and back. I know it sounds feeble, but it was summer and she made it interesting by falling off a horse a few days before and placing her plastered leg on the opposite train seat while picking a number of spirited arguments with me. I was beginning to feel hunted. So why was I liking it? When one afternoon I found that my briefcase in the St Giles office was filled with cornflakes I began to wonder if this was a suitable liaison. So did her parents. They didn't know about the cornflakes but they were beginning to realise that we were showing preliminary signs of being an item. I was ten years her senior; I was one of her father's staff; and he was having enough problems at St Giles without a conflict of interests at home.

At this point she conferred a signal favour. I was invited to accompany her and her little brother Laurence to the stables near Livingston where on Saturdays she went to ride her beloved horse Martine. As a signal favour it was a signal failure. One of my blind spots is horses. The magnetism of the horse escapes me. Even less am I gripped by all the things that go on around a horse. I'd always appreciated the clerihew, "I know two things about the horse, and one of them is rather coarse". I wasn't sure what that might be, but to a rarefied sensibility like mine the paraphernalia of washing, cleaning, cleaning out, massaging, brushing, polishing, not to say stroking and patting that seems necessary to appease the horse's vanity before you deal with feet, tail, and then all that leather! The overwhelming sense of gameyness left me not so much cold as hot under the collar with the alienation of pure embarrassment. To crown it, she was devoting her entire attention to the horse and none at all to me. It was a very fine big horse; even I could see that. Much bigger than me. So why had she asked me? It was later that I realised that she had been sharing something which to her was sacred.

It was a costly exercise, though, in terms of public relations. A St Giles elder phoned the manse to ask if Dr Whitley was aware his assistant had been seen consorting with his daughter? Consorting? If only! Anyway, the cat was among the pigeons. My boss had a man-to-man talk with me. Elizabeth was very young, easily impressed by a man of the world like me. Huh! I thought; how could so many mistakes be crowded into one short sentence? Easily impressed, indeed! I felt it was with the utmost difficulty that I was making any impression at all. Young? She was the most mature nineteen-year-old I'd ever had to argue with. And me a man of the world! I'd no idea what a woman's body looked like— this was pre-girlie magazines and Page 3.

When Elizabeth on one early date apologised for being tense and made mysterious references in some coded language, it gradually dawned on her that I hadn't the foggiest notion what a period was, let alone P.M.T. Between bursts of insane giggles, she explained it to me as to a child. I was. I was a complete innocent.

Mind you, if her parents had known that, they might have been even more alarmed.

I know, I know, how was it possible to be so ignorant? Not so hard. It was a different world back then. When, much later on, I first saw Elizabeth à la nature, I was utterly astonished; I'd had no idea the female body was so interesting. As regards what unbelievably young boys and girls get up to these days, we didn't attempt that till the first night we were married and then laughed so much we fell asleep. Well, it had been a long day.

11
Warr and Peace

I'm aware of having said more often than is safe for credibility that such and such made all the difference, or nothing was the same again, or everything changed. It reminds me of trips to the Highlands with a number of overseas students from the New College residence where I played the role of the Rev Mr Eager, the knowledgeable guide in E.M. Forster's *A Room with A View* though I hope I was less sententious.

On these journeys I was inclined to make use of the concept of "The gate to the Highlands". Some of my clients were surprised; they'd thought they were already at the gate to the Highlands. Wasn't Edinburgh such? I would allow the point: yes, South Queensferry could perhaps be described that way. At Stirling I would sigh with satisfaction and say, "Ah yes, but now we are truly at the gate to the Highlands". Similarly at Perth, Aviemore (or Glencoe and Fort William if on the A82). Inverness was so clearly the genuine gate I normally concluded the tease there. With one exception. A tall vigorous American with whom I had a passing acquaintance invited me to accompany him at his expense on a tour of the Highlands and explain what was what. He was a decent guy with one limitation which Americans have difficulty overcoming. They are so used to long distances that, thinking Scotland a miniature bit of territory, they miscalculate journey times.

David (not Dave Harned) explained that the tour of the Highlands would take two days, and the one overnight would be in Skye. I demurred. It was a long journey. He was much amused. He prodded the atlas. "At home I'd drive to Skye between breakfast and lunch." He'd already booked a B and B on Skye. He reckoned a two-day trip would take in Skye and the Highlands. In view of which I was startled to see him staggering out to the car after breakfast with two gigantic tartan-covered cases suitable for a month's voyage on a cargo ship.

The hired Volkswagen Beetle had nice tartan-covered seats. We set off. I did the "gates" sequence, of course, and then after Perth we were on the A9 pointing to the mountains. This was the old twisting A9. Soon we were stuck behind a seamless convoy of caravans, lorries and under-powered cars slugging it up to Dalwhinne at a remorseless thirty-five miles an hour.

David couldn't believe it. It took four hours from Perth to Inverness. We had a late lunch. David recovered. "Right," he said cheerfully. "That's the worst over. Skye's just up the road. Let's go." I maintained a straight face but in a cavern of my soul permitted myself a smile. Schadenfreude is good, but with several hours of misery in which to anticipate, it is a delicacy to be savoured. This being nearly fifty years ago, we were soon onto single track tarmac with passing places. High Noon was performed on a regular basis. We were averaging ten mph. The Achnasheen fork was a significant gate to the Highlands. Naturally at Kyle of Lochalsh I told David this was the gate to the Highlands. We queued for hours for the tiny ferry. The sun was low in the sky; soon it was behind the Cuillins. It turned out the B and B was still a long way as a crow walks.

By now David was dog tired and the Beetle was developing a talent for veering into the ditch. At length we came to a farm road with a sign indicating we were almost there. It was now dusk and raining. The farm road forked and we took a grassy track which came to a dead end before a wooden gate. On the other side of the gate was a wet field. On the other side of the field was a cottage. David got out and stared at the gate. "This," I said, "is the gate to the Highlands." I thought he would hit me. We left the car and opened the gate. I walked smartly over the grass; David stumbled squelchily with his mammoth pieces of luggage. The door opened and we received a great welcome. "Ach," said the lady of the house, "but you made very good time."

The dinner was stupendous. David was mollified. He even made a joke. "Now," he said, "I have discovered that it is sometimes not better to travel than to arrive."

We took an extra day to return, and this time he actually looked at a bit of the Highlands.

There is, of course, no gate to the Highlands. The Highlands themselves are a gate to whatever one is looking for in one's heart. It had never occurred to me in the decade now ending that I had been looking for the gate to two such conventional things as a wife and a job. But when I found myself with both, it felt at last like arriving.

A few pages back I ventured the comment that Harry Whitley was having problems with St Giles. Or you could say, and a number of St Giles and Edinburgh notables did, that they were having problems with him. I was to have problems with all of them, but at first I was pleased to be back.

You will recall that I had previously spent five years haunting the place as assistant organist, a part-time job which had given me access to the power of the organ. Now life had made an honest man of me and I was not only to be paid a full-time salary—not much, but dependable—I was to have access to the power of the pulpit. There was another bonus. Tom Scott and I would share the power of the Vespa! Yes, St Giles had acquired a motor scooter to speed the assistants on their way; I now had access to the internal combustion engine. It had been a long way round from the power of the organ, the bicycle and the steam locomotive in childhood Fraserburgh, but as one threaded one's way stylishly through Edinburgh streets, the scooter leaning to port or starboard in the Roman manner, it wasn't hard to feel part of a Fellini film. Except that we didn't have soutanes to flutter behind us.

During our last year together at New College Tom and I had speculated about the future. The next step was to be attatched to a minister to whom one would be articled, like a junior in a hospital or law firm. We looked around. Who was worthy of our talents? It didn't take long to decide. Whitley, the new man at St Giles, seemed the best bet. St Giles had two assistants; we might even finish up together. We graciously invited Dr Whitley to be our lunch guest at the university union. Over a pie and pint we put the proposition; we'd looked round Scotland, and we were prepared to have him as our boss. He guffawed, then gazed at us speculatively, an uncomfortably searching look. "It won't be a bed of roses, you know. There are forces gathering. They want to keep St Giles as a museum. I have been asked to make it a place of life. That is upsetting Edinburgh already. Are you up to this? Think about it." In his decisive way he had accepted us. He judged that we weren't playing games. He was a man of his word. Tom, who left the college a year ahead of me, became junior, then senior assistant. I repeated the process a year later.

There was one personal sub-plot. After two summers directing the Iona Community music, I was invited by Ralph Morton and George MacLeod to become the Community's first music organiser on the mainland. I would go to the New York Union Seminary to study choral music at the associated college, then come back to Scotland to co-ordinate music in the Community parishes—the kind of job John Bell has done in the last two decades. It was a wonderful offer. One snag: my mother was becoming frail. I was the only sibling who could keep an eye on her by living with her. If I was an assistant in an Edinburgh church we could share a flat. In my little room in Iona Abbey that summer I made up lists of pros and cons. It had to be con. I said no to America and Iona music-making, and yes to my mum. No martyrdom; nobody could have decided otherwise. So it would be St Giles.

Harry, over his pie and pint in the union, had had reason to warn us; and if we'd known the true gravity of the situation we might have bade him a fond farewell and scuttled. No, I think not. I believe we had courage. But we were still idealists; we hadn't yet encountered the full force of naked power-lust. I won't call it evil, because that is to descend into the arena of manipulative language which lies near the heart of the problem. In each of the five jobs I was to occupy from 1960 to 1988 I was to meet this syndrome: a male clinging to the power to control that on each occasion had to be resisted. The St Giles job was different from the other four in that I was still the apprentice, not the master; but I was intimately involved in the nexus of nerve-endings beginning to jangle throughout St Giles and the Edinburgh establishment.

The basic facts are so simple there that there is no point either in embellishing or concealing them. Charles Warr had initiated the process of calling a colleague and successor. That was a dodgy process in itself—the Kirk's culture and structure did not sit easily with collegiate ministries, namely two ministers of equal status running one charge. It nearly always ended in tears. The idea was quite different from the more recent development of team ministries where sharing is the bene esse of the arrangement. Warr assured both Whitley and senior elders that he wouldn't stay for long, just ease his successor into the situation and then hand over.

It all seemed straightforward and above board and no doubt at that stage it was. I was in the St Giles organ loft on Harry Whitley's first Sunday and heard Charles Warr's enthusiastic endorsement of this exciting new ministry from the West of Scotland. The problems that ensued constellated round various factors, each of which by itself might have been surmountable but taken together blew up in everyone's face.

First, the two men had diametrically contrary styles of conducting worship. Whitley had no less high a view of worship than Warr, but he had an intrinsic belief in the power of the spirit to blow a fresh wind into worship as well as life, and he had a gift for humour, for movement, for lively utterance. He adored children and integrated them into the worship, taking them trotting round the church to hear stories about the weird and wonderful articles of furniture or statuary adorning the place. He had a live lamb in on Passion Sunday, candlelit processions on Candlemas, and, of course, a mass of moving foliage on Palm Sunday. When there was a children's address he might begin, "Now you'd better listen to this because it will be over the grown-ups' heads and you'll have to explain it to them at lunchtime."

The bottoms of some of the devout shifted uncomfortably; they didn't realise that such informality and movement was actually nearer the Anglican and Catholic tradition than Dr Warr's atmosphere of static reverence. The congregation divided. Some of the older members, though not all, were disturbed by what they felt to be a disrespectful interference with their habitual piety. Warr had been their spiritual guru for half a lifetime and was still around taking half the services. They reacted emotionally. One genteel elderly Edinburgh lady spat at the Whitley family in the street. Excretia was posted through the manse letter box. (Warr now lived in a grace and favour house in Moray Place.) Nobody suggested that the senior man would encourage or condone such behaviour. What he could do was go. He didn't. He stayed—for years.

Harry Whitley had been called and inducted as the High Kirk minister and moderator of the kirk session. Charles Warr was still Dean of the Thistle and Chapel Royal. It seems incredible now that the scope for confusion in such a division of powers had not been foreseen. But of course, what can with goodwill be made to work may be turned into obstruction, given fundamental problems. As Dean, Warr retained a central role in many important services and functions affecting Scottish life, the Edinburgh establishment, and royal occasions; he was well known and liked in royal circles.

The scope for trouble was thus unlimited. Take the cathedral diary. Who was to referee a dispute when the dean wanted to book the cathedral for a "special service", and the minister on the same day for a congregational one? Indeed, who was to decide when each would preach? Couldn't the two men just meet and toss a coin? I've seen the correspondence. Some letters would curdle the milk as it came out of a cow's udder. The difficulties were such that the kirk session eventually took responsibility for a preaching rota; and that was humiliating for everyone.

This now being a public scandal, the Edinburgh establishment took sides. And being Edinburgh there are no prizes for guessing which side many of them came down on. One of the most powerful figures in Scottish public life visited Harry and put it to him in these terms: there are ways of doing things in the Edinburgh circles in which you are now moving. Do things our way and the highest honours will come your way. Do things the wrong way and there will be trouble. I wasn't present so I can't quote actual words, but I had it from Harry's own lips that he showed his visitor to the door, saying he would not be blackmailed in his own home.

Many of the Edinburgh establishment were Episcopalians, and even among those who were not, it was common to send sons to English public schools where they were confirmed into the Anglican communion. In the present ecumenical environment, not an eyebrow would be raised by anything so commonplace. Alas, the then Episcopal Bishop of Edinburgh felt he should be given greater recognition. Harry liked Bishop Kenneth and I can vouch for the fact that he made repeated efforts to befriend him. But others were sowing seeds of paranoia in the bishop's head. The bishop invited me to tea. He seemed kindly and civilised, but when he began to pump me about my "controversial" boss, and I declined to play ball, he became sarcastic. "You think you're a clever young man, don't you?"

Finally and climactically, Harry's preaching was strikingly topical, and prophets are not popular in their own country. His social gospel was not as politically defined on the left as George MacLeod's, but he was one of MacLeod's young men, indeed one of his closest confidantes. What did people expect Harry would preach about? The loveliness of daffodils? This was the minister who had made waves as an independent councillor in Port Glasgow, who hobnobbed riskily with the local Catholic priest, and when he moved to Partick regularly left dead rats at the Glasgow City Chambers until they did something about the state of Partick housing.

Harry was master of the ten-minute sermon and tough on his assistants if their preaching strayed beyond ten minutes. As a result, each message got through, and Scottish journalists began attending St Giles to pick up a story. So Whitley headlines regularly appeared in the press, and not only on major issues as when he came out against Polaris in the Clyde, or in support of Scottish independence. Not every minister, struggling alone in his parish, is so saintly as not to feel wistful to see another receiving attention, and few understood the pain and pressure the High Kirk man was undergoing.

The Warr struggle to retain power was a sad business and went on for several years. I had been quite fond of Charlie Warr before Harry came. He seemed a quiet, agreeable man who wouldn't harm a fly. Admittedly neither would he set the heather on fire, but that ability is not given to everybody. He clearly loved the flummery in his position, but also he got on well with the pious elderly. When I came to see at first hand the destructiveness of his later behaviour, it was a revelation about the corruption of power. In the end you can say he was sick in the head with the fear that if he became bereft of his position and influence his life might be empty. Or you can just say he became a bad old man.

My mother offered me a completely tangential perspective on the modus operandi of the elderly Charles Warr. As assistant matron of a prestigious Edinburgh nursing home, she associated on a naturally gossipy basis with prestigious Edinburgh surgeons who were paid large sums to plunge the knife into prestigious Edinburgh citizens. On hearing that her son was assistant organist at St Giles, one such surgeon creased with mirth and told her the following story.

Driving from Mallaig to Fort William (single track with passing places) he encountered an obdurate car. It refused to budge. Out of the recalcitrant vehicle emerged a woman of character. It was Mrs Ruby Warr. She addressed the surgeon, "Will you please give way?" "No." "Do you realise who my husband is?" "Madam, if he was the Archangel Gabriel I would expect him to observe the courtesies of the road. He only has to retreat a few feet into a passing place. I am happy to wait here until he does so."

After a unconscionable time Dr Warr retreated.

Some months later, Warr, in for surgery, eyed his surgeon.

"Have I met you somewhere before?"

"It's possible; for example on the Mallaig road."

As Charlie Warr groaned, "Oh, my God," the anaesthetic overcame him and the surgeon plunged the knife.

I have never found Edinburgh less than fascinating, but I've never been sure about its fundamental human values. In the case of the Warr-Whitley fratricide, the people I blame are those who stood aside and let it happen, or actively stirred the pot. It was all very Edinburgh, I fear, not least when the Episcopal establishment, and its bishop Kenneth Carey, supported by the Kirk establishment, hounded John Tirrel, a young Episcopalian priest, because Harry had invited him to share in the dispensing of Communion at St Giles. You'd have thought Harry was proposing devil worship or fertility rites on the altar. It was a simple Christian gesture. But to these church politicians it was verboten: against the "rules" drawn up by the ecumenical strategists who ruled it to be against the Holy Spirit. Their rule (which naturally the Holy Spirit must adhere to) was that church union must be "organic". Thus was a young man's career destroyed. Harry begged Tirrel to save his career and desist, but the young man had seen a vision and stood firm. After various ultimatums his vocation was obliterated.

It was the most rotten ecclesiastical fix I ever came across. In writing that I know I'm not exaggerating. The distinguished (Episcopalian) theologian Donald Mackinnon, then divinity professor at Cambridge, briefly became involved in "The Tirrel Case". I interviewed Mackinnon in Aberdeen in 1987 for the TV series *The Quest*. In a break between filming he said it had lain on his concience ever since that he had not done more to protect John Tirrel and Harry Whitley from "spiritual slander". As I write, "organic" ecumenicism is no longer fashionable. The Holy Spirit got the timing wrong.

Harry and his family suffered over this period, but the children were resilient and passionate supporters of their father. Harry's wife Betty, a journalist and church historian in her own right, had seen spiritual corruption before—in the Scotland of John Knox and the covenanters about whom she has written with authority and humanity. In the manse she kept an open table to all and sundry of every persuasion and none. It was at such a Sunday lunch that Tirrel and Whitley met.

Was it all worth the struggle? You could say so. A majority of the St Giles session saw what was going on. Some apologised to Harry for the morass. Most were loyal to the minister they had called; many were loyal beyond the call of duty. When he retired, he left a young and lively congregation and sound finances. St

Giles did not have to come under the provenance of the National Trust as Glasgow's cathedral had to in order to guarantee its future.

Harry had one piece of advice for his assistants: go and break your heart in the parish. He didn't add: and save your soul, but we knew that's what he meant. And so he worried that I was dodging parish work when at the end of my two-year stint at St Giles I was asked to become Scottish secretary of the Student Christian Movement.

I wasn't dodging; I had a high view of parish work based on my father's commitment. But I had also inherited my father's doctrine of "the call". It just so happened that the SCM called me before any parish showed interest. It would be a job based in Edinburgh, so I could continue to share the flat with my mother, who was building up quite a track record with the orthopaedic departments of Edinburgh hospitals; she had her hip joint replaced many times. Also, the year before, I had become a founder member and leader in Scotland's first Telephone Samaritans project, operating in Edinburgh, and was glad not to give up that work, demanding though it was, including night duty.

In addition, it did not escape my notice that as the SCM job involved travelling to staff meetings and conferences in London, it would enable me to keep contact with Elizabeth, now entering her third year at the Froebel Institute's residential college at Roehampton, London. We were now engaged. The wedding was fixed for the following July. I had to pinch myself to check that I was really going to allow myself to be tethered to the mast of the good ship marriage. But it was so. One evening, walking with Elizabeth from Tollcross to the Cameo cinema it had become known to me in a flash of absolute clarity that she was the only person with the strength and spirit to stand with me for a lifetime. As I write, it is three months till our fortieth anniversary. How can she conceivably have put up with me?

12
London Zoo

Afer our first London night at a boarding house near Victoria Station, we took a Greenline bus out to Bushey, a village near Watford. The removal van was there, dwarfing our house. It didn't take much to dwarf it. We were number one in a terrace of erstwhile servants' quarters adjoining an erstwhile great house, now a grammar school. Our domicile was modest. Think of a thin slice of Nimble bread. It was so modest the removal men had given up trying to get the bed up the doll's house staircase. That night we slept on the floor. The next day a crane arrived and squeezed the bed through the upstairs window. Almost immediately I was magicked away up the M1 in a three-wheeled vehicle with a canvas roof to a weekend SCM meeting in Birmingham. And just married! I certainly sensed Elizabeth's absence. But enough sentiment: this is about a job.

In retrospect I'm embarrassed that I succumbed so easily to the lure of London and with my new wife trod the well-worn road south. But the salary, though not princely, would exceed that for the Scottish post; and they would buy a new tied house for us. So what of my mother for whom I'd given up Iona music? I'd never remotely considered imposing a wife on my mother, or vice versa, nor would my mother have considered it, though in fact she got on famously with Elizabeth and they became close friends during her remaining twenty years.

I would not have joined the SCM if I hadn't believed in it. It was a world-wide movement, its headquarters in Geneva, but exerting an influence on every continent. Students, after all, were supposed to spell the intelligent future of the planet. In contrast with other Christian student organisations, the SCM was committed to an intellectual agenda. The "student" element in the equation was serious: it meant study: study of the Bible, yes, and theology, but equally study of the world, its social, ethical and political issues on a broad front requiring scrupulous analysis.

I do not regret one second of my time with it, though for me personally it ended in disarray. That intelligent activity of the Holy Spirit which created the World Council of Churches had its first breath of life in the Student Christian Movement; and the best people at the top of the Church of Scotland, those with the broadest and most generous outlook on the Gospel working in the world, were in my time mostly those who had been inspired as students by the SCM.

The year before, up in Scotland, my task had been to organise the SCM branches in Scottish universities and colleges. That was interesting enough, and had begun to groom me in management skills. But a cloud no bigger than a man's hand had loomed on the horizon. His name was Ambrose Reeves. Ambrose was a bishop of the Church of England and had just taken over as general secretary of the SCM in unusual circumstances. It was he who had decided to bring me to the London headquarters as assistant general secretary with responsibility for study material, conferences and the magazine. It sounded just up my street— "pamphlets" remember, the word that had frozen the Cambridge don's face?

Everything about my boss broke the mould. That is probably why he chose me for a central role; he thought I broke the mould and that therefore our brains, if not our hearts, would beat as one. I actually did like the man, even when our working relationship broke down completely; but I can't say the same for Elizabeth. She was suspicious of him from the moment they first met. I thought that a little unreasonable of her, but when her suspicions turned out to be wholly justified, I'd begun to learn that my wife's many assets included remarkable antennae about people. Over forty years her score on bull's eye people judgments is uncanny.

My score isn't bad, but I've been bowled out more than once after ignoring a wifely caution. Ambrose had been Bishop of Johannesburg. It's a blunt reminder of age when one realises that the Sharpeville massacre is beyond the memory range of most people. South Africa's apartheid system was then the supreme moral issue for liberal opinion, churches, and students and specially for students.

After the Sharpeville massacre, Ambrose flew round the world raising public and governmental awareness of what had happened. It had been an impulsive move, and some thought he should have stayed in South Africa. To most he was a prophetic figure issuing a wake-up call to the white world. But now he had no job. His worldly goods were stored on a Southampton quay. He was an embarrassment to the Anglican church who had no diocese for him. I never found out who pulled the levers, though I could make intelligent guesses, but in the Anglican way, lo and behold, the excellent young general secretary we had, who had hired me in the first place, was found a parish; he wrote us a diplomatic letter saying that an exceptional situation had arisen in which a man of charismatic vision was available to lead the SCM into a new stage in its pilgrimage.

Golders Green was pleasant and prosperous, and up one leafy road was a large leafy villa. It was then occupied by the SCM HQ staff, and included a space large enough for the ruling body, a general council of students from all over the UK, to deliberate. Here I took command of a spacious room overlooking through casement windows a leafy car park. And here I met the fragrant Miss Denny. Ecce, la secretary! Miss Denny was a sport. Yet there were two shadows engrained on her soul which rooted the English rose in tragic seriousness. As a WAAF officer in the Second World War she had fallen in love with an airman. Before they got married, he was killed. He had remained the only one. The other and more immediate shadow was that she had formed the firm opinion that Ambrose Reeves was a man shrouded in darkness.

Ambrose was obsessed with the one issue of apartheid. Though small, even elfish, he was a charismatic speaker who inspired students up and down the country. As a personal crusade there was nothing wrong with that: it brought to life political awareness dormant in many a complacent student. But obsessions carry a heavy cost. The bishop became committed to turning the SCM into a one-issue movement. To that end, staff who didn't support such a policy were treated badly and eased out (we now call it constructive dismissal) and, even more worryingly, I became convinced that he was responsible for the disarray in the organisation's finances.

When the bishop told me face to face that he'd rather pull the SCM down about his ears than change tack, I decided to act. While Ambrose was at a conference in Vienna, I called a meeting of the general council. I outlined the danger we were in. There was a debate and a vote. I lost. I realised that I was out of a job, but I was still concerned about the objective problem. I submitted my resignation on one condition: that the Bishop of London headed an inquiry into the management of the SCM. The inquiry found against Ambrose Reeves, he left, and the SCM picked itself up and renewed a more modest existence. But it was never the same again.

I had no animus against Ambrose, and strangely he bore me no grudge. Our farewell was affectionate. Lynette Denny was right: he had a Conradian darkness within him. Perhaps it did arise out of Africa, but the SCM was not suitable for him to use as therapy. The clever Anglican fixers who had arranged his appointment were the guilty men.

Before Elizabeth and I crossed the channel for a summer holiday in Brittany, I took a call from a senior figure in the Church of England. He was known as a brilliant man with a brain larger than Kent and well-honed diplomatic skills, but my ear blistered as he let fly. To say he was incandescent is to take a minimalist position. He was very nearly screaming. How dare I, went his rant, challenge a bishop of the Church of England! And then the threat: I would never again hold down a serious job. A few days later, I still felt shattered by the fury of that phone call.

What that senior churchman had not known was that I had already embarked on another job: one with more serious influence (and a more serious salary) than the one I had just left.

It did seem rather miraculous. Just after I'd burned my SCM boats, Penry Jones phoned. He was a big Welshman, Christian layman, eloquent speaker, and had been industrial adviser to the Iona

Community. He told me he'd been appointed the first religious officer for ITA, the Independent Television Authority, which was charged with supervising the output of the ITV companies. Now ABC wanted a successor to Penry as the station's religious adviser, and they'd asked him to offer suggestions. He had put up my name. As a speaker at a couple of SCM conferences he'd seen me organise and compere the evening concerts, and he'd been impressed.

So it was that on a roasting morning of 1964's summer I found myself on the way to the Teddington ABC TV studios on the banks of the Thames. At last, I was about to sniff the aroma of real power, twitch to the seduction of the executive shirt sleeve, succumb to the smell of business machismo. The aroma turned out to be sweat. On this blisteringly hot day and despite the Venetian blinds, the closeness of the air on the ground floor of the executive suite drew the four of us into an unforeseen intimacy. Throughout the vicissitudes of the following five years I never quite lost that sense of being drawn into a family of interest, a sort of low-level mafia. Even when enmeshed in bare knuckle conflict or hung out to dry after a tactical reverse I was to find ITV an exceptionally agreeable working environment, and it began that day at my interview.

It didn't feel like an interview, more like the kind of conversations I'd been led into during my abortive pursuit of Oxbridge scholarships; except that these TV interlocutors were like dons who had actually grown up. The biggest was Lloyd Shirley, whose bulk lent authority to his Canadian twang. As head of features, he was to become my immediate boss. Lounging like a lizard in the chair behind the desk was Brian Tesler, the programme controller, a slighter man with a bright round face and a well-ironed light blue shirt. The third man was the joker in the pack. Corporate ambiguity hovered over George Brightwell's spare frame. He had a sardonic face but the eyes were slivers of shrewdness. He alone was dressed like a City gent, with dark suit and tie. He was obviously the administrator, the enforcer, the fixer. I liked them all.

The idea of becoming part of this world was an improbable

absurdity, so I wasn't in the least tense. I was amused at the presumption of this escapade and perfectly happy to enjoy a fragmentary encounter with creative piracy; even in this first meeting with the thrusting young brats of commercial television, I could sense an entrepreneurial jollity in the air—at the opposite extreme from the antiseptic intensive care wards of the BBC I was to tiptoe into a decade later.

On my first Monday, I arrived at the Teddington studios and was escorted to Lloyd Shirley's office. He was sharp and not one to mince words. When I declared my hand to the extent of saying it would be good to get rid of the Sunday evening "God slot" because it ghettoised religion, he clicked his teeth like sawn-off shotguns and put me right.

"Without that slot you'd be dead," he explained amicably.

I was happy at ABC, Elizabeth was happy teaching, and we had good friends, so I was surprised to be assailed by a duodenal ulcer sufficiently painful to make me obey the doctor's instruction to lie in a darkened room for half an hour after I got home every evening. I felt a complete idiot, but with medication it became manageable. I never took a day off work. It has refused to go, but it seems to hold no grudge against me and we have remained contented companions to this day.

We were fortunate. Our six London years were in the sixties. The swinging sixties can be caricatured, but we were there – and I can tell you that they were an absolute delight uniquely lit up by hope and happiness.

Hope is an indispensable ingredient of happiness, and to illustrate that I'll select not the young armada of King's Road mini-skirts, the blithe dotty films, the brave kitchen sink dramas, the art college rebellions, or the escalating Vietnam protest movement. Instead, I'll lead you gently to the doll's house front door near Watford.

We are standing in anticipation. Alongside is our neighbour, a widow who has voted Labour all her life, has drudged, canvassed, done the empty cold halls thing forever, and several times made the journey to Russia, not as a communist, but as a conscientious trade unionist. So what are we anticipating? Within our eyeline is a railway bridge. It carries the west coast main line from the north to Euston. On this train (our neighbour has done her research) will be a pipe being smoked by Harold Wilson. Yesterday he was Labour leader. Today he is Prime Minister. Having been overnight to hear the result at his Huyton constituency, he is returning to take for the first time the reins of power at No 10.

On the dot the train zooms over the bridge. We pointlessly wave. I turn to make some flip remark to our neighbour; and I'm choked. The tears streaming down her face are of joy. That's hope.

I keep having to remind myself that it was different being young, because nothing else can explain how we managed to enjoy life so much when employment was insecure and work was rackety and all-encompassing. ITV offered work which was fun, a jolly atmosphere, and opportunities for experimentation, but it never promised a safe haven for life.

Because in the early days of ITV, people were driven by creativity rather than a pecking order in a career structure, I felt the ambience amazingly free from backbiting. Only youthful resilience had kept my morale buoyant in the St Giles power struggle; and then I had been plugged into the vortex of a power struggle with Ambrose Reeves in the SCM. I had begun to wonder if this was what the adult world of work was all about; had I given up music for inevitable power struggle? So this daily experience of enjoying work in ITV aroused in me a new exhilaration.

Our banker, Rae Elliot, ex-Westminster Abbey choirboy and best friend of St Giles' Herrick Bunney, took us out to lunch and suggested the time had come for us to invest in a house. So we bought a new Wates house on the edge of Ham Common, near Richmond. I could now walk to work. It took ten minutes to stroll across grass to the Thames, across Teddington Lock, and up to my office.

To complete the idyll I had bought a half-Siamese black kitten for ten shillings in Teddington High Street for Elizabeth's birthday, and a month later for my birthday she had negotiated the arrival of a black and white collie puppy from a farm south of Glasgow, travelling to Euston by the night sleeper. We named them Sancho, as in Panza, and Quixote, as in Don.

After three months in the new house, two events collided: I was offered a new contract as executive producer and the week arrived for ITA to announce the new ITV franchises, which might mean that I would have nothing to executively produce.

Foreseeing this night of the long guillotines, I'd arranged for some overdue leave. I wanted to be as far away as possible when the news came out, and I wanted it to be an environment of such serenity that I would be indifferent to the trivial matter of a career going caput. Only one place to go: Sutherland. Not only Sutherland, but as far away in Sutherland as it is possible to go other than squatting in the Cape Wrath lighthouse – a fishing village called Kinlochbervie, quite near Cape Wrath, at the end of a road, jutting out into the Atlantic.

We arrived, booked into the little hotel, freshened up, appreciatively sniffed the air, and repaired to the lounge for restorative tea by log fire. From the depths of an armchair, a voice boomed, "Ian!" It was the religious adviser to Anglia Television. He explained he had wanted to get as far away as possible pending the franchise decision, and had chosen Kinlochbervie as guaranteeing no contact whatsoever with anyone from the world of television, let alone religious television.

Amidst much hearty laughter we agreed to ignore each other except for the odd tincture in the bar. A codicil was added: on the evening of the franchise announcement it might be more than one tincture.

It was a bigger ITV upheaval than expected. New companies were created, others were axed. What affected me was the major London-based weekend franchise. Half of ABC became Thames (the rest dissolved). Rediffusion was axed, but some staff went to Thames, and all its engineering staff and resources went to the new London Weekend Television, LWT.

There was to be a year before the carve-up was to be implemented on air, but in preparation time that wasn't much. Decisions had to be made about staff. We returned to London knowing that we had a year of security as ABC worked through its last year. But after that? As the new boy on the block, I wasn't over-confident.

I assumed LWT, launching a fresh menu of weekend programmes, would choose a new religious executive. Such an assumption was bolstered by the fact that, with one exception, the creative and managerial leadership of LWT, integral to its bid for the franchise, consisted of senior BBC staff. The one exception was the programme controller, Cyril Bennet, who was programme controller of the now embittered Rediffusion. He was a boisterous, shrewd, news and current affairs man. Having him embedded as programme controller of an echelon of ex-BBC top brass in LWT was a mistake which would end in disaster.

In post-Thatcher, post-modern, post-old Labour Britain, what I am about to relate may strain credulity. The management of ABC TV, a capital-based profit-making outfit, faced with its own extinction, took responsibility for resettling those of its staff who faced redundancy. Particularly striking were the activities of my new boss Michael Redington (Lloyd Shirley's successor as head of features), who had been one of a consortium which had bid for a franchise, and failed. He had nothing to look forward to. Yet in a spirit of selflessness he devoted his energy and time to easing his staff into jobs in the new set-up. Not "Get on your bike in the market-place" but "Now where would you contribute most creatively?"

So it was that through his good offices I found myself in a quiet restaurant facing an elegant cigar. The cigar was the head of children's programmes at the Beeb, now to head up children and religion at LWT. The cigar had a commanding voice, a smile the size of the Grand Canyon, and a tendency towards monologue. That alarmed me, until, cigar giving way to food, monologue gave way to dialogue, as one might expect of a future president of the Liberal Party. Doreen Stephens was magisterial in her womanliness, in that respect like Thatcher, though in no other. She was as intrinsically liberal as the future PM wasn't. I decided, by the end of the evening, that she was a good egg, and I was right. I don't know what she made of me, a wee timorous Scottish beastie, but she decided to hire me. A couple of weeks later in a noisy restaurant, this time for lunch, I found myself facing two cigars.

Cigar one, the slim one, introduced me to cigar two, a blunt instrument. This was Cyril Bennet, programme controller. It was a rollicking kind of lunch, more, I thought, according to his wish than hers, then he was up and away leaving Doreen and myself to chew over what had been said. Without wishing to be too wise after the event I think it is the case that I detected a lack of communion between him and her; or was it a mismatch between ITV and BBC? Or was it both?

Have you ever tried to save your life on a merry-go-round spinning out of control? You have? Then you know what the next year was like for me. It was possible, just, to breathe, eat, and wave to Elizabeth as I passed, but the rest of the week was divided between doing a Groucho Marx walk across the grass to ABC at Teddington and a bumper-to-bumper crawl round the North Circular to Wembley where LWT was painfully emerging into life. Having bought the Ham house to be only a pleasant walk from work, I had now cleverly contrived to put a three-hour round trip of crouching behind a car wheel between home and desk.

And there was a problem. I couldn't drive.

Enter Mr Grist.

Mr Grist was a retired police driver who ran a one-man driving school.

"Getting from Ham to Wembley by public transport is impossible," I explained to him on the phone.

"Mmm," he hummed, "I could think of a more inconvenient journey but it would take me time."

I realised that Mr Grist did laconic. That was reassuring. "I've got six weeks before I start work at Wembley. Can you get me through my test by then?"

"Mmmm. If we book the test today and if you're very good or very lucky, it isn't impossible."

He didn't just do laconic on the phone, he took it out on the road. After an hour of doing clutch, gear, and steering around the byways of Ham, he puffed his pipe and said, "Mmm, are you an organist?"

"I thought you had been a police driver, not Sherlock Holmes." I gasped.

"Your hand and foot co-ordination is unusually good. Ah, here's the Kingston bypass, just keep going." He puffed contentedly as cars and lorries suddenly swarmed around us like maddened bees. What helped was the car, that lovely old classic, the Triumph Herald. Apparently made of wood and leather, its lock turning was on a sixpence, the controls clunked like a Leipzig baroque organ, and Mr Grist was puffing his pipe beside me, so I felt invincible. Either he was a hypnotist, or his personality was honed to impart relaxation.

My family still describes my driving as "majestic" (i.e. slow): thirty five years on, Mr Grist is alive and well in me. Incredibly, I passed. I bought a Vauxhaul Viva, Elizabeth and I did a spin to Cornwall and back at the weekend, and on the Monday, as cockily over-confident as every new driver, there I was swarming with the best of them in that vile funnel of carbon monoxide, the North Circular Road, which was no road but a maze of interlocking rat runs, in no way circular, and spent very little time going north. I soon learned that if I rose at four and left the house at five I could cut the journey from ninety minutes to forty five; but there was nothing to be done about the evening journey except suffer it.

In my last eight months in London I worked exclusively at Wembley, but in the ten months before that, half the week was devoted to Teddington, where we still had to produce a full quota of programmes for the ITV network. Many were recorded or went out live on the Sunday, so home life was limited, but we worked around it. I might dash home for a lunch or supper in between work, or Elizabeth would join me for a drink in the riverside pub or a meal in the studio restaurant overlooking the river. It lifted my day when, at last going home of an evening, I would find her with Quixote waiting at the lock. Sometimes Sancho was there too: he loved loping in and out of the long grass.

In that last spurt at ABC we must have produced something like seventy programmes, excluding the regional epilogues which we arranged for transmission on Saturdays and Sundays. These required regular attendance for recording at Manchester's Didsbury studios.

One Saturday Elizabeth came with me, to spend the night at Manchester's Piccadilly Hotel and view my first TV epilogue, recorded already and transmitted only in the north. When the time arrived for me to study my face on the screen for the first time, the continuity announcer apologised for my absence and explained that I was indisposed. Sitting in the hotel room, Elizabeth said I looked perfectly well to her. I phoned the London continuity announcer and asked if they could let me know which particular disease I had.

"Being wiped," came the reply, followed by a snigger. "And what should I take for it?" "A stiff drink."

I have given no account of our programming. For better or worse, this is a narrative about my life, not a treatise on television. In any case nothing is more stale than lists of fondly remembered achievements and famous people. Suffice to say that, backed by generous budgets, a brilliant design department, bold and original directors, and an astonishing freedom of format and content, we came up with an unceasing flow of novel programmes.

There was a children's slot, a "serious" slot which had original drama with scripts by proven writers, and ambitious music programmes from the Hallé Choir to Duke Ellington. Naturally we also did probing discussions, in one of which David Jenkins, long before he was Bishop of Durham, made his first TV appearance. The interlocutor in this long-running *Looking for an Answer* series was the journalist-historian Robert Kee, one of the most distinguished thinkers I ever had the priviledge of working with.

I lived in London because I had been invited, first by the Student Christian Movement, then by ITV. But I hadn't exactly struggled against it. My father would have described it as a "call"—meaning from God. But I was human. I was capable of being seduced by the concept of power; and obviously there was more power in London then there was in douce, dreich and colonised Edinburgh. But I loved London not because it was powerful but because it was loveable. Sociologically, it was a zoo of vulnerable human tribes. Municipally it was a string of villages on two sides of a river bank. Spiritually it was a festival of self-expression. Politically it was a theatre. It was a breeze to be there for a while, but I never forgot where my roots were: in the land of my fathers. Therefore I turned down prestigious job offers from the USA and Geneva. I was still awaiting a "call" from Scotland – to a parish. I would have felt a fool if such a call had never come. Thankfully, out of the blue it did.

I was summoned to Peterhead, the most easterly point at which Scotland juts out into the North Sea, and eighteen miles from the Fraserburgh in which I was born. This was a real call: it had the stamp of authenticity. I was in one bound free from the chimera of so-called centres of influence. We were being invited to respond as a free man and woman to the only centre that matters: a call to care.

Between accepting the Peterhead call and leaving London I was living in two worlds. Once a decision is made to leave a place, that place imperceptibly fades like the Cheshire cat into unreality. There's a theological word for this psychological process: eschatological. Christians live eschatalogically, that is, under the shadow (or in the light of) the last things. In the case of Peterhead, I saw the situation literally in the context of my end. Having thrown all other possibilities away for the sake of a commitment to a Scottish call to a parish, I now found I would be back on the bare rocky coast of my childhood.

I pictured my ill father slowly climbing the steep pulpit steps in Fraserburgh, and thought it entirely plausible that I would also die in harness after a couple of decades battling through long dark winters. You may think that melodramatic, but as my father had never deserted a post without a pressing call, I did not intend to; I didn't foresee a further call that would justify my leaving

Peterhead. I had asked only one person's advice, my father-in-law's. He was unequivocal. "Go. The only thing that can save the Kirk in our day is preaching." So be it.

13
Winter Journey

A King's Cross platform on a bitterly cold evening in early February 1969 was not at the time a romantic place, however much one may invest it with sentiment in retrospect. It was the occasion of our leaving London.

My brother Alan was there, to carry things as well as to bid us farewell. Dog Quixote and cat Sancho were apprehensive, though at this stage quiet.

We were tired. Over the previous two days our worldly goods had been packed into two pantechnicons from the old Aberdeen removal firm Shore Porters. We expected them to turn up at the empty Peterhead manse the following day. The train we were boarding was an overnight motor-rail to Aberdeen. Our Vauxhall was this night the only vehicle attached to the rear of the train. The animals were deposited in the guard's van (remember those?) and we took up our sleeping berths in the adjoining coach. Alan waved sadly, we waved back bravely, and that was it. In a jiffy we were jolting into the King's Cross tunnel.

As Elizabeth assembled a picnic and nightcap in the cabin, I looked long and hard at her. Was I being fair? I had not thought myself a male chauvinist but the fact was that she had followed me in my career, I had not followed her. She'd married me, gone with me to London, faced possible unemployment, and given up her teaching career to support my work. London had been fun, but now she was following me away from London, almost certainly for ever. And to what? A cold place and a hard job, with no prospects. There had been no argument, no disagreement.

When the call to Peterhead had come, she had been as keen as I had at least to visit the place. She didn't know the north-east at all, so I had grimly warned her: no scenic beauty, no balmy Gulf Stream, no hills, no trees, bitter winters, working all hours, and little expression of gratitude from a dour people. When we'd driven up for our recce, we'd gasped as we turned the corner. It was a halcyon August day, Mediterranean-balmy. The sea all the way up had been painted blue. The marina, a bay enclosed by the red sandstone harbour wall the same colour as the town, was radiant in a rainbow of yacht sails. The church, which one of the elders showing us around apologised for—"it's just a big barn"— was a Georgian structure reminiscent of Fort George, brightly restored inside, with splashes of high colour in the form of cosmically themed windows recently installed by Pluscarden Abbey monks; the sun shining through them created an ambience which then, and every time I entered the building for the next five years, I revelled in.

Most compelling of all was the nature of the people we met: warm, bright, direct and humorous. As we drove back to Edinburgh that evening, Elizabeth asked, "Why did you tell me all those lies?" There was, we'd agreed, one disappointment. The elegant old manse, overlooking the bay, was not to be ours. They had sold it and bought what they called a "townhouse". Well, it was a house, and it was in the town. What it lacked in style it made up for in space, being multi-roomed with the kind of huge kitchen you eat in if you wish to feel grand—so we did—and a bathroom in which a regiment of Gordon Highlanders could have washed simultaneously. Thankfully it wasn't the kind of minimalist "modern" manse in which so many congregations, having sold the original, install a new minister; the main criterion being that it's easy to heat (i.e. small) with a cupboard in which sermons can be written if one's elbows don't stick out. It was, therefore, that shining image of a happy sunbathed town that we had held before us through our last cold wet months in London. Silly of course, but helpful in stiffening the sinews of hope.

So yes, we were united, but should I have so easily accepted her sacrifice? As the Deltic-hauled train swayed towards Peterborough and we nibbled and sipped, I reflected for the umpteenth time how lucky I was to have this person on my side. Courage is not only a *sine qua non* of creative work but of living. In the first five years that we were now rushing away from, it had not been all roses for her. There had been two miscarriages, one as we toured Germany, France, Switzerland, and Italy on a summer holiday visiting friends. She insisted on going on with the visits, and none of our friends ever knew the mental and physical distress she was in. The other miscarriage occurred on the day we were giving dinner and a bed to Dr John Marsh, principal of Mansfield College, Oxford, a notable theologian, and senior member of the ITA religious panel. Elizabeth wrote to him afterwards to apologise for the meal not being up to standard, and explaining why. He wrote back the gentlest of letters.

Less important, though animal lovers will understand not insignificant, had been two animal frights and one tragedy. Quixote almost lost sight in one eye after a horrific fight defending Elizabeth from a hound of greater size. And Sancho had incredibly survived a ghastly Hogmanay in Ham. We kept vigil all night as he was clearly in a desperate state, his spine paralysed and in terrible agony. At dawn on New Year's Day, with epic convulsions and a smell of burning rubber he passed out of his system, intact, a large rubber snake which we hadn't realised had gone missing. These two four-legged friends of ours hurtling north, were now succumbing to panic only a few feet away in a roaring, shoogling, lonely, friendless space. We paid regular visits through the night, but the most alarming one was as we passed through York. Echoing round that curved canopy, there ran the blood-curdling concatenation of Sancho in full howl. Sprinting in dressing gown into the guard's van I saw a trembling Quixote frantically licking Sancho's face. Oh, hell. Was I being fair to these helpless craturs? Obviously not.

The animal tragedy had been on a different scale. When I described some of my ordeals in dating Elizabeth I referred to Martine, the beautiful bay, part-thoroughbred beside whom I counted for little. I didn't actually mind because they were so obviously soul-mates. Not for nothing was the horse known as "mad Martine". At local gymkhanas crowds would gather to watch Paddy Blackwood, the acrobatic horseman who owned the Muriston stables, jump Martine. This attracted crowds because of the delicious anticipation of even Paddy being thrown. Elizabeth turned out to be the only person who could tame her; though tame doesn't cover it. They were equals: they communicated. When they escaped from a hunt, they would let rip together. Elizabeth's descriptions of the freedom in flying across lonely moorland in communion with landscape, wind, and a noble creature at full stretch enabled me, an unhorsey person, to catch a glimpse of primitive Gothic, Shelley's west wind in pure wildness.

We were in London when Paddy died and left Martine to Elizabeth. After much effort, partly through my sister Etta who arranged stopping-over places down England, the journey south was arranged. Near us, Ham House made fields available. It was a dream coming true. The week before the transfer, a thunderstorm frightened Martine in her field. She jumped the hedge—no problem—but a careless roadman had left barbed wire in the ditch. It pierced her skull.

That was another time I was in awe of Elizabeth's strength. She didn't complain or decline. It had to be business as usual, cheerful to all our guests.

In sleepers one doesn't sleep, one rolls in and out of tunnels of sensory deprivation. Somewhere in the depth of the night these tunnels join up so that, nudged into consciousness by a signal box light flashing past or a particularly clattery counterpoint of points, one wonders idly which planet one is on. In February there was the additional womb factor of perpetual darkness. Edinburgh, despite Elizabeth's family and my sister being only twenty minutes away, passed like the tremor of a duvet. Wakefulness crept in at Dundee. It was still dark, but by the light of that under-estimated city, and the winking lights of Newport across the Tay, one could see the weather was clear. Thank goodness for that. We'd be in Peterhead by lunch-time. My interest began to stir. Could it even be thrill? London had been a gem; but a small gem; it was a city, vibrant but quite wee, viewed from the air. Scotland was huge. In every direction it stretched to infinity. I felt my lungs opening, my spirit expanding. I was in a genuinely foreign place: my home.

Forty-five minutes later, the attendant knocked at the door. Two doll's house trays with doll's house teapot and tea biscuits. "This is Montrose. The—ah—weather has changed a bit." We jostled to snap open the blind and stare out. "A bit?" We were gazing blankly at a white-out.

Somehow the train managed to grind through a Tolstoy-sized blizzard and sob to a stop before the Aberdeen station buffers. There was a whistling sound. It was the wind. There was a smell. It was the herring, its aroma permanently distilled at the harbour adjoining the station. And there was a cat crying. It was our cat. Sancho needed a pee. Owing to the points at the car-unloading bay being inoperable because of frozen snow, the car couldn't be unloaded. Therefore we were unable to gain access to the cat's litter tray. Being a well-brought-up cat, he refused to do the needful in his basket, no matter what the pain. The station staff leapt into action. Although they had operational problems of their own (no trains) they rushed hither and thither like mad things. They brought sand reserved for putting out fires. Sancho declined the sand. They brought grit reserved for de-skidding the iced rails. Sancho declined the grit. In desperation they assaulted the points. Blow-torches, boiling water, for all I knew candles, were applied. At last the points moved, the car was unloaded, Sancho had access to his tray and with an aura of bliss, our cat condescended to urinate.

Sancho was relieved but we were not. The station staff, now treating us with a kindness I wish every asylum seeker received at Dover, kept us abreast about our forward travel. It came down to a simple fact: there wouldn't be any. The road to Peterhead was blocked. There was one road out of Aberdeen still open, if we hurried: the road to Old Meldrum. Maps were brought. Elizabeth dug out from her emergency bag a *Signposts* travel guide. At Old Meldrum was a country-house hotel. We repaired there, a sentence of whose euphemistic brevity I am proud. The last skitter up the hotel drive was a miracle of faith over adhesion. We slewed to a halt at what looked like a sketch of a door. The world was white, but peeping out from roof-high drifts were what might be fragments of windows. Not hopeful, we rang a bell. Footsteps. There was our angel; Brian, aged sixteen.

Yes. Come in. Tea, no problem. Dinner, no problem. Large

bedroom, for cat, dog and yourselves, no problem.

It had been a real castle. Our "bedroom" was possibly the original banqueting hall, stretching in every direction to the horizon. It was not warm. Cats being heat-seeking missiles, Sancho found the patch of floor faintly heated by the tangential, as distinct from central, heating. We all crouched round it. The public rooms, on the other hand, were well heated. Brian said he wasn't allowed to serve alcohol, but in his opinion this was an emergency. We concurred.

Apart from us he was the only human being in the besieged castle. No other staff had been able to get through the drifts, and the owner/manager/chef was stranded somewhere far away. But not to worry (seeing us twitch at the thought of the chef being stranded far away). He, Brian, was being trained as the sauce under-chef. Would chicken with brandy sauce be acceptable for dinner. Was he joking? We fell upon it.

After cooking and serving, Brian retired to his room high in the tower. We were now in virtually sole possession of an ancient castle submerged in the worst storm for years with no hope whatever of meeting with our new home, our congregation, or all our worldly belongings, possibly by now buried upside down in a snowdrift. Was there really a place called London, or had it been a dream?

At what one could laughingly call dawn, we looked out hopefully. Oh no! Someone had stolen the car, or, could that slight bit of white lumpiness be it, several feet under? When we asked brightly for a cooked breakfast, Brian said, "Oh, yes. Would chicken with brandy sauce be all right?" We settled for toast and frozen Frosties.

The telephone lines weren't down, a major godsend, and the Peterhead people were happy that we were safe. In their opinion we had acted sensibly. Conditions round Peterhead were impossible. The police estimated that two hundred vehicles were lying abandoned on the Aberdeen—Peterhead road. Bill Macdonald, session clerk, had contacted the Shore Porters removal firm. Our two vans had had a rough time but were secure in Aberdeen. It was now the weekend. We'd all see what could be done on the Monday. My induction to the charge, followed by the "social" (ceilidh) was not till the Wednesday.

So we bunkered down. Brian was meticulous within his limits. He even became adventurous over his hot stove; he tried chicken with whisky sauce.

In a generous gesture of comradeship, Elizabeth's brother Michael, a doctor in Aberdeen, fought through the snow with his wife Valerie to join us for dinner on the Sunday night. They were impressed by the chicken in brandy sauce. By Monday, snowploughs had cleared the roads for one-way traffic. We were in Peterhead by lunchtime, and at 2pm welcomed our pantechnicons. Not a single item was even scratched.

14

A Shattered Head

I don't have the second sight as my cousin Helen of Garve did, but I suppose some genetic trait of Highland intuition survives. So any job for me is essentially its people. Abstract analysis of what happened next, and then after that, and what policies were involved, or administrative structures and decisions, let alone blow-by-blow accounts of who won this round, and who that one, leave me as uncomfortable as if exposed on a rock with the tide out.

What can the difficulty then be in writing about Peterhead? A parish minister's job is nothing but people, and my five years there teemed with people as the North Sea used to teem with fish. All I have to do now is let them swim on to my onboard computer and download onto the page.

The problem is confidentiality. In my case, it was knocked into me by a manse childhood that the rule is absolute: keep your mouth shut. I can't therefore share my rich store of memories about Peterhead's fabulous people. Those who opened to me their door or their heart were entitled to believe it wouldn't finish up in a book.

One exception is Mac: Bill Macdonald. I extract him from anonymity, not only because he was the king-pin of the Muckle Kirk—that should entitle him to extra protection—but because he and his wife Millicent became close personal friends, and if he were still around I can hear him in the Buchan lilt expostulate, "But man, that's terrible what you've said! And why did you leave out the story of..." As likely as not it would be a story against himself.

When Harry Whitley wanted to cut the tumescent arrogance of us assistants down to size he would say, "A parish with a bad minister and a good session clerk: fine. Ministers come and go. A parish with a great minister and a poor session clerk: disaster." I had a great session clerk.

Mac came from the Turriff area, farming territory inland from Peterhead, but he had adopted Peterhead with a ferocity of love which knew no bounds. Wherever you went in the town, he seemed to be there; even if he wasn't visible you could feel his energy crackling under the town like the New York Metro.

His day job was the TSB bank. Technically, he managed it. More like, he infested it. It was strategically placed at the centre of Broad Street, acting as a citizens' advice bureau, legal advice agency, job centre, financial consultancy, youth co-ordinator, senior citizens' tea and sympathy depot, and ecclesiastical confessional.

As his house was over the bank, Millicent was available for a bit of TLC—when she herself was not out and about. I seldom missed a day without calling in at the bank. We both found it helpful, I the chairman of the board touching base with the chief executive. But I went regularly for a different reason: to extract energy from him.

It was a pit-stop which frequently kept me going, as it did so many others. And he wasn't even a town councillor! If I was to be diligent I would do some research to compile a list of all the committees, boards, societies, and activities he was on, but that wouldn't convey much. For one thing, he was never just "on" anything. Smallish though he was—which helped to make it all tolerable—and no matter where he was in the room or hall, his flailing brain dominated the gathering like subliminal bagpipes. Till eventually, unable to stomach any longer the slovenly thinking around him, he would erupt, smashing a fist repeatedly into the other hand till his forensic outrage became a tide of molten lava engulfing the assembled company. What was invigorating to me (because I was usually not competing), but galling to his peers, themselves not deficient in energy, was that Mac was nearly always right, damn him.

When he was not right, and it was a matter involving me on a church matter or over a person we both knew (he was a Justice of the Peace and deputy sheriff), I found a surefire way of dealing with it. Giving him twenty-four hours to get off the barricades, I'd ask for a half-hour chat. We'd meet either in the manse, or on his territory over one of Millicent's suppers served, as was the Peterhead way, on dreadnought trolleys armed on every deck from bow to stern with pastries, pies, sandwiches, scones and cakes.

After suffering mutual damage to our superstructures and settling low in the armchairs, Mac and I would review our little problem and invariably—I stress invariably—resolve it. He was a man in whom theatricality and rationality fought each other to a standstill, whereupon the fundamental quality of love flooded his heart and took command.

He was a very great man. A metropolitan notable might smile condescendingly at such greatness being attributed to a small-town figure; but that would reveal a lack of discernment so chronic as to disqualify such a person from any comprehension of greatness whatsoever. I write this with feeling, because when we left London some friends and colleagues had asked, "But who will you talk to up there?" Elizabeth and I found more natural intellect, street theatre, and compassion in Peterhead than anywhere else, and over much of rural and small-town Scotland I expect it is the same.

I believe that few people grasp what an immense job every parish minister faces. To me it is amazing that so many of this frequently patronised profession climb so many mountains, plumb so many depths, survive so many dead calms, and batter through so many storms to the end. Every minister has to evolve strategies for mental and physical survival. I was lucky in that I had Elizabeth, young and resilient, with the insights of a manse daughter, to share problems with.

One simple tactic in self-defence was that we made Mondays work-free zones. Emergencies apart it was an iron rule; but the corollary was that we had to remove ourselves physically from the town. I don't want to go on at what may seem tedious length about this, but I can't overstate the significance of such a partnership. I may have become over-dependent on companionship as a result of being virtually an only child owing to the age gap with my older siblings, and then losing a home at thirteen, but I doubt if I am that peculiar. I positively enjoy solitude and there are situations, e.g. writing, which make me intolerant of disturbance. Well, perhaps that's it. I'm intolerant: intolerant of being alone when I want company, and intolerant of company when I want to be alone. In other words, an egocentric monster, a typical human male.

No, I want to dig deeper.

In Peterhead it was a rare week that did not involve me in two or three funerals. That was not unusual in a town of 15,000 where, as the main parish church, we attracted the floating voters who needed assistance through the rites of passage of baptism, marriage, illness, death and unexpected tragedies.

Although every minister has to develop some professional detachment or face breakdown, there's a limit to which you can thicken your skin without losing the sensitivity to suffer with the people who need you. There was no crematorium then in the town, so nearly everyone was buried in the bleak cemetery which sloped up a hill facing the North Sea. Many was the dark afternoon in a winter month when a north-easterly whistling straight off the sea with horizontal rain or snow would whip away my words round the empty grave and lash the numb faces of family and friends in black.

If that was the third such occasion in forty eight hours, and I had spent hours sharing shock and distress in several houses, I would crawl home, empty, a walking wounded, scarred by doubt that in the end love was anywhere in the cracks and crevices of fate. Also I was cold and wet. Then I would walk into the big bright warm kitchen where Elizabeth was waiting with a pot of tea, hot cheese scone, and—this is the point—the instant recognition as to whether I needed to talk or needed not to talk. I daresay I would have coped if she had not been there; but the strain would have been greater, and cumulatively so.

It worked the other way. She had been unceremoniously press-ganged into the presidency of the Woman's Guild. It was a mammoth guild; the hall was always overflowing at its meetings because women from all the other churches came to let their hair down, there being lots of fun and very little "religion". Controlling those pullulating hordes gave my wife a useful training in public speaking, at which she became a dab hand. She had been warned. When I had preached before the vacancy committee in Cults Parish Church, we'd met afterwards for a confrontation with the committee. It had been a tough grilling. We were given two test questions: one to her, one to me.

Hers was a googly: was she for or against gambling at church events? Ouch! The Church of Scotland was divided on this issue. There was no way she could know which in this company was the right answer. The faces, specially of the women, were strained. Clearly it was the $64,000 question. She decided to say what she thought: she could see nothing wrong with it. A sigh of relief soughed through the rafters. She was in. If I survived my question, we were both in.

"Can you shout?" shouted a big burly man. "This is a small church with a microphone. Our church is big with no microphone." There was only one answer. Having won on gambling, I gambled on shouting. "Oh yes," I remarked quietly, "I can"—I turned the volume up—"SHOUT!" Laughter all round, followed by a slap-up lunch at the Atholl Hotel.

I gather vacancy committees are not like that now. More's the pity.

Anyway, we were warned. Elizabeth shouted at guild meetings, but in a refined St George's Edinburgh kind of way. And in the pulpit I bellowed, to some effect, as I thought. At my second session meeting, one elder put it straight. "Could you manage to shout a little less loudly? Two or three of the older members say you are frightening them." Most of the session nodded, gratified not that I had been rebuked, but on the contrary that they had chosen the right kind of minister who could scare the hell out of the flock.

Shouting was indeed not my style. It's difficult to shout jokes. I learned to master the acoustic. Audibility is not about noise, but focus.

Elizabeth enjoyed the guild meetings, but not the guild

committee meetings. The committee of thirty was as big as many guild memberships. Here she simply couldn't believe what was going on. What was going on was a frank exchange of views. It wasn't only the men of Buchan who called a spade a highly adorned shovel. More than once, the young damsel of the manse arrived home—late—in tears after a committee agenda had gone up in the smoke of a verbal punch-up.

What really got to my wife was that the very next morning in a shop she would bump into two women who the night before had all but scratched each other's eyes out; and here they were chatting as if they were lifelong friends—which of course they were. It didn't take long for us to learn that these people loved drama. Every incident in a day was street theatre. Life in the town was a soap opera, and they were not only the actors but the script writers.

A year in, I received a deputation of four older elders, notably argumentative ones. They regretted that meetings of the session were much duller than they used to be. The session clerk, treasurer, and I always seemed to have things cut and dried. I hardly ever expressed an opinion, I just chaired the meeting. They were never given a chance to work up a head of steam before the meeting—Bill Macdonald as session clerk kept matters confidential till the meeting. When I took votes, the majority always won. Worst of all, the meetings were short, they got home long before bedtime. It took me some time to digest the fact that these weren't compliments, but fervent complaints. Then the penny dropped. I wasn't shouting enough. But most of the session approved; they quite liked getting home not in a state of collapse.

Why should a god, a horse, a rat, have life,
And thou have no life at all?
Thou'lt come no more, never, never, never, never, never!

As a schoolboy I had been overwhelmed by these words as George Booth in his Shakespeare classes at Fettes had dragged us mentally kicking and screaming into the dark. And as a student I had shuddered alone at a winter matinee in Edinburgh's Kings' Theatre as Donald Wolfit, heading a touring company, had shredded himself and me in the *King Lear* storm scene. He had invested Lear's despair not only with power but with that pitiless bleakness which is at the centre of pity in the tragic Greek and Shakespearian sense.

Now here I am on my own blasted heath, a moor for which the word bleak might have been invented, on a hill above the village of Gaimrie. I'm looking north over the village to the pounding North Sea, a sea whose grey heaving mass is so malevolent it chills the heart, but which one can only see when there is a break in the sleet enveloping us, icy half-white stuff driven by the gale and slapping the faces of our little huddle of men.

I am only about three weeks into Peterhead. I've already conducted several funerals—February is a killing month for the elderly in God's waiting room—but this is of a different order. We are burying, in the place where he was born and had his childhood, a young man who a few days before had put a shotgun in his mouth and pulled the trigger. The human figures supporting each other are expressionless. Suicide stalls the engine of compassion; bleakness is all. There are no explanations.

The journey from Peterhead to this terrible place had taken an hour, the black hearse leading as in a gothic dream, myself in the undertaker's black Volvo, a handful of family cars dolefully following. The undertaker, a burly man much loved in the town, and I had already struck up a conversational friendship, but today we had been silent. The weather and the occasion clamped our spirits.

Round the empty grave, I struggle to clothe words in the hope of the New Testament, but my spirit longs to pour out the darkest words from the Old; those places where the psalms gouge out hopeless songs from the bottom of the pit. I feel my father and his father fighting in my breast to cry out through me the nameless protests of all the dead of all the years before venturing on incantations of the Christian hope. I try to express both parts of the equation, but for whom? Is anyone hearing? I doubt it. The whistling wind whips away words. Shouting is no good here. The storm smothers all life, even hopeless life. The deed done, the suicide and the life that led to it buried together, we climb into our vehicles and go away across the bleak dead moor. My soul swings on a black thread in the swaying black Volvo.

Over an early meal I don't say much to Elizabeth, but she knows it wasn't good. We talk about other things. She has a meeting at seven. On the way out she places on the kitchen table a large book. I hardly notice. I'm ruminating. I haven't yet stayed in on an evening. I've been visiting, getting to know people in their home or activities in the hall or at meetings. But an echo from the void inside me tells me that tonight I have nothing to offer. Uneasily I boil the kettle for fresh tea, and see the book. It is new to me. I sit down and look at it.

I think of Yeats' cloths of gold, though this cloth-bound volume is not under my feet but in my hands. The cloth is of light gold irradiated by darker gold sunflowers. I remember why, during a programme I had produced in London, the Dean of Guildford had cried out, "You can't fuck a flower", because he felt the art students heckling him on behalf of the flower power philosophy of the musical *Hair* ("Let the sun shine in") were failing to connect with the real world of power, violence, suffering, evil. Here I am in a northern winter darkness at the end of the sixties. It was a shattered head I had buried today; no sun shining in.

Two words are embossed on the cover in a third tone of gold: "News Cuttings". I can see that the fifty or so pages are of thick cream parchment. I open the book. On the first page Elizabeth has glued words of mine on a card I had enclosed in a package I had given her on New Year's Day only a few weeks ago: "Ian invites Elizabeth to an exploration of what London can offer that Peterhead cannot."

I press my elbows on the kitchen table, hold my head, dig my fingers into my forehead.

It had been a wonderful fortnight, spilling glory. A plethora of suns had shone in. The package had contained tickets for Covent Garden, the Festival Hall, the Albert Hall, the best plays in town. We had agreed months before to give our date of availability as a clear two weeks after my finishing at London Weekend TV, so that we could have two weeks of freedom in London structured in. Parties had fitted spare slots. In taking leave of the city we had come to love, we turned it into the festival that in a broad sense over five years it had been.

Unknown to me, Elizabeth had quietly collected reviews, photographs, farewell notes, memorabilia, and linked them with diary entries of her own; and waited for a moment to let me remember alone. It was her gold casket of jewels.

I trod gently on the dream.

The first pages bulged with press cuttings of the party David Frost (aged twenty-nine) had thrown on 5th January for 2,000 guests at Alexandra Palace, TV's birthplace. Elizabeth's entry is factual:

Arrived about 11pm. I wore my scarlet and gold caftan and Ian his red waistcoat with gold dragons. Reached the front door at the same moment as Judy Garland. She is tiny, almost invisible between large red floppy hat and red shoes. She and entourage entered the Great Hall in front of us and David greeted her with a hug. We slipped in behind and stood drinking in the thunderstorm of canned music, roaring machines and neon lights. We jumped when David descended on us from behind to shake hands and greet us by name. How can he remember 2,000 names? He and Ian talked for a few minutes about David's controversial Enoch Powell interview—he kept thanking Ian and blessing him. Diana Dors was puffy and new husband looked wet behind the ears. Almost walked over Ronnie Corbett at the Candy Floss Stall. He's even tinier than you think. Heard Cilla Black's laugh as her dodgem smashed into a scaffold. Kingley Amis in smoking blue velvet very attached to a young man. Lulu's hair redder than Ian's waistcoat. Yoko Ono and John Lennon looked identical neuters. Roy Kinnear came on to the dodgems and his girlfriend almost fell off. Also on the dodgems was Norman St John Stevas (he's been dizzy for three days since). Christopher Martin [ITA Religious Officer succeeding Penry Jones], was a young Mr Pickwick, black velvet jacket and floppy bow, tiddly enough to kiss me, so I dared him to go and kiss Fenella Fielding equipped in yellow chrome and vast false eyelashes. We lost Christopher after that. Stirling Moss spent his whole time trying to hold up his girl's backless, almost topless, outfit...

Gaimrie. The sleet, the sea, the grave, the pointlessness, the shattered head...

Next page: Klemperer conducting at the Royal Festival Hall. Klemperer had saved Mendelssohn from the patronising treatment of most conductors, making the "Scottish" symphony a brooding structure; and he'd utterly transformed the Hebrides overture. Here is a cutting from the review of our concert by the *Telegraph* critic John Warrack:

It is this quality of order imposed on sensation that made Klemperer's readings so fresh, far more vivid and satisfying than just a sharper exhilaration. How often the Hebrides overture has sounded like a "wish you were here" postcard. Klemperer made the crescendos not waves surging against the roof of Fingal's Cave, but a more fundamental force. This was tone-painting raised from aural snapshot to the level of highest art.

As I sit at the Peterhead table, something stirs in me ...structure, force, art... If I am to live with real life tragedy, I must meet it head on and ride it, as Klemperer had ridden the orchestra to make Mendelssohn real as life. I must find the essential music of Peterhead, not by evading the dark but by embracing it.

Even so I hesitate to turn the last pages in the book, both dying to plunge into the most golden memory of all, yet fearful that in doing so my courage will fail.

I turn.

The pages blaze at me. The burning sky, the universe an open furnace. Every star an Inca city. The spheres of heaven open-mouthed. The pages are empty, but for one heading: "Covent Garden, *The Meistersingers of Nurenburg*, by Richard Wagner, conductor George Solti."

Elizabeth has left the pages blank so the sun can shine in. In the mid-sixties we had travelled to Bayreuth to see *The Ring Cycle* in the Festival Theatre which Wagner designed himself for his operas. That had been a fairy tale, strolling in evening dress up the avenue in mid-afternoon, returning to our boarding-house under the moon; in between there had been two long eating intervals from which we were summoned by trumpets (no pate de foi gras). *The Ring* completed, we'd climbed (by rail tunnel and cable car) the 10,000-foot Zugspitz. From the top, silver Alpine pinnacles glinted from horizon to horizon like a planetary pipe organ. It had been a dizzy experience.

The Meistersingers is different. It's about the earth and conflicts of human values, not legends of the gods. It's conventionally called Wagner's "sunniest" work, and with reason. But the sun's intensity involves dangerous power. It causes cancer. Even less than Mendelssohn is it a picture postcard. From the prelude to the peroration of Act 3, it is an exercise in the power of art, appropriating the complexity of Bach's counterpoint, the open joy of Handel's major chords, and the flowing weight of Brahms' beard, finally alchemising these traditions into the gold of Wagner's sound world.

The last act is a tumult of such happiness that having reeled out of Covent Garden on the Tuesday night, on the Wednesday we got tickets to go to *The Meistersingers* again on the Thursday night. I sit now at the Peterhead kitchen table, seeing and hearing it again and again until Solti's manic energy, broadening out into the apotheosis of Act 3, calms my pulse.

By the time Elizabeth returns home, I am drained, but resolved. I know what I have to do. My first Peterhead crisis is over.

What I have to do is celebrate the lives of my parishioners from birth to death. I have to descend into the shadows of the orchestral pit to provide the support which enables them to live out on life's stage the threnody of their daily doing and being, in the theatre of being alive. But since my principal tool will be not music but words, it is in the pit of word-making that I must work. They have called me to be their word-maker, their bard, their celebrator, their

Greek chorus. I am to be, however inadequately, their mastersinger, attempting through the mechanisms of art, word, and liturgy, to be a rainmaker, a rainbow maker, and when life and happiness fail, and clouds blot out all light, even there I have to forge words to carry them through.

It's an absurd, an impossible task, but it's one I can understand and to which I can totally commit. Yes, I will work at letting the sun shine through, and with help from a cosmos forged in a blaze of light there will be not only light in it but love.

In October James died. He took only one day to be attacked by a mystery virus, to be catastrophically ill, and to leave us. He was eighteen. He was also the only child of Bill and Millicent, my session clerk and his wife.

Neither before nor since did I see a community so stunned by one death. James Macdonald was to the town a young Jimmy Stewart, Hollywood's Mr Nice Guy. He was universally popular, bright, cheerful, courteous, straight. One week before he died, he'd gone with his dad to Aberdeen to check out the digs which he was due to occupy in a few days for the university career which to judge by his school achievements would have been distinguished.

Because the Macdonalds lived over the bank in the town centre it wasn't a private drama. The mystery bug struck in the morning, in the forenoon many saw the stretcher carried down into the ambulance which rushed James to Aberdeen's Royal Infirmary. The Aberdeen labs worked flat out to identify the virus but there was nothing like enough time: by the evening it was all over.

While I was in Aberdeen with the parents, Elizabeth was hosting a gathering of all the town doctors in the manse. It wasn't an organised event. Every doctor by instinct separately made his way to the manse as being emotionally the nearest they could get to the empty bank flat, but also because as a group they were pole-axed by the devastating public demonstration of their professional impotence. Elizabeth gave tea and snacks to the doctors, keeping entirely to herself the irony that while she did what she could to comfort them they were unable to comfort her, for they didn't know that during the night she had had another miscarriage, fortunately the last.

The Muckle Kirk was packed by school and community for the public farewell to James. Never was *Guide me, O Thou Great Jehovah* more rousingly sung.

Not that it matters, indeed it sounds trivially self-referential, but I guess that funeral, the first of many such public rites of passage, was when I found my true voice. Now I had no sense of imposing myself as an outsider on a community's life. These people needed me. I had to say the right things in the right way. I truly was their word man, and though all words are inadequate, I had to avoid the ones that are more inadequate than others. Any minister will tell you how awe-ful a moment it is when he or she walks into a church packed with grief.

But it's that huge mass which lifts you and everyone else. You let the eddies of pain provide the strength. As a plane needs a headwind to take off, or a surfer needs the threatening wave or a climber needs the force of gravity to energise, the preacher finds the eagle wings spoken of by the poet who wrote in the psalms. It is a mystery, but without it no footballer could play, surgeon operate, firefighter leap into a fire, conductor conduct, actor act, leader lead, or minister pray.

15
Centre of the Universe

In our second Peterhead autumn I had my nervous breakdown. I
have to say it was one of the neatest, smoothest, tidiest
breakdowns I ever came across, though as I've never had
another one, empirical evidence is limited.

We'd had a perfect summer holiday: two weeks in a tiny cottage
in Cullen's picturesque harbour, and two weeks in a rented house
opposite Gruinard Bay in Wester Ross, the latter owned by Bill
Mackenzie who had been governor of Peterhead prison and was
now in charge of Barlinnie. In balmy weather, I'd read the three
volumes of *Lord of the Rings*. Over three decades before it became
a global film property, I was enchanted; its open confrontation
between light and darkness in a context of pilgrimage uncannily
reflected what we were experiencing in our daily parish
switchback of joy and sadness.

Our monthly parish magazine would look old-fashioned now.
Printed on good paper by the local newspaper, I was encouraged to
write a substantial essay as the centrepiece. I found the Tolkien
style infecting my prose as I sought to find a language which
would reflect the heroism of ordinary people in conducting and
surviving the ups and downs of their lives.

The rest of the magazine bulged with news of church activities
returning in the autumn. I think it was while surveying this
plethora of functions about to explode in my face that I felt a
sudden vacuity of the brain. Elizabeth was in the house so I asked
her if she would accompany me in the car. I drove up on to a
lonely piece of moor where we often walked Quixote. I parked the
car, switched off the engine, and said, "I think I'm having a small
breakdown. I feel well, I'm not stressed, and my mind is clear. But
suddenly I can't make decisions. Either I can't, or I'm so allergic
to decisions that I won't. Would you please take over and make all

my decisions? Let's say for two weeks, then I know I've got that period to relax. I will continue to do everything while you pull the strings. That way, nobody will know."

She didn't fuss, agreed at once, and for two weeks she ran the parish, scheduled my every move and told me what to do and when to do it. As I was otherwise perfectly well, I seemed to everybody to be a normally functioning person, and not a single thing went wrong or failed to be done.

After two weeks I said thank you very much and picked up the reins. Nothing like that has happened to me since, though later at the BBC I was to employ a mental trick distantly related. In the second of my sixteen years at the Beeb I resigned my post, but never told anybody. That way I was able to turn up, draw my salary, and do the work without feeling snared in a bureaucratic trap. I never withdrew that phantom resignation. It played the role of a fat cheque in the back pocket and a great comfort it was.

The relationship between pastor and people has well been compared to a marriage or, in modern terms, a partnership. I was fortunate in that my other partner, Elizabeth, understood this. Otherwise she might have cavilled at the loss of holidays, weekends and weekday evenings and nights.

And what about losing Christmas Day? The schedule went like this. Half-past midnight till 2am: post-watchnight service vigil with Bill and Millicent Macdonald, a tradition begun the first Christmas after James died. It was a special moment for all of us. They'd lost their son, we remembered our miscarriages. But, lifted up by the midnight service, we were quietly happy together. In my subsequent BBC years they returned the compliment every Hogmanay immediately after my 1am epilogue, perversely called *Prologue*.

Mac would come on, "Man, that was terrible, your worst yet. Didn't understand a word. You're looking awful, you'll be needing a tonic. And where did you get that tie?"

On Christmas Day, a brief morning service was followed by lunch at the Cottage Hospital, an excellent medical and minor surgical facility run by a majestic matron. The patients were lavishly indulged after I said grace and a doctor carved. Afterwards we repaired with the staff to their rest-room where blue lagoons (don't ask) were polished off with escalating animation. We had to be temperate as at 3pm the next call was a Christmas service and tea at the main home for the elderly, where I had to renew my shouting as many inmates were deaf. I also played the piano with festive force. Every Christmas turned out to have curiously mild weather, so we finished off the day with a long walk on the moors.

One Christmas, I had to fit into these commitments the funeral of a young farmer's son. A funeral at Christmas? Yes, my instinct was to cry out that this was a day for celebrating birth not death, but fortunately bit my tongue, realising how academic such a thought would seem to a family who had specially asked for the funeral to be in the context of seeing the hope of God in a baby. This is what parish life is about: give and take. Passing on whatever insights are given to you, and receiving back insights flowing from the heartaches of the people.

It wasn't a funeral, but something even more heart-stopping, that turned another Christmas into a gateway to hell—it is impossible to ignore the visual and musical echo of the scene in *Don Giovanni* where the statue of the commodore walks on stage.

Tom Galloway, our organist and friend, wasn't a great drinker— of alcohol. But he drank of life with his whole being open to everybody and everything. He was in charge of the music at Peterhead Academy. Every one of the 1,600 pupils adored him. He was a big man, tall, broad, bursting with bonhomie, and hilarous invention. As was said of the late John Smith, he would start a party in an empty room. He had one deficiency; he lacked an arm. Just before I met him he lost it through cancer.

Being a brilliant musician, he had rewritten Bach's organ works for two feet and one hand, and his playing on Sundays was spectacular and profound. His car driving, was, if not profound, certainly spectaular. His daughter told me of being a passenger while he drove half-way up Ben Nevis steering and smoking with his one hand. Three years later the other arm had more or less vanished. There was some kind of residue wrapped in bandages.

His last public appearance was just before he entered hospital for the last time. The academy choir and orchestra were performing Handel's *Messiah* in the church, and Tom was going to conduct. The doctors insisted he was not to conduct. It was obvious: he couldn't. He had nothing to conduct with. As usual, with complete good humour, Tom paid no attention. The church was packed. The tall torso entered and faced his singers and players. It was the most searching performance of the *Messiah* I have ever heard. An almost dead body displaced by mind and the music of the spheres. And at its heart, a suffering man—Ecce Homo.

Grant us, O Lord, an unquiet night and a true end.

If life in general is a mix, in a close community sadness and cheerfulness are inextricably mixed. Just walking down the street was pure street theatre. Boisterous characters felt free to say what they liked to me and I felt free to make whatever retorts came up my back.

We had friends of all sorts. The town's brightest lawyer was Jock Smith, whom I had known as a child in Fraserburgh. He'd been at Fettes, slightly ahead of me. As a solicitor he did many unsolicited acts of kindness, so that when the oil came to Peterhead and he and I had vigorous debates on the pros and cons of the encroaching developments, I realised he had a vision for the town which may have been more people-centred than the issues I raised in the pulpit and in local newspapers.

The doctors and their wives were a lively bunch who dispensed hospitality at the level of dinner rather than high tea. And we formed a relaxed attachment to John and Rosemary Sewell, when they arrived to stay opposite us half-way through our stay. He was doing research for Aberdeen University into the social effects of the oil boom; she was a social worker, responding to the needs of the vulnerable day and night with a wholeheartedness which I often thought put us clergy to shame. John, latterly Lord, Sewell advanced through COSLA to be minister for fishing and agriculture in the first Blair administration.

We were not, therefore, isolated from the wider world. If I've given an impression of being cut off, that is because being cut off is what I expected. Instead of which I found that Peterhead was civilisation – with Aberdeen only an hour down the road.

Then just down the road from Aberdeen was London. I was appointed chairman of the Scottish religious panel of the ITA which entailed regular meetings in London. I became fond of the mini-steak baps on the night sleepers there and back, so that I only missed a day of parish work, and was much cheered by the amazement of ITV executive friends that not only had I survived the inconceivable ordeal of living outside London, indeed as near to the Arctic as one can get without sleighs, but I was looking more healthy and bouncy than they were.

The Scottish panel met in Glasgow. I had no premonition that Glasgow would soon become our home city, but I loved its buzz, and going there meant by-passing Edinburgh, always an encouraging thought.

I haven't mentioned Edinburgh for a while. Should I not have been traipsing there every other week in order to coagulate with the hundreds of other peripatetic ministers and elders from Shetland to Stranraer meeting in the committee rooms of the Whitehall of the Kirk, 121 George Street? Oh, yes, I should, but oh no, I didn't.

From childhood I'd been fitted with a 121 bypass. Starting with my father, continuing with my uncles, and extending to every minister that entered the Fraserburgh manse, I observed a clinical condition one might describe as the 121 shudder. If, in a forgetful moment, some kindly old, or idealistic young, dog-collar let fall from his lips the fateful number 121, eyes would roll and general shuddering take place. My father, uncles, etc. did their duty. They even took their place on the rota to attend the General Assembly.

The effect of the Assembly on my father was so pronounced that my mother prescribed a week of convalescence. As an Edinburgh Royal Infirmary trained nurse, her regime was draconian. She put my dad on a building-up diet of his favourite fry-ups, imposed rest periods with novels and magazines and insisted on a course of Guinness to alleviate post-Assembly tristesse. After about a week he would emerge one morning bright-eyed and bushy-tailed, all traces of Assembly amendments to counter-motions and revised deliverances wiped from his memory cells, and exhilarated at the prospect of once again meeting real people.

This recurring malaise I proposed to avoid. I slightly lapsed in that I did attend some committees as a toe-in-the-water-dipping exercise, but was so bitten by verbal crabs, stinging jellyfish, hardboiled lobsters and procedural basking-sharks, I retreated to the dialogues I genuinely enjoyed with the Peterhead characters categorised as sick and housebound who had more energy, wit and wisdom between them than a thousand committees. I also represented the Presbytery of Deer at one General Assembly, but when I reported back to presbytery as truthfully as I could, a couple of senior ministers worried that I lacked reverence for the supreme court of the Church. Oh good, I thought, I've not yet been infected.

But in Peterhead our metropolis was not London or Edinburgh or Glasgow; it was Aberdeen. Those Londoners who were surprised to discover that Scotland had universities might have difficulty believing that Scotland also had culture. Should I press the point that as a boy I attended my first opera in Fraserburgh? Admittedly it was *The Gondoliers*, but the orchestra was advertised as "...containing members of the Scottish Orchestra", which prompted an uncertainty about what else it contained.

Scottish cities, of course, boasted not only theatrical life—Aberdonians were natural actors—but beautiful theatre buildings, and Aberdeen's His Majesty's Theatre was (still is) a gem frequently packed with bus parties. One should explain that no north-eastern group, association, company, or guild was ever so happy as when it was in a bus. Buchan roads were on a summer afternoon or winter evening clogged with buses songfully proceeding between X, Y, and Z and back. When the then ground-breaking musical *Hair* began a run in Aberdeen, the omnibus pace heated up. As guild president, Elizabeth had to go. As dutiful husband, I agreed to give her moral support. So many humorous remarks were made about the manse decanting to the theatre to view an orgy, we had no doubt what we were in for; and so it proved. The guild was draped round the circle's front rows to observe us: any suggestion that we were blasé would gravely disappoint, so we worked valiantly at being shocked. We obtained some assistance from the smoke bombs.

A cultural frisson of a different kind was prompted by a phone call out of the blue from Douglas Templeton, assistant dean in New College. Douglas was devoted, not only to his dog and students, but to his three remarkable children, and a remarkable wife, Elizabeth, who as a female theologian is globally known to more ecumenical archbishops than anyone since Julian of Norwich. Douglas writes theological books of subversive insight which are crammed with more jokes than Dundee cake has raisins. In my youth he drove me over the Alps on my first visit to Italy and later introduced me to T. S. Eliot's *Four Quartets*.

Need I say more? Well, yes, because the subject arose over this phone call to Peterhead. He was being visited by two ex-Cambridge University friends; could they all come to Aberdeen and meet up? Of course, but on the night in question Elizabeth and I had tickets for the opera. If they could bear to support a little provincial effort, I would provide extra tickets. This was naughty of me, but I felt a tease coming on.

At Aberdeen we met the train, Douglas, and his two southern guests, eminent in London aesthetic and scholarly matters. They were tired, but being polite, indicated they would be glad to support what they took to be a local charitable amateur effort. And the opera? When I said *Cosi Fan Tutti* they looked apprehensive. A local attempt to murder *Merry England* or *The Mikado* was one thing, an assassination of Mozart was another. The beautiful theatre was a surprise to them, as were our seats in the centre of the stalls. Reading the programmes began to destabilise their pre-suppositions, but there was little time for discussion before the curtain rose on what, pace *The Ring*, many would say was the most perfect production ever staged by Scottish Opera: *Cosi Fan Tutti* led by Janet Baker. At her peak, she sang with that kind of gossamer delicacy which makes you want to weep; and Alexander

Gibson, also at his peak, conducted with a wicked wit. During the
interval there was an air of being stunned. After the performance
my guests were too happy about the experience to put me up
against a wall and shoot me.

These and other diversions were by and large shared by both of
us. There was, however, one activity which I gradually realised
Elizabeth was pursuing, if not exactly in secret, then most
definitely without my involvement. She had a habit which was
developing beyond recreation into addiction: attendance at roups.
In Buchan a roup was an auction, after a death or a property
changing hands, often at a farm or country estate. She had always
loved auctions for their theatricality, but the Aberdeenshire rural
roups riveted her with their colourful personalities, not least the
Doric eloquence of the auctioneers, and the unbelievable bargains.

At that stage the city dealers from the south hadn't discovered
this honey-pot, and even with her self-imposed ceiling of a fiver
per roup, it was remarkable what was brought home. The green
baize divan which, as I write, still stands in our downstairs front
room bay window, to enable Chelsea, the current collie, to bark at
other dogs who have the effrontery to walk along the public
pavement, cost one pound sterling at a Buchan roup thirty years
ago. It might have cost more, the life of two humans and a dog.
The spouse had gone off with Rosemary Sewell to the roup. The
divan could only be accommodated by leaving the small Renault
hatch-back's fifth door open to allow the divan to stick out the
back. Rosemary drove while Elizabeth sat with her nose squashed
against the windscreen, our collie Quixote crushed on the floor,
and on my wife's knee two oil-lamps, filled with paraffin, while
exhaust fumes through the open fifth door nearly overcame them.

All travel was an adventure then. Health meant being fit for any
risk. Safety was guarded against by not going out in a small boat
in more than a Force 12 storm. Aberdeenshire roads were life or
death lotteries. Fishermen drove cars as if they were boats, farmers
as if they were tractors, undertakers as if they were overtakers.

And then the oil came, and Texans drove cars as if they were
supersonic oil-rigs.

16
A Bribe

When the oil came! It sounds like a ravening beast in from the sea. And so it proved, though by myself I wouldn't have foreseen this. Like everybody else I welcomed the work and prosperity promised by North Sea oil and all that its ancillary development would bring to the town.

I said everybody thought that way. The exception was Pat Strachan, the wily, idiosyncratic editor of the *Buchan Observer*, Peterhead's weekly thunderer. His was a lone voice proclaiming that the oil would disintegrate the culture and integrity of the community, and that the European Common Market would spell the death-knell of the fishing industry. Pat was that rarity, a true prophet, a fact proved also by the fact that nobody paid the slightest attention to him.

The well-educated laughed at his frequent writing up of events in Doric, including his reports of my sermons; for he jaloused that in my own way I was raising in the pulpit issues about the core values of the community. I regarded myself as doing a reasonably competent job in that respect, but my self-satisfaction received a rude awakening when one afternoon a stranger appeared at my door. My name had been given to him by a couple of TV people in London and Aberdeen.

"Come in, have tea," I said. He left about twelve hours later when we had talked each other to a standstill. He pitched it at me and his pitch was strong. I took it on the chin because his command of the facts overcame my arguments. It's difficult to shake off an argumentative Australian who has his teeth in one's ankle, specially when he is a documentary film-maker working all over the world for government information departments, and thus knows more than you or I will ever know.

His challenge was a wake-up call: Peterhead with its hinterland was the next place to be raped by the oil industry if it just said yes and rolled on its back. As a community leader I must do what I could, if not to stop it, at least warn the people and urge conditions which would limit the worst effects by maintaining some leverage against the oil companies and developers (as Shetland did).

I didn't submit to his perspective. Against his professional pessimism I deployed my personal optimism. But he was wearing me down. He could produce chapter and verse from one continent to another of the communities he'd seen collapse when a short-term bonanza went off like a space-ship which has laid waste one planet before moving on to another. I was glad of an evening meal during which Elizabeth took up the cudgels; but it was afterwards, fuelled by Glen Grant malt, that he turned me. It was simply done, but brilliant: he turned against me my theology, my ministry, my *raison d'être* in the community. To my protest that I was not a community leader, just a non-political preacher, he countered that I was therefore one of the few in the town with no economic vested interest and was free to preach values other than profit.

When I quoted the parable of the talents, and even, to my shame, the very parable Margaret Thatcher was later to deploy in the General Assembly, that of the Good Samaritan who was able to help the mugged traveller because he has created wealth enabling him to help, my stranger countered with blows to the head from Jesus' withering remarks and stories about the tendency of the rich to store wealth up for themselves.

I rested my case on the fact that despite three foreign-based factories and the fishing, Peterhead had a low economic profile, and asked, "How in moral terms can I campaign against poor people increasing their income and lifestyle?" That was when he landed the killer punch. "I presume you're not in this job to be popular. I presume in the context of eternity your preaching takes the long view. I'm telling you any benefits will be short-term. In thirty years there will be disillusionment. It's important that people can look back and see that someone spoke the truth. It'll be important that someone spoke up for values other than greed."

I winced. Who was this guy? It was straight out of the Old Testament: a stranger turning up from nowhere and delivering a message to the jugular. I didn't know if he was right or wrong on the detail. What I did know was that he was making me face the nature of my call to the pulpit. He sensed my wobbling. He added: "Just ask questions."

We talked a lot more, but I was no longer challenging him, I was picking his brains. After he walked out the front door I never met nor heard from him again. That happened thirty-two years ago. Four months ago we heard from a friend that Peterhead is now a sad town, with the oil and the fishing running down.

In my remaining eighteen months I did what I could. I preached, held meetings, spoke at inquiries, wrote articles in the *Buchan Observer* and headline-grabbing centre-spreads in the *Press and Journal*, Aberdeen's daily. I took part in TV debates and successfully moved the Kirk's Church and Nation Committee to enquire into the situation. At an international oil exhibition in Aberdeen Elizabeth and I stood protesting at the entrance. We made use of the fact that Elizabeth was a great-great-grand-daughter of Paraffin Young, Scotland's first oilman, who pioneered the extraction of oil from shale, and was featured in the exhibition. Such Green protests are *de rigueur* nowadays but then they weren't, and against a public mood of excitement that for once Aberdeenshire had met its destiny in a bonanza, I felt more than a passing empathy with King Canute.

Yet the process made me admire and like the people all the more. Most of them disagreed with me, yet they remained not only loyal and friendly, but understanding. They respected my stand, were proud their minister was involved in local issues, and never lost their pawky touch in joking about my latest headline. And to be fair to myself I was careful never to be judgmental. I had stood where they stood. It was another who had forced on me an alternative focus; there were reasonable arguments on both sides. Nevertheless, I didn't think of giving up, because I had reason to think I was right, or rather that the stranger in the night had been right.

Two disclosures fortified me. Grampian TV, who made excellent documentaries on the subject, told me that I was top of one oil company's list of hostile targets. And I was personally nobbled. The town provost took me to have a drink with one oil company's top man who had flown over from Texas. He was a kindly silver-haired man who spoke softly. He straightforwardly tried to bribe me. "The church is always short of money," he said. "You are here to do good, help the disadvantaged, spread the Gospel. Even if you're right, and unwanted social consequences flow from the oil, all the more will the community need a strong church to make its witness with many more resources than you now have—buildings, facilities, staff, money you need, welfare and educational programmes. All that we ask is that you don't get in the way. Save your breath. It's going to happen anyway. Let's make it comfortable for everyone, and you can have more success than you've ever dreamed of."

I couldn't believe my ears. Now I understood how the Town Council had been picked off one by one over a Gaelic whisky in the bar. Not by a crude appeal to greed, but by suggestions for expanding the prosperity of the community, a process in which of course their special talents would find unprecedented opportunities for constructive business.

I'm not sure, but I believe I laughed, the approach was so preposterously brazen. What I said is beyond recall, but I suppose I tried to explain that the church had a different agenda. Anyway, thank you very much, but not.

He seemed genuinely surprised. He'd made an open-ended offer, one no sensible person could refuse. And all I had to do was relax. He sighed, smiled, and said, "I only wanted to assist you in God's work."

At last I had met power, naked and unadorned. And how could one recognise it? By the smile. I never saw a serpent smile until then.

Stephen had a different smile, more like a grin which before long developed into a chuckle. We called him Stephen because he arrived on St Stephen's Day. That was a cheery thought: Stephen, you may remember from your last speed read of the Book of Acts, was stoned to death by religious vigilantes egged on by Saul of Tarsus. We also called him Stephen because nobody on either family tree had that name and we were determined to avoid temperatures being raised by hereditary scrabble.

It proved quite impossible to make him unhappy. Naturally, we tried. Well, I did. I made funny faces. I sang execrable songs. I jigged up and down (those were the days!). I threw him in the air. I even caught him sometimes. All to no avail; his cheerfulness was inexorable. What was wrong with the child? Did he need some special inoculation? At that, he obliged by a few days of wall-to-wall projectile vomiting. But our doctor, Gavin Taylor, cured that at once and wall-to-wall cheerfulness broke out again. It was like living with the Teletubbies, chortle chortle, chuckle, chuckle, and even the sun giggling. Long before he could speak he chatted nineteen to the dozen—we shall never know what he was saying. He was baptised on Pentecost. Elizabeth's father, my ex-boss Harry Whitley, with Elizabeth's mother, came up for the weekend to do it. Harry and Stephen entered into a competition in the cheerfulness stakes; they made each other laugh until one or the other choked.

On the Sunday, we were not drunk, it being but eleven in the morning, but it would be playing with words to deny that we were riotous. The north-east champion Irish dancer danced himself into a fury and threw his bonnet into the packed church. Harry danced a reel with young Sunday school kids in front of the altar (let's not stand on ceremony and call it a communion table). Other Sunday School members dropped thousands of pieces of red paper from the galleries—they may not have been actual flames of fire, but they made almost as much mess. And when smothered in water, Stephen jiggled up and down in pleasure.

It was one of those rare moments caught in the words, "Rarely, rarely comest thou, spirit of delight."

Only six months later we left Peterhead, a moment far from delight. The story of how that happened belongs to the next part of the narrative which carries me back into broadcasting and us as a family into the main part of our life. I had thought my work would end in the cold but admirable north-east. I'd been wrong.

17

Battery Hen

A few months into my Peterhead job the charismatic Aberdeen minister George Reid had phoned me. Intellectually he was no slouch, but it was his oratory that hit the jackpot. His rich voice could culminate in the most musical scream I ever heard. It was scary stuff; when he got going in the Assembly it burned the varnish off the rafters. In the Assembly debate on the Wolfenden report (legalisation of homosexuality) his denunciation of the Assembly's sour resistance had been a lonely and brave declaration. And here he was agitating my Peterhead phone.

"Mr Mackenzie, I'm the chairman of Grampian TV's religious panel. We'd like you to do some epilogues." I grimaced. I'd been vaguely aware that at some stage I might have to face this kind of situation, but in the hurly-burly of parish business it had receded to the back burner.

"Er," I said decisively, "that's very kind of you but I've left all that behind. I've given up television in London in order to do a parish job in Scotland." I could hear the moustache bristle. "My dear chap…" was all he could muster. I sensed a combination of bafflement and outrage. Drawing himself up to his full vocal range he embarked on a tenor fusillade with full orchestra. The burden of this euphony was that with my TV experience in the south, it was my plain mission to place myself at the disposal of the church in this important field.

I was in a cleft stick. To agree now was to start on a slippery slope and betray the career choice I had most painfully made. On the other hand I didn't want to offend a senior man I admired by sounding holier than thou. A clever tactic occurred to me: I said I would discuss it with my session clerk and phone back tomorrow.

"My dear chap," he said with worrying satisfaction, and we

replaced our phones amicably.

I walked into the bank and as always Mac invited me conspiratorially into his office. I recounted the phone conversation and waited for him to nod agreement at my refusing to go whoring after the doubtful glamour of spouting clichés long after Buchan farmers and fishermen were in bed dreaming of fat cows and glistening herring. Alas, it turned out that my clever tactic was too clever by half. The tactic misfired, turned round in its tracks, hurtled straight for me, and blew up in my face. Mac looked appalled. "Man," he groaned (his equivalent of "My dear chap"). "You canna say no."

We argued stoutly for quarter of an hour. But I was hoist by my own petard. I'd said I'd consult the session clerk. I'd done so. And the session clerk was clear. To say no was impossible. I must say yes. At once. Immediately. Straight away. Now. The congregation, the whole town, would be scunnered if they knew their minister had turned down the chance to represent them all over the north of Scotland. "Man," he cried, thumping a fist into the palm of his hand, "don't you see—you'll be visiting your own people in their homes."

The next day I phoned George Reid. "My dear chap," he cried. And that is why, one thing leading to another, five years later, I was to leave a job I thought I was committed to for life, to turn up at a hell of a job in religious broadcasting. Thank you, Dr Reid.

In the late spring of 1973, nemesis came out of a clear sky. Coming home for lunch I encountered a thoughtful Elizabeth. With a casualness that didn't deceive, she named a Grampian TV cameraman/director with whom we had become friendly. He'd phoned to ask if we'd seen the job advert in the papers; if not, it was worth a look. I was uninterested, but Elizabeth had found the ad and gave it to me. There was a BBC vacancy for religious broadcasting organiser (Scotland) based in Glasgow. (That was then the title for what became head of religious broadcasting in Scotland.) It was the post Dr Ronnie Falconer had occupied for nearly three decades until recently retiring.

I was mildly interested only because of an incident a few weeks back. A BBC production and camera crew from Glasgow had interviewed me in Aberdeen harbour about my attitudes to the oil boom. The religious producer had been James Dey, deputy to Ronnie, and now his successor. James had asked me the relevant questions about oil during the interview, but otherwise his conversation had revolved round BBC office politics, a subject with which I couldn't engage. He'd been asked if he would apply for the post of head of programmes, Scotland, but also he was being canvassed for the post of head of religious programmes, television, in London. And yet he'd only been in the top religious job in Glasgow for a year or so. What should he do? He was so demented by indecision that he was consulting me, a complete stranger.

Judging by this ad, he'd jumped to London; I really didn't care. I was now so immersed in Peterhead that I would have been as fascinated by stories of managerial musical chairs in Jenners store. But now the phone rang. It was George Reid. "My dear chap," he said.

At tea time the phone rang again. It was Ian Pitt-Watson. Now this did interest me, because anything Ian P–W said was worth hearing. He was a gifted choral conductor who had founded the Edinburgh University Singers. But preaching and parish pastoral work were his priorities, pursued in Forfar and the huge congregation of New Kilpatrick in Bearsden, Glasgow, before he became professor of practical theology in Aberdeen. In this phone conversation he was characteristically persuasive. He knew what he was talking about; he was a regular broadcaster who served on the BBC's religious advisory committee and was a friend of all the BBC staff likely to be involved in the latest move.

As I would expect he had the wit not to insult me by assuming that I would jump at the idea of going to Glasgow. Rather the opposite, as he acknowledged; why should I swap a big pastoral challenge among real people for a foetid office and endless days and nights away from home? That was the first claw sinking in. Moreover, after my creative programme-making in ITV in

London, I would probably find the straightforward transmitting of worship and *Songs of Praise* lacking in stimulus. A second claw. But my career path had equipped me in an unusual way to match ideas, TV experience, and parish work with a job in Scottish broadcasting which required a fresh look. Third claw. All he begged was that I give the matter some thought.

Impatience made me decisive. This was getting silly. I contemplated the image of James Dey in Aberdeen harbour dancing on a thousand pros and cons over what to do next. By a serendipity Elizabeth's parents were due at the weekend so that her father could douse Stephen with water and declare him baptised. I was not going to let the BBC job deeve me. I'd put it at the back of my mind till Sunday was over. Then I'd ask Harry Whitley's opinion. After that I'd forget about it. This was a dead cert. Before I'd come to Peterhead, Harry had been categoric. The future of the Kirk lay in preaching. Here I was, preaching. I'd go on preaching. Subject closed.

Huh! On the Sunday afternoon, I drove my parents-in-law into Aberdeen to catch the train home. Nobody had referred to the BBC, but I knew Harry would have spotted the ad; he missed nothing. After an inspirational morning service in the church I was confident that he would restate his faith in the parish ministry. I asked his opinion. Sitting beside me in the car he puffed at his pipe. "Well..." he said. I tensed. "I don't see much future for the institutional church in its present form. The hope is that small communities will pursue their own vision. They will need something to keep them in touch with each other. Broadcasting may be that link. I think you should go for that BBC job."

I felt stabbed in the front. Before the train left he looked me in the eye. "I may be wrong. But there's no harm in applying."

Which is what I did. But not before doing a reality check. On the Monday I phoned John Lang, head of the whole BBC religious broadcasting outfit in the UK. I made an appointment to see him in London on the Tuesday morning. I pictured him grinning on the phone like an angler getting a bite. I listlessly chewed my mini-steak in the night train buffet and as we pounded down the east coast I felt a climbing plant stealthily enclosing my feet, legs, heart… it was a dream.

At 11am in Portland Place I was handed a cup of coffee as John Lang surveyed me. We knew each other; when I was ensconced in London ITV and he was the new boy on the block as head of BBC's religious radio he'd stood me lunch at the Athenaeum. I liked him but I was determined at this point not to yield an inch.

"Your ad was brought to my attention. I'm considering it. I gave up London and broadcasting for my present job, and I'm very happy there. I won't risk rocking the boat in Peterhead by applying for this post if there is no point, so I need to know if it is already sewn up. Will it go to an internal BBC application?"

"It will be an open board," he said. "But why are you considering it?"

"Because of the wording of the ad which struck me as unusual. It referred to serving the whole community of Scotland."

His gaze intensified. "Ah. I wrote the ad. And I wrote that phrase with you in mind."

I suspected the veracity of this, but on the other hand it was a hint as broad as Regent Street.

To clinch it, he added: "Things need changing up there. More coffee?"

The next day, back in Peterhead, I called on Mac at the bank, told him the story, and said that people I respected had advised me to go for it, and leave the rest to God. As always, Mac exhibited grace under pressure, carefully hiding his disappointment. He had got me there; now it was possible that after less than five years he'd have to start all over again. We agreed to tell nobody until the board made its decision.

I think it was in July that I made my way to the board in Queen Margaret Drive. A suprisingly large number of faces round the conference room table stared at me. What had they expected? A giraffe? I recognised only John Lang, who did all but wink. It soon became apparent that the other man who mattered was the head of programmes, Pat Walker, a figure of quiet sagacity who, through a beard, voiced appreciation of a TV series I'd presented from Peterhead called *Jesus and the Circle*. It had been largely improvised with children, and Pat expressed approval of the risk that had involved. The controller of BBC Scotland, Bob Coulter, had eyes which looked through one but he seemed happy with my answers to questions.

Others whom I thought were less sure about me included a representative of the Broadcasting Council for Scotland who stressed the importance of traditional values. I replied that nowhere in the world were values more traditional than Peterhead, yet they had apparently not found themselves under serious threat from my values. I so did not want this job that I was carefree if not downright reckless. When John Lang, throwing a lifeline for me to display creativity, asked for examples of programme ideas, I retorted that since I might not get the job I had no intention of giving away ideas that others might use.

Afterwards I walked to St Mary's Episcopal Cathedral, read the psalms for the day and a collect or two, and committed the decision to God. Then hotfoot back to Peterhead, more convinced than ever that there lay my karma.

Day after day, decision came there none, until one afternoon I was phoned in quick succession by Douglas Aitken and Ralph Smith, radio and television producers respectively under Ronnie Falconer. Each had applied for the post but wanted to congratulate me and assure me I would be made welcome. A couple of days later, having heard nothing offical from the BBC, I phoned Glasgow where a harassed assistant explained that there had been a hold-up in paperwork owing to holidays. This first impression of the Beeb's bureaucracy was not encouraging.

The following Sunday I announced my change of work first to the kirk session, then the congregation. I said I regarded it as much a call as theirs had been; that I saw the broadcasting task as an extension of the parish one; and that I would try and relate decisions about programmes to what Peterhead people had taught me. It was all true but I was not enjoying this.

Nor did I enjoy house-hunting. Leaving Elizabeth and Stephen to look after each other, I spent two days driving around Glasgow and its hinterland. We'd agreed that we'd want to stay either in Glasgow's west end, within walking distance of the BBC (and the area of the city known to Elizabeth) or right outside Glasgow; half in and half out seemed pointless. Elizabeth was clear on one matter: on no account would we live in Helensburgh. From all she had heard it was posh, stuck-up, and wealthy, in short the opposite of Peterhead. With this diktat ringing in my ears it was inevitable that the house I eventually decided to recommend to my wife was in Helensburgh.

But not until I had exhausted all other possibilities and myself. Me and my Renault did the grand tour: west end, Clarkston, Giffnock, Pollokshields, Newton Mearns, Barrhead, Paisley. Not a stone was left unturned... and put back again. After two days of this purgatory I needed a break so before returning to my B and B I drove out to Helensburgh to get some fresh air. I parked the car and sat in the square. Gosh, this was rather pleasant, decidedly pleasant, extremely pleasant. For the first time in forty-eight hours I relaxed; something like peace stole over me. We couldn't stay here of course? I knew it was imagination calling, but it felt like the town calling. I examined photos in an estate agent's window, and went looking. There was a rather nice terrace. And here I am, thirty years later, writing in the end house of that terrace.

After an emotional evening service on our last Sunday in Peterhead, one man had a particular message to deliver to me. He and his family had been the only members to vote against my call when I'd preached to the congregation five years before. Mac had been torn, mortified that the vote hadn't been unanimous, but thrilled that a family had exercised its democratic rights. When I became minister, the protesting man explained that it wasn't personal, but my theme had been that Peterhead was the centre of the universe and since that was obviously daft he'd voted no on intellectual grounds. Now I was leaving he had to confess I was a true prophet. Since the oil had come to Peterhead it was after all the centre of the universe. I considered explaining to him that what

I'd meant was that everywhere was the centre of the universe but I thought better of it. What the hell, why look a gift horse in the mouth? In five years I'd made one convert.

On the Sunday evening we had our last supper with Bill, the best session clerk a minister ever had, and his winsome, witty Millicent; said goodbye; embraced; cried.

The next morning, on the last Monday of October 1973, for the second and final time, I went south out of Buchan, that bare, spare land with its brown earth, loveable people, ever-moving sea, and vast skyscapes. It had given me birth, childhood, uniquely fulfilling years in a true community in the company of a young wife, and now a son and heir. There was no joy in this departure, only sadness.

Moving from Peterhead to Helensburgh was never going to be easy, but I had completely failed to foresee the force of the change. After all, both were medium-sized towns, both on the Scottish mainland, both less than an hour's drive from a major city. A change, but no change.

Wasn't I the geographical and ecological innocent? For once I hadn't made lists, I hadn't done a reckoning. I was too concerned about a change of job to give weight to a change of environment.

The environment repaid my indifference in three ways: it cluttered my eyes, deluged me with water, and sent me to sleep. The clutter was eye-boggling. In place of long straight lines, distant horizons, empty sea, infinite sky, flat empty land, the eyes suddenly had to grapple with a visual display inducing aesthetic dyspepsia. The brain was bombarded by objects: hills, trees, bigger trees, bushes, flowers, even in November an ocean of wet autumn leaves, God, not another mountain, yachts, huge yachts, yes, laid up for the winter, over some garden walls loomed a yacht, submarines (not in the gardens, but the British and American Polaris bases were just round the corner), clouds— clouds?—yes, the mountains seemed to spout clouds like Vesuvius smoke—dogs—dogs?—yes every other Helensburgh citizen was walked past our window by a large dog, often two, and one man just up the road carried a cat round his neck, toilet rolls—toilet rolls?—yes, Edward Heath's winter of discontent was upon us, with its three-day week emptying the shelves in an orgy of panic-buying, and one fine upstanding citizen walked past our window carrying pillars of loo rolls sufficient to last a parliamentary term. Two toilet rolls are company, this was a crowd. But everything was a crowd. My eyeballs screamed and demanded overtime.

Then the deluge of water. People born and bred on the Clyde called it rain. We had come to take for granted the dryness of the north-east. When in Peterhead it did rain it could be fierce and when it snowed it threw you on your back, and the winds, unobstructed by objects like hills and trees, made seagulls fly backwards, and oh yes, it could be cold, even in July; but records showed that for dryness Peterhead competed with Bournemouth. For wetness Helensburgh competed with the Niagara Falls. Specially in November, which is when I began as a commuter to try my hand at negotiating the flood waters to Glasgow. At first I couldn't compete with the rugged tanned men and women of the Clyde who, deprived for the winter months of their beloved yachts, expertly pitched, rolled, tacked and yawed their off-road vehicles through the swirling waters of the A82 and A814. Eventually I learned from their tricks how to make it to Glasgow.

And being sent to sleep? I acknowledge that to be on the verge of an exaggeration. But for a year I had to struggle not to doze my way through the day. It was the Gulf Stream, you see. The climate was—is—extraordinarily balmy. It is virtually impossible to feel cold, except during the occasional icy snap but when one of those arrives to bathe one's eyes, one joyfully submits to the magic of Helensburgh's multitude of trees sparkling, glittering, night and day a forest of white. You don't call that being cold. You call that fairyland.

And, since I'm now drifting into the affirmative, I must blow a fanfare of silver trumpets in favour of Helensburgh's spring. In thirty years, I can recall few springs and early Clyde summers when the darling buds of May did not blossom in weather so blue-sky'd one held one's breath. For that spring festival one gladly pays the rest of the year's Danegeld of rain, specially as it is often banished for two or three weeks in golden October so that the majesty of the trees which climb up the hill on which the town stands can climax in the tone poem of what Americans so wonderfully call the fall.

While I'm about it, why don't I summon a flotilla of gold trombones to send soaring above the Arrochar Alps a fanfare for Argyll? Until we came to stay here I'd regarded Argyll as a poor man's alternative to the real Highlands from which genetically I had sprung. Ignorance is not bliss, it's blindness. Now my eyes were opened—spectacularly. Nowhere is more wonderful than Argyll. I was tempted to write that nowhere is as wonderful as Argyll, but having fallen hopelessly in love with so many parts of Scotland I realise that geographical promiscuity can breed an excess of rhetoric, so I proceed with caution. Nothing can gouge from my sub-conscious a primal worship of Wester Ross and Sutherland, but Argyll is blessed by a holy union: the trinity of mountain, loch, and island. At the risk of over-specificity, I'll go one step further; even when it rains, Loch Fyne reigns.

Rae Elliot, our saintly London bank manager, once told us that when buying a house one should not underestimate the "turning the corner" factor. He meant that if a particular property had the effect of lifting the spirit when one turned the corner and saw it at the end of a hard day, that was worth paying more than might be justified on paper. The same test can be applied to a workplace at the beginning of the day.

Helensburgh blithely passed the evening test. Turning the corner after Dumbarton and Cardross to see spread below the Clyde basin, the mountains beyond, and the town nestling between, freshened the fevered brow. However, the BBC building off Queen Margaret Drive failed the morning test: blitheness did not occur, or not enough of it to cause the lark in one's heart to soar. The sense that glad morning had come was elusive.

Broadcasting House was to become my day-home for a

considerable chunk of my life so I don't want to speak too harshly of it, but damning it with faint praise is a contrary risk. Let me attempt ratiocination on the subject. First, one should separate the exterior effects from the interior. I like open territory, the sea, rivers, a flowing highway, roads over moors, the shoulders of hills, mountain passes. I like sky, horizons, vistas. I like movement, however minimal; a breeze blowing in the grass will do. I dislike cul de sacs. Hamilton Drive, just off Queen Margaret Drive, was not then technically a cul de sac (though the BBC section of it now is) but it felt like one. As one turned off the human bustle and traffic of Byres Road and Queen Margaret Drive, one was suddenly up a creek. The Beeb lay on one side, like a ship in dry dock, or a beached whale, while on the opposite side of the narrow road an embankment and tenements rose steeply to create the effect of a ravine.

Once I was inside I found that my office was a box in a row of boxes on the ground floor allocated to the religious department, looking across at the embankment opposite. The claustrophobic effect was aggravated in winter by lack of daylight and on a hot summer day by a lack of ventilation. Opening the window admitted only stifling still air. After the piercing fresh air of Peterhead, or even the balmy zephyrs of Helensburgh, spending hour after hour in this chicken coop was to give me a lasting sympathy for the battery hen.

The poultry analogy resonates. Anyone who has observed a procession of hens across the farmyard (the only thing missing being a banner proclaiming "The only thing to fear is the feral") will perhaps understand why after a couple of weeks I began to feel a bit trussed in by the religious department procession to the canteen for coffee, lunch and tea. They were only being kind, taking me under their many wings, but there is such a thing as being smothered by caring.

Every now and then Douglas Aitken would manifest at my door his proconsularity, having journeyed west from the Edinburgh radio province which he administered. He had a warm vocal personality which, frequently heard on air, endeared him to a generation of listeners, and he was unsparing in his assurances that, although they considered themselves already to be running a tight ship, any ideas I might bring on board would be treated sympathetically. What could I do but bow gratefully?

I evaluated the human resources. The first thing that was obvious was that they were all tired. On the TV side they were seriously overworked, with a swollen workload of outside broadcasts as well as studio programmes. James Dey had gone to London, Andrew Barr was temporarily (though it became permanent) transferred to London. My impression, confirmed by John Lang and James Dey, was that Ronnie Falconer had overstrained them on a hamster wheel of relentless activity which had left them with no spare energy or mental space for fresh thinking. My first aim was to reduce the workload and that meant reducing the number of religious programmes even further than already planned.

Then I pondered their skills. On the radio side Douglas, senior producer, played to his strengths which were radio scripting and speaking, a passionate commitment to topical relevance in the interface between religion and politics, and a willingness to go anywhere at any time. Stewart Lamont was new, witty and fired by journalistic instincts. Father Bill Anderson was a spiritual man with a sharp brain and classic literary background. He was the most meticulous of all producers. On the TV side Ralph Smith was not only theologically accomplished but had the most experience in O.B. direction and, given a major challenge, e.g. a big event in a cathedral, could match music and architecture with a craftsmanlike command of both. Michael Simpson was at his best with children, of whom, being blessed with a large and beautiful family, he had plenty experience.

These producers shared one quality which from Ronnie Falconer's angle had been an unmitigated strength but from mine constituted a worry: they were all devoted church people, male, and all but one ordained. There was experience and commitment here which I must respect, but both the experience and commitment were limited by a particular ecclesiastical and broadcasting tradition.

To sum up the situation, it seemed that the team I had inherited was well trained to fulfil the remit of the public service aspect of religious broadcasting in Scotland, and also from time to time conduct experimental forays which they thought appropriate along the interface between the churches and an increasingly secular society.

There was a snag, however. Whereas they were fully skilled and motivated in the first area—worship, hymn singing, theological and ecclesiastical discussion—they were, through no fault of their own, less equipped by background and training to make programmes which would go out and hook, or intrigue, or even just surprise, the vast number of Scots who would no sooner go to church, sing a hymn, or consult a minister, than fly to Mars.

The solution seemed obvious. This dedicated core would continue to supply the public service religious requirement. I would try to persuade them to explore new territory and different techniques to engage the unchurched. And in due course I would look for additional talent in non-clerical, and possibly non-Christian areas.

To reassure the staff (a new boss is always a worry), stabilise the department, and get things going, I wrote a memo to my line manager, Pat Walker—in the BBC of those days, modelled on the civil service, memos were the main form of nourishment. I proposed a clear structure: under my supervision Douglas would be in charge of radio output, Ralph in charge of TV.

Pat, a quietly civilised man, took me aback by sending me a yelp in memo form. On no account, it said; you are to take full charge of the television output and radically change it. I realised this wasn't so much a rebuke for naivety as an expression of visceral anxiety that I might betray my essential brief at the outset. I went to see Pat. His manner was, as it always would be, infinitely comfortable; he once told me his main job was first aid and bandages. But the message was clear: let programmes for the next year take their ordained course (his face was so deadpan you never knew if jokes were intentional). My task was to think grandly about the future. I left the room feeling ever so slightly less ungrand, like a junior minister advised by Sir Humphrey that there was no immediate need to do anything unduly courageous.

But Sir Humphrey was not his usual perceptive self there. There was every need to be courageous, and that sharpish. Sir Humphrey, Pat Walker, and I had failed to take into account the dog that had not barked. In fact this particular dog had wagged its tail at me. The Kirk, which, through the Church and Nation Committee, had welcomed my appointment, was not only going to bark, but to bite.

18

"Do You Believe in God?"

t first I was quite unsuspecting. One morning, a knock at the door. Here, all joviality, was this well kent face, good-looking, with boyish grin and avuncular manner. I was delighted to see him. If not a mate—he never quite let go of that sense of authority which had made him a de facto bishop to hundreds of Kirk ministers—I regarded my distinguished predecessor Ronnie Falconer as a friend.

In the course of discussing and making many programmes with me from Peterhead, he had stayed many a night in our manse, eaten many an Elizabeth meal, drunk many a Speyside malt, shared many a confidence. And after I'd been appointed to the job which he had created and occupied for quarter of a century, he had written me a remarkable letter. Its first part had gone beyond generosity into being effusive about the BBC's choice. He was relieved I was to carry the torch, because he knew that I believed in Scotland and the Kirk and would stand up for them.

The second part of the letter was rather a surprise. It consisted of pen portraits of the staff who had been his colleagues and were to be mine. There were, as one might expect, warm compliments, but intertwined were comments of a satirical nature. I was impressed that he was entrusting me with such material. He was right to trust me; I never exposed the letter. But my unease about it began to crystallise into reflecting that it revealed undercurrents of tension that I had not suspected.

Anyway, now here he was in the office which was once his. His big desk had gone—I'd given that to Ralph as an inheritance—but he settled comfortably in a chair. After general chat, we got down to business. He had brought me some programme suggestions for next year, the year I was beginning to plan. The most substantial was a series of lectures given by him on the subject of preaching through religious broadcasting, illustrated by archive TV footage. Though there had been a certain amount of this kind of thing leading up to his retirement, it wasn't a bad idea, other things being equal. But other things were not equal. I had been given a strict brief, recently reinforced by the head of programmes, to branch out into new kinds of TV religion, not to look backwards. This was to be my first year of designing a new brand of schedule and Ronnie, more than anyone, would know that all the balancing acts involved in sorting out ideas, resources, budgets, staff and slots made this moment far too early in the process to make firm commitments. I was careful not to reject his proposal, but in a professional way to thank him and say I would consider it alongside other ideas, possibly in a different form, for example a single lecture.

I was completely unprepared for his reaction: he was visibly shocked. He looked at me in horror as if in front of his eyes a reliable friend had metamorphosed into a snake. Quickly mastering himself, he made a couple of other suggestions, one of which I took up immediately, partly because it was a perfectly good idea, and partly to ease the atmosphere. Ironically this proposal of Ronnie's was to become a famous *cause célèbre* and set off the alarm bells in the top echelons of the Church of Scotland that in me the Beeb had acquired a loose cannon.

We called this programme *The Anderston Talk-In*. The subject was that hardy annual crisis: the Kirk is short of money! Ronnie recommended two Glasgow inner-city young ministers to lead it: David Graham, minister at Anderston, and Johnston McKay at Bellahouston. I concurred at once. I'd known Graham when he was a radical student on the editorial board of the SCM magazine *Breakthrough* which I edited in London. When I say "radical" I mean he would not only argue the hind legs off a donkey, he would argue off the left front leg and the right front leg, before pinning the tail to the rear end of a bucking stallion.

Johnston McKay I knew through St Giles where he had supported Harry Whitley in a four-year assistantship. Johnston was more subtle; he'd just place a bomb under the donkey and stand back. In other words, both were ideal for a quiet philosophical meditation on the box. Not!

On the night, they performed up to expectation, but the explosion came from elsewhere. Erik Cramb, then ministering in Glasgow's east end, delivered a withering diatribe against wealthy middle-class churches who did nothing to help working-class or new housing estate churches and communities who were financially on the ropes. This speech did not lack clarity, but for colour Erik threw in the phrase that in this context Christians in Bearsden and Morningside were on their way to hell. The colour this phrase gave rise to was a choleric flushing in the faces of middle-class Kirk Christians watching the programme. A correspondence raged in the *Scotsman* and the (Glasgow) *Herald* for over a week, and the mail-bag in my office simmered like a boiling kettle.

I was frankly incredulous that one phrase, however colourful, would set off such general pandemonium towards the end of the twentieth century. It suggested a national church far from sure of itself, indeed on the defensive. And there was no doubt who was being blamed—not Erik Cramb, obviously just a mad young leftie. No, it was the BBC. I should have known better. This would never have happened on Ronnie Falconer's watch!

If I was left in any doubt how twitchy was the church I was going to have to deal with, the last scintilla was removed by an official visit from the moderator, Andrew Herron. I was one of the guests at a lunch given by the controller at Queen Margaret Drive. *The Anderston Talk-In* came up for exhumation. Andrew Herron had been a pawky Glasgow lawyer who, after doing theology, became a pawky Glasgow Presbytery clerk and was now the pawkiest moderator ever to appear on stage, screen, and Assembly, where he had them rolling in the aisles. But today all was gravitas. I remember his climactic judgment exactly. "The Kirk still has confidence in the BBC," he pronounced solemnly to Bob Coulter, the controller, and then added, looking meaningfully at me, "but if that confidence is lost, it will be difficult to regain." He nodded sagely. We were all suitably crushed.

From then on Ronnie and I met periodically but usually as part of a group round a canteen table. Civilities were always observed, but I could never get used to the eyes staring out at me between eyebrows and moustache. They were angry.

It began to filter back to me from sources outside the BBC that he was advising churchmen that, sadly, I was not up to the job.

This was an uncomfortable situation for everyone concerned, not least because Ronnie was a close friend of my aunt and uncle who lived above Drumnadrochit; Ronnie took family holidays in the cottage next to their croft, about which he had made a film. He was also a supporter of Elizabeth's parents, and they thought highly of him because he seemed to be a sturdy defender of Scotland's church and broadcasting interests.

Elizabeth and I, still homesick for Peterhead, discussed ditching the BBC and looking for another parish, but dismissed that option; surrender was not in our vocabulary. To us it was clear: I had taken on this job, not through any ambition of mine, but because serious people had urged me to make serious changes; and I had not even begun to implement any changes. To double-check, however, I reported to Dalwhinnie. Where? You heard me: Dalwhinnie.

There were five publicly known things about Dalwhinnie, and one private. The public facts were that it boasted a distillery, a hotel, a railway station, and a telephone kiosk; and that it was near the highest point on British railways, the Drumochter Pass scraping the clouds at 1,484 feet. The privately known fact was that on occasion God and I met there, by the shore of a wild little loch. Readers who can't swallow this don't have to. They can rationalise it as my finding the environment conducive to a clear-headed dialogue with myself. On this occasion it wasn't God who turned up but Jesus.

I came home that night with a clear message. I had been appointed to explore spiritual experience with all the people of Scotland, not those of a particular creed or church, still less church leaders of power and influence. I was to serve all the people. Hearing that instruction on what was effectively the roof of Scotland cleared my head.

Which was just as well, because shortly afterwards Bill Cattenach summoned me to his Murrayfield manse. He was then the minister of St George's West, a notable preaching station in

Edinburgh's west end, but he was also chairman of the BBC's Scottish religious advisory committee. We were meeting so that I could take him through the agenda of the next meeting.

Suddenly, over coffee and biscuits, he barked: "People tell me you don't believe in God. Is that true? Do you believe in God?"

I considered walking over and thumping him. This will surprise my friends who would not think of me as warlike. But I had been taught the rudiments of boxing at Fettes. Then I remembered Dalwhinnie, so I took a deep breath, smiled sweetly, and said, "Yes, as it happens, I do believe in God."

"Right," he said. "Next point."

It would be historically careless to dismiss all this as paranoia. I have in my possession a letter written to me by Stuart McWilliam two years before he died. Stuart was an eminent preacher of grace and wit at Wellington Church, the Glasgow University church on Gilmorehill, and later at Killearn; and at the time I'm describing was a member of the BBC advisory committee.

Twenty-five years later he wrote two letters from his retirement home in the sylvan Trossachs village of Gartmore. The first expressed appreciation of a radio programme I'd presented. I wrote back and made a fleeting reference to possible misunderstandings in the past. That unlocked an elegiac response from him which moved me deeply and had a powerfully healing effect on my memories of the troubled first years at the Beeb.

He wrote that he wanted to apologise for hasty and ill-informed judgments he had made about me. I had been briefed against, and he'd had no reason to disbelieve what he was told by reputable sources, but he had long since discovered them to be false. We Scots and we Christians, he concluded, have a poor record in thinking the best of people. We met in his village pub for a long and fascinating lunch. I owe him for drawing a line in the sand. He was indeed a man of grace.

Before I set about the task I saw clear before me, I consulted one other person. Nelson Gray was in charge of STV's religious output, which was of considerable quantity and had a directly emotional impact. I picked up his invitation to meet, and after showing me round the STV studio at Cowcaddens he gave me lunch.

I immediately relaxed. Being back in an ITV environment was like being let out of school. Nelson, a Congregationalist, was an archetypical streetwise Scottish evangel (not evangelist), hiding behind a gruff wit a lively theology and strong social conscience; Tom Allan and Ian Fraser come to mind as others of that ilk. Nelson seemed to know the BBC inside out and gave me two specific pieces of advice. Think far ahead. Decide where you want to be in five years' time and plan accordingly. The BBC is very slow, so don't expect much movement in less than five years. On the other hand, if you can't achieve your aims after five or six years, perhaps you're in the wrong place. Secondly, find one person in the BBC you can trust, confide in, and if possible work with.

I pondered these tips. Nelson was obviously a shrewd operator who thought in practicalities. And his first point about patience in a slow-moving bureaucratic machine convincingly echoed what Jim Buchan, Grampian TV's buccaneering programme controller, had said to me before I left Aberdeen. "You can do almost anything in the BBC so long as you learn to use its systems. It needs patience. The BBC doesn't have a bureaucracy; bureaucracy has the BBC."

As I walked away from Nelson's reassuring company, I resolved to look for that one person. But I made another resolution. I was not going to postpone change for five years. I was now primed, armed, forewarned and watch-your-back-warned, inoculated, equipped, dressed down, and hyped up, and I had a road-map to show me exactly where I was: between a rock, a hard place, and a swamp. The situation was not good. Advance!

And advance I did—into the swamp of the General Assembly. I should have known better. When assistant minister at St Giles I had written a piece in its magazine about the Assembly and had titled it "A Choked Drain". I wasn't trying to be rude: the article was about archaic business procedures. But St Giles didn't like it;

elders grumbled about showing disrespect to the supreme court of the Church. I could never quite get my head round this reverence for the Assembly, but I put it down to three factors: people were proud of a (relatively) democratic Kirk; in the absence of a Scottish parliament it was the next best thing; and even rebellious Scots wanted someone to defer to. In the absence of bishops and archbishops, the Assembly filled the role of totem-pole. There I go again! I should have not written totem-pole, I should have written that the Assembly was uniquely guided by the Holy Spirit. But I'd seen enough of how the Kirk's manipulators pulled the levers of power behind the scenes to have doubts about how often the Assembly spirit bloweth where it listeth. Occasionally the rank and file rebelled, and that could be splendid, but that was despite, and not because of, the best laid plans of mice and men in the marbled halls of 121 George Street.

The relevance of this is that in the BBC I found General Assembly coverage to be a totem-pole; indeed in terms of resources it was the totem-pole of Glasgow's output. *Songs of Praise* and worship programmes were the religious department mainstay, but the outside broadcast commitments required for these events were complementary to the requirements of the sports department and every effort was made to make locations mutually convenient. Whereas the Assembly coverage stood on its own.

It was this state of affairs that I called into question. To my relief I found that within the corporation (you hadn't fully sunk your personality into the BBC unless you called it the corporation) I was pushing at an open door. Bear two things in mind: nobody would have dreamed of querying our daily radio Assembly coverage which was professional, comprehensive, and relatively inexpensive, despite tying up audio and production staff for nearly two weeks; and, secondly, it was nearly two weeks. In those days the Assembly lasted for ten days.

The cost of tying up a television camera crew and scanners for that period was prohibitive, not to mention the hours of relay lines to videotapes and editing facilities in Glasgow which also tied up news staff and engineers to make selections for a nightly TV programme. This would have been a grotesquely inflated commitment even if what was being shot and edited was perpetually fascinating. But the most obsessive Assembly aficionado would not claim that all or even much of the Kirk's internal business was riveting material for the average Scottish viewer, and this, even more than the cost, is what worried me. Not every day was Church and Nation day and not every moral issue led to debates of high quality.

By chaining engineers, craftsmen, and producers to their positions through days of drudgery we were supporting a broadcasting culture in which the work was a chore, religion was a bore, and the stewardship of rare TV resources seemed of little account. This was so obvious that I found almost nobody in the BBC to disagree (though Pat Walker, in his role of Sir Humphrey, sniffed the wind, raised an eyebrow and said I was courageous). How right—as always—he was.

As Bagehot might have expressed it, the established Church of Scotland had its effective parts and its dignified parts. Any attempt by that other national institution, the BBC, to reduce the quantity of Assembly coverage (nobody ever suggested eliminating it) was seen as hurting the Kirk's most dignified part. I'd expected some resistance followed by discussion and negotiation. I did not anticipate a howl of rage. I assumed that church ministers would be rational, not that they would declare war. Nor did I expect Ronnie Falconer, now convenor of the Kirk's publicity committee, to take command of a war against the BBC in 121's underground bunker.

He tackled the campaign with zest, as every presbytery clerk in Scotland was to discover; he now had evidence that I was betraying my church. When I pointed out that I was not employed by "my" church and that I had spiritual broadcasting obligations to non-presbyerian Christians as well as to non-Christians, agnostics, and atheists, I was only driving another nail into my coffin. The arguments were long and wearisome and were only finally resolved, as is often the case in the sweep of history, by new technology. The advent of lightweight video techniques made flexible and inexpensive treatment of the Assembly possible on a sensible editorial basis. The O.B. circus left town, and the

Assembly reformed and abbreviated its procedures. It had been a battle I could not afford to lose, for it was the public fulcrum of a vital battle within the Beeb.

The dogfight over, the Assembly was a catalyst which cleared the air. People now knew where they stood. The Kirk leadership—by and large, there were of course intelligent and benign exceptions—was worried about me as someone apparently bent on dismantling a Kirk-supporting tradition. But the BBC's managers, both in London and Glasgow, backed me, because they understood my strategy and knew I needed time to deliver on it.

Leaving aside the technical ramifications, and the jargon, I can precis it in a set of propositions. The religious TV output should engage with viewers outside church walls. It should be measured by the same professional standards as the rest of the output, in drama, documentary, and current affairs. To achieve that required a shift of resources from outside broadcast-oriented events to film motivated by creative imagination. In studio, there should be a proper design budget. (Incredibly, religion had been given no design budget. Studio sets were "on the house", i.e. knocked together out of bits from the programmes of other departments). There would have to be major incremental steps in budget ceilings, but to the extent that the above changes would make many programmes more expensive (e.g. film was labour and time intensive) the total number of religious programmes in a year might at first decline. Finally, we would have to increase staff numbers and look for different kinds of producers skilled in film and experimental studio work.

Neither my bosses nor I were stupid. We realised this degree of change would take time and would have to be proved at every stage. At the technical level we had to achieve credibility. Even more daunting was the philosophical debate in which it seemed everyone in the BBC joined, from the Broadcasting Council to the most junior security officer. That isn't a rhetorical flourish. One of the most invigorating theological tournaments I ever participated in was at the Broadcasting Council. Alastair Hetherington, then controller, relished an argument and you could see him goading the Hebridean, theologically conservative Farquhar Macintosh at one end of the table and Kay Carmichael, the socially radical agnostic at the other, to clamber into the ring and hammer each other on to the ropes on the question of what constituted a religious programme. And at the bottom end, probably the most successful series we ever made (certainly in terms of our ratings, beating the BBC religious department in London into the ground) was the *Yes, No, Don't Know Show,* which arose out of a discussion I had with the youngest security officer. I asked him to my office to tell me what he thought we should be doing.

In his book *Inside BBC Scotland,* Alastair Hetherington, controller from 1975 to 1980, writes:

> *Paul Streather went on, building...to the Yes, No, Don't Know Show with Kenneth Roy. These two together were very effective, with Roy, hitherto a news man, proving to have a pleasant way of moving up and down a studio audience, encouraging people to speak their minds as they wished but not for too long.*
>
> *These programmes, however, were shock-horror to some of BBC Scotland's religious advisory committee. They objected first that some of the people taking part were not Christians and had said some blasphemous things, second that the Christian religion was not always winning the votes in the debates, and third that it was chaotic, not intellectually sound. At the same time the audience figures were rocketing. At my meeting with the Church and Nation Committee, this time accompanied by Ian Mackenzie, when asked about these programmes I reminded them of the much higher audience figures. Did they think it all bad? There was, I think, not much response.*
>
> *Ian Mackenzie was doing his utmost to bring a new and wider understanding of a changing world—changes that some of the more senior Church of Scotland people did not recognise.*

In the end we won the argument because we made the programmes. When I tried in meetings to explain that all religious language is metaphor and therefore images are all important in a visual medium, many looked blank. But when they saw Paul

Streather's films their eyes were washed clear and they saw reality. When Les Mitchell staged themed studio extravaganzas with the Falkirk Youth Theatre, critics rediscovered their humanity. When Les, Helen Alexander, and Stuart Miller constructed entertaining formats for serious *Voyager* debates, they attracted viewers not because they were '"religious". James Cox, veteran BBC journalist, rated Les as BBC Scotland's best studio director. When all our staff, old and new, worked together on the complexities of *Coast to Coast*, a long-running interweaving of OB hymn-singing and documentary films, communities up and down Scotland recognised that we were in our time being faithful to the old tradition of meeting and exploring the spiritual diversity of the nation. When we maintained traditional word programmes, for example *The Spirit of Scotland* lecture series which elicited a demand for eight thousand copies of the transcripts, it was evident that in giving a high profile to visual virtues, we had not abandoned our commitment to words.

When Jim Hunter, head of music and arts, became head of programmes, his visionary drive gave us resources and slots that enabled us to opt out of most UK religious output. Since our ratings were rather good, this process created something of a riot in London, whence I was summoned to explain myself. Our Scottish religious advisory committee retaliated by summoning Colin Morris, head of religious TV, to Glasgow.

Colin, temporarily forgetting his opposition to colonialisation in Africa, tried to lecture the committee, a surprising misjudgment which sent him back south with more fleas in his ear than a distressed hedgehog. Ronnie Falconer would have enjoyed that. And even more, if Ronnie had not died, would he have enjoyed the two years when, with Jim Hunter's passionate support, we did wall-to-wall live TV Assembly coverage, with modern techniques and journalistic values, spearheaded by the same Kenneth Roy whose presenting skills and forensic brain had turned the *Yes, No, Don't Know Show* into a ratings-winner.

By this time we had proved that selling the Kirk and the nation short had never been on our agenda. And our budgets were twice what I'd inherited.

19
Life's a Party

Sixteen years into the job, aged fifty-eight, I had a serious heart attack at almost exactly the same age as my father, elder brother, and elder sister. But whereas they had died, I, as the alert reader will perceive, didn't. However, taking advice from my family, I left the BBC eighteen months before retiral age. There was a rather splendid farewell party in Studio One, one of the grand original features of the Queen Margaret Drive buildings. Studio One was the home of the BBC Scottish Symphony Orchestra which has in recent years achieved astonishing new standards of exciting concert-giving, and it gave me a buzz to finish my BBC career on that particular spot, playing on one of its grand pianos to accompany a raucous set of verses which appeared to emanate from me.

It was a lovely party in studio one so it was, chust sublime. There were so many people there that I loved. Let me be a camera circling the room.

Who to start with? In a circle there is no start or finish. My eyes gravitate (forgive me, this is family) to Stephen, the son and heir. In a sacrifice so gargantuan I can hardy believe it he has for once in his life condescended to dress smartly. As a consequence he looks stunning. He isn't just a son, he also happens to be one of my tiny group of best friends. It is, for instance, he who convinced me I should retire early to "do your own thing".

There across the room is Elizabeth, but I've said more than enough about her, and there's more to come.

Now, however, my eye strays. Only a few feet away is a tall slim girl. She's only fourteen (I happen to know this) but she is beautiful, cool, poised, alarmingly attractive. She is my daughter. I haven't mentioned Alice up until now. Well, the trouble is, you can't just "mention" Alice, you have to give her floor space, stage space, star space. Her personality demands it. She arrived in our life three years after Stephen. Stephen welcomed her, in fact Stephen named her. We offered him a list of possible names and unhesitatingly he chose Alice (her mother's middle name).

Unfortunately, although we welcomed Alice, she did not always welcome us. It turned out that she had the emotional volatility of a prima donna. Sun out, all chuckles, smiles, hugs. Sun in, Apocalypse Now. But when the sun shone in, it was worth the tears. I was regularly reduced to jelly when, meeting the family at Central Station returning from a visit to granny in Galloway, Alice would hurtle along the platform to jump headlong into my arms. She rejoiced easily, she hurt easily. As an Aquarian, her brain would usually sort out her problems. But not always. At her christening, for example, David Reid, our first minister and friend in Helensburgh, did the needful, with all appropriate panache. But Alice did panache better than David. As the baptismal party exited, she reached out to seize from a Sunday School child his hymn-book. It took much subsequent negotiation to return the hymnary to its tearful rightful owner.

But focussing on family is bad manners. Who next?

I've asked a few special people to pay me tributes. You're joking! You've written a book (so a reader shouts) desperately trying to convey the impression of a sane, modest, dispassionate author devoid of any trace of egotism, and suddenly you put that image in jeopardy by disclosing that at your bowing-out ceremony you choose people to praise you? Yes, m'Lud, guilty as charged. After a decade and half of brickbats and elephant traps, this is catching up time.

I have chosen well. Episcopal Bishop of Edinburgh, Richard Holloway, ex-Moderator Robin Barbour, ex-head of BBC Scotland's music and arts department, Keith Alexander, are not the sort to dispense cosy vacuities. Keith, indeed, was an icon of mine. We founded a club of two which did not meet frequently enough (I could never have enough of his company) for a sandwich lunch in the Grosvenor Hotel to exchange intelligence, gossip, and jokes about bureaucracy. But more. At one programme review board, Keith declared our religious department output was producing more artistic films than his. Keith, not only was that unbelievably unpolitical of you, but mended a heap of wounds.

And, last but not least, a tribute is paid by my mother-in-law, Elizabeth Young Whitley. This sounds like family again, but I've asked her to the party not as family but as herself, social worker, politician, journalist, Green prophet, broadcaster, a writing stylist, and above all a historian with a long view of Scotland. As always, her speech puts together sharp words of perception with a light touch. She is one of Scotland's under-rated intellectuals.

My memory of that farewell party makes a kind of carousel in my head on which the turning circle of those who were there merges with those who were absent because they had moved on or, in the case of Paul Streather, had died in a tragic road crash. The diversity of programmes eventually achieved had depended on diversity of talent, interesting people producing interesting work that attracted other interesting people, creating a critical mass to generate fresh ideas. But a critical mass is not stable. Talent steps on and off the carousel. One is just grateful for each contribution so long as it lasts.

I see faces, hear voices, recall work. I've already listed several, but not some whose individuality won't fit any list. Donald MacDonald, islander, left his Partick church to make radio programmes of genius, a genius touched by the instability of his oscillation between constructive mischief and dark depression; a loving, lovely but ultimately lonely man.

Another islander was May Bowie, half Ayrshire, half Colonsay. Pharic Maclaren, the drama head who made *Sunset Song* and *Para Handy* told me May was the best drama assistant he ever had. Remembering Nelson Gray, I asked her to help me. After some years of being the brilliant organising energy behind our expanding range of programmes, she reluctantly acceded to my request to direct and produce. I guessed that her grasp of the force of metaphor deriving from her Celtic background could make pioneering use of film, and indeed that's exactly what she did in *Gates to Space* and the twenty six-part film series *The Quest*. When some theological intellectuals dismissed the films of May and Paul as making a naively literal use of visual metaphor, I contented myself with thinking that the reductio ad absurdum of that thought process would be to burn every poem ever made. An image is an image is an image. It either works for you or it doesn't. You can't defend it with logic, and if you analyse it you paralyse it.

Jock Clark, son of the actor Jameson Clark, took on the Herculean task of editing *The Quest* as well as many of Paul's films. Participating in that editing process was intellectually the most satisfying element in a broadcasting life. The standards of engineering and crafts in the BBC Scotland of that time were of the highest. I was lucky to benefit from them before the multi-tasking revolution began dismantling precious in-house traditions.

I now go below deck to salute the terrible twins, Alison Annand and Liz Robin. Alison was the omni-competent PA who organised *The Quest* over its two-year production of twenty-six films, with an even steeliness and pleasantness which oiled the wheels of crews on location. She then went off to have these qualities recognised as associate producer in the comedy unit. Religion had always been associated with sport (yes, yes, the other religion) but not with comedy until the gifted maverick education producer Gordon Menzies (supported by Pat Walker who was often around when subversion was in the air) introduced Rikki Fulton to mock the afflicted on Hogmanay.

Liz, the other terrible twin, was the sister of Fiona Robin who had been Pharic Maclaren's production secretary in drama before running our *Voyager* series. (It was Fiona who, on the basis of my intake of canteen fluids, first suggested I had diabetes). Liz joined *The Quest* project halfway though to help me edit vast acres of transcripts. Half of this had to be done after my heart attack when I was mentally and physically under par; I simply couldn't have done it without her. But what made Alison and Liz terrifying in combination was their capacity to work each other into flights of lunacy. Nobody reading this account of my misspent life can doubt that I am perpetually torn between a belief in silliness and lurches into solemnity. *The Quest* was in essence so solemn that these two practitioners of loopiness kept me sane, specially during and after my cardiac adventure.

If this was a book about the BBC I would enjoy writing word sketches of scores of colourful characters who triumphed over the bureaucratic machine by remaining themselves. I savoured them in passing encounters, but I recognise that because I was so busy fighting my corner I didn't exploit the clubbable potential of Queen Margaret Drive's Kafkaesque madhouse as I had the ITV circus on the Thames. Nevertheless when they sat round the conference room table at the programme review board, one could observe them framed in that formal setting as characters in a Scottish portrait gallery.

Yet another islander, the lugubrious Finlay J. Macdonald, deployed a mordant wit which could have stung like a wasp if it were not for the enfolding velvet voice. Fred Macaulay was the Gaelic head. Vying for resources, he and I conducted a lengthy jousting of memos, outdoing each other in irony, until head of programmes Pat Chalmers, with Inverurie eloquence, slapped us both down with a memo which read "This correspondence is closed. Paper is expensive". Christopher Irwin was a head of radio so sharp he cut himself every time he opened his mouth; and Stan Taylor a head of radio so generous he said he actually understood my film *Gates to Space*. Controller Pat Ramsay, like Nelson, was selective in what he saw, and in control of a finessed line of humour. And Pat Walker, who had held every top management post, indeed every post except head of paper clips, was a thoroughly amusing chairman of the programme review board. I was hypnotised by the skill with which he once quite deliberately worked the entire drama department into a lather of rage by suggesting that in a drive for economy it was quite unnecessary for them to have catering facilities on location.

For all its flaws, I reckon I caught the Beeb at the tail-end of a golden age. Its most interesting thing – certainly the most interesting thing to happen in my time cobwebbed within the BBC in Scotland – was called Alastair Hetherington. It has to be said that neither Queen Margaret Drive nor Scotland rose to the occasion. As distinct from the BBC in London, which sank to the occasion with penumbral aplomb.

Not that Alastair was my kind of person. From the moment I saw in the *Daily Record* a nearly full-page colour photo of a tall rosy-cheeked man striding up a Scottish mountain I recognised in our new controller everything I would go to considerable lengths to avoid meeting in a corridor. And that sense of alienation persisted till the last time I saw him. But not being a complete nitwit I've usually been capable of perceiving that not being like me does not constitute *a priori* grounds for someone not being entitled to my respect.

Indeed, from what I know about myself, the more someone is unlike me, the more valuable he or she may be. When clergy, notably of the evangelical variety, wax glibly about God the Father, Son and Holy Spirit, the more one suspects that if they were to actually bump into one of these "can do" characters on the street, dismay might exceed rapture. Alastair Hetherington was "can do" incarnate. He was a force of nature.

To be truthful about BBC Scotland, few of its staff pretended to be forces of nature. Not many set off in the morning thinking "Today I will change the world". Most were content to exercise their skills in a reasonably comfortable working environment with a view to getting home in one piece that night, having a good sleep, and doing more or less the same the next day. So when asteroid Hetherington landed WHOOSH on their patch, blowing away all the familiar procedural landmarks, a degree of twitchiness was to be expected.

I was torn. Not at first. At first I just ducked. My office window looked directly on to the Hamilton Drive pavement, and when at midday a rattling window led me to look out and see Alastair and Pat Chalmers (whom Alastair quickly perceived as another potential force of nature—he later became controller) pounding athletically towards a dialectical sandwich in the Botanical Gardens, my impulse was to dive under the desk.

But I became torn. I was fond of a couple of the Glasgow managers, especially Pat Walker, my immediate boss. Pat knew the BBC inside out and achieved much more than he was given credit for in encouraging creative talent, but when Don Quixote from the *Guardian* rode into town ready to lance every dragon in sight, Pat's irony was powerless to deflect the charge. Alastair Hetherington was an irony-free zone on legs, and every bureaucratic mechanism that Pat was adept at manoeuvring to keep London on side was to Alastair a red rag to a bull. Nostrils flaring, the Hetherington caber was hurled. That's why I was torn. I wanted Alastair to win his battles without people I liked being hurt. It was an impossible equation. They got hurt. And because underneath, like Don Quixote, Alastair was an innocent abroad, he too was hurt. In the end, fatally.

In the above observations I may have been led into caricature—more cartoon strip than Hogarth—but they do reflect the general impression as one lifted one's head momentarily from immediate problems to catch a snapshot of dramas on the managerial stage. I was still immersed in fighting my corner vis-à-vis the Kirk establishment, but by the end of the Hetherington five-year regime I had a truer reckoning of the strategic situation.

It was both more complex and more simple than I had at first envisaged. The emerging conflicts were to some extent a matter of personalities, but the main problems ran deeper and wider. I was weary of my own difficulties being attributed to personality clashes and so I was wary of the Hetherington upheavals being diagnosed at that level; it could be an intellectually lazy way of avoiding judgments on underlying issues. In any case, even at the personal level, most people behaved like grown ups, civil in discourse, honest in argument, and working hard to make the BBC machine work even when under strain. I wasn't aware of direct conflict, for example, between Pat Walker and Alastair; it was more of a case of the controller bypassing the head of programmes to act out the role he was familiar with as a hands-on editor operating on twenty-four hour deadlines.

There would have been more direct conflict with Alec Brown, Scotland's head of administration. He was famous for designing the then new Queen Margaret Drive extension in which he was awarded the largest room outside the chancelleries of Europe, with a desk at one end behind which one expected to find Hitler, a.k.a.

Charlie Chaplin, playing with a balloon in the form of the earth. Alec must have seemed to Alastair's force of nature an offence against nature, the can-do confronted by the can't-do.

Being socially well house-trained (and a man who always treated me with kindness), Alec saw things from the perspective of a skilled bureaucrat who, at the drop of a hat, could produce more elegant reasons for not agreeing to any suggested course of action than a fertile rabbit could produce baby bunnies. To be fair to Scottish staff, when Alastair, a fast taker of decisions, said something must be done *now* (a bewildering concept in the BBC), local managers were sometimes right to say it was undoable.

Although he learned at speed, the dynamic newspaper editor at first had a slender grasp of the nuts and bolts of engineering. Specially in a centre with limited resources, it took some dexterity and no little patience to resolve competing technical demands in a television schedule. The overarching problem was resources incommensurate with the pretensions of a broadcasting system serving a Scottish community increasingly conscious of nationhood. London was failing to back adequately the devolution agenda.

One memorable year, Alastair wrenched the annual plan from Stan Stratton's competent logistic grasp and tried to do it all by himself over a weekend. In my interview as head of religion, he offered me the earth. I had to tell him I couldn't handle the earth: I didn't have the staff. He promptly offered me more staff. I had to point out insufficient studio, O.B. and film facilities. I still benefited; I got a lot more programmes than the normal planning process would have given me. The Hetherington methods were not subtle, but they got things moving.

If Alastair hit his head against what he felt to be a wall of negativity in his own building, the administrative mountains he faced in London made the Cobbler he easily climbed in the Arrochar Alps look like a molehill. To an increasingly tetchy corporate machine Hetherington was not a force but a disorder; not an accelerator to be balanced by a brake, but a spanner in the works liable to wreck the machinery. And this is where it gets interesting. The fate of the Hetherington experiment in BBC

Scotland throws the whole devolution experiment into glaring relief.

In the BBC laboratory, the theory of devolving some power but not too much was tested to destruction. It could not work. Why? Because it was designed not to work.

As he reveals in his book *Inside BBC Scotland*, Alastair grasped this point too late. He should have made it a condition of accepting the job of controller Scotland that he had the status and effective power of a member of the BBC directorate. Whereas, at the end of the day, he was a branch manager. Was that arrogance? Why should he have had more status and power than previous Scottish controllers? Because he was being given a more important mission, based on a new political situation. The devolution connection is crystal clear. When he was offered the post, the illusion was created that he would have real power. That illusion was created both by the motive behind his appointment and his apparent mandate. It was a sleight of hand manoeuvre. Because the first devolution referendum was impending, the BBC was nervous about the possible fall-out of a yes vote leading to a push for independence in broadcasting, amputating the BBC's operations north of the border. So Alastair was sent north to behave in a sufficiently independent way to make a formal break-up seem unnecessary.

As it happened, thanks to the fiasco of the percentage hurdle, the referendum vote was negative and London could sigh with relief. Except that—shock horror—Alastair had by now been unleashed in Scotland. And the cannon wasn't just loose on the deck, it was taking over the ship. If the new controller had been a traditional BBC type, he would have behaved like an English gentleman, touched the forelock, smiled ironically, and said, "OK chaps, I see that the need for the charade has evaporated, I'll revert to the status quo. London rules—OK."

But Hetherington was no more an English gent than his father had been when running the great University of Glasgow. Both were sons of Scotland, equipped with Scots blood and intellect. If they had forelocks, nobody had taught them how they were to be touched. Alastair was in his actions, as in his prose, startlingly straightforward. He'd been mandated to make Scottish broadcasting more independent? Very well, he would do it. The mandarins in London realised too late that their sleight of hand had been all too brilliantly slippery. Well, not entirely too late. They could always sack Hetherington. So they did.

I have personal knowledge that the failure of the Alastair experiment was not due to his personality. I know from hearing it from the lips of subsequent controllers and heads of programmes that the abiding problem was the centralisation of power in London. In the last resort, men as diverse as the very gentlemanly controller Pat Ramsay, the headstrong Aberdeenshire controller Pat Chalmers, and the feisty head of programmes, Jim Hunter, found that if they pursued Scottish interests beyond a certain point, the London door was banged firmly in their faces. Scottish devolution must not be allowed to become real enough to lead to independence: that was the agenda, and we see it now writ large in a Scottish Parliament held on the leash of powers reserved to Westminster: including, ironically, powers over Scottish broadcasting.

Yet the experiment was not a complete failure. Hetherington's blast of wind liberated talents, harnessed able outsiders, enhanced the range and authority of Scottish broadcasting journalism, gave courage and support to producers such as myself, and pushed forward radio devolution within Scotland. People even turned up to meetings on time.

The day after Alastair left the building, there was a great silence. Some upstairs managers may have felt relief. For programme makers who had dreamed of a Scottish renaissance, it was a silence smelling of death.

20

Seer

Nobody forgets their first experience of George MacLeod. Mine takes place in St Cuthbert's Church in Edinburgh, in a world so far away I can't believe it existed or that I then did. The Second World War has just finished but douce Edinburgh seems untouched. On a Sunday morning little stirs. A dilatory rat scurries back to Princes Street Gardens after its Saturday night binge in McVities. But now behold the human race. Here appear people, multi-hatted and umbrella'd. Also me, in my teens, going to church with my mother. In the mists swirling in the swamp below the castle floats the spire. In our hundreds we descend silently into the graveyard, past the resting place of De Quincey, into the mausoleum which swallows us into the vast space of its piety, the organ quietly playing, female perfumes mingling. Edinburgh's bourgeoisie is ready for worship.

But not ready for George Fielden MacLeod. I am awaiting my usual Sunday treat, an Adam Burnett sermon. Dr Burnett, collegiate minister of St Cuthbert's, is a prince of lyrical preachers, the Adonis of the poetic sermon. So my soul is quivering in the pew tuned to his lyre. But the beadle emerges, entirely bereft of Dr Burnett. And what is this striding in?

My mother whispers: George MacLeod. Who? After routine devotional exercises the interloper is introduced. He swaggers to the pulpit. I'm sorry, but that is what he does. He swaggers. Every bit of him swaggers. His legs swagger. His spine swaggers. His jowls swagger. His eyebrows swagger. He is the swagger made flesh. He mounts the pulpit like field marshal Montgomery commandeering a tank. During the last verse of the hymn he glares at us like a brigade of tanks aiming its guns. Apprehensively we sit down.

I would like to describe what happens next, but I can't. I'm too busy trying to survive. Cowering within the carapace of what I have hitherto taken to be my soul, I am aware of certain things. This is not a sermon. And this is not religion. And this is not about God. It is not a sermon, it is a speech. It is not religion, it is politics. And it is not about God, it is about man. And it is not comforting, it is frightening. Apart from anything else this guy has no idea how to behave. Like a demented baby he is throwing everything out of the pram. He bites great theological chunks out of the pulpit and spits them at us. He throws statistics about poverty and hunger though a stained glass window. He hurls scriptural bombs at the gallery. He flings socialist thunderbolts at the ceiling, sets hellfire to the chancel, reduces the church soporific to rubble, burns my whole religious position to the ground. And then he has the nerve to walk calmly down the pulpit steps and back to his seat. Next Sunday, fortunately for the blood pressure of Christian Edinburgh, Dr Burnett returns to comfort us with quotes from the poets.

By the time I next hear Dr MacLeod I am grown up. Well, I think I am. I'm a student, and I edit the *Student*, the Edinburgh University magazine. The General Assembly is in town and this is a special youth night. St Giles is packed with yoof because the preacher is George MacLeod. But whereas the St Cuthbert's bourgouisie had goaded him into a full-scale bombardment, the mass of young potential spread before him in St Giles moves him into mood-music. All the challenges are still there, two-thirds of the world is still starving, inasmuch as you drop a nuclear bomb on one of the least of these my brethren you do it to me, but there is a gentleness to the pleading. At the end, if a pin had dropped, it would have sounded like a meteor hitting St Giles.

Afterwards I catch up with him and ask if I can print part of his address in the magazine. He doesn't know me from Adam, but, "It's the usual rubbish", he says, hands me the script, and disappears into the crowd. I look at the manuscript and am astounded. My illusion that he adjusted the sermon because he was moved by the congregation is exposed. Not only is every word there exactly as read, but everything else is there, down to the most minuscule piece of stage direction and point of expression.

Not only every comma and semi-colon; not just every bracket and every pause; not just every underlining; not only every important word in capitals, but specially vital words are in *red*.

As I stand there in Parliament Square digesting this document I have the first rudiment of comprehension that in George MacLeod I am confronted by a serious phenomenon; not just a spirit of extraordinary inspiration but a brain of dedicated perspiration; not a charismatic maverick but a diligent worker, a committed craftsman, a professional artisan, a person of meticulous organisation, a disciple of exactitute, an artist. As a lazy student I feel subdued into a rare humility.

It was from that moment that I began to reform my ways, not because of the message in the MacLeod sermon, but because of this hard evidence that no amount of inspiration is a substitute for attention to detail. Here in my hand I can see a brain of serious intent in the business of communicating with other brains. George MacLeod is not just a romantic, an adventurer, a Celtic word-spinner, a mystic, a poet, a comic, an entrepreneur, a warrior, a prophet, a seer. He is something more dangerous, something so insidious it is capable of not just rocking boats but sinking them. He is an intellectual, but worse, an intellectual pretending not to be. He is a Christian spy risking his mind in the world of shifting ideas. Where ignorant armies clash by night there will be George in the midst. No-man's-land is to be his chosen home and we all know the name of that No-man's-land is to be Iona.

Nobody can forget their first sight of Iona: simultaneously unbelievable, and yet suddenly the only thing worth believing. There it lies on the edge of the known world, naked yet formidable, inviting one to cross over into a different dimension. Except... that's all words. When you first see Iona, it's wordless.

And then, as with so much reality, when you cross over you're suddenly in the realm of cartoon (cartoon being another word for myth). Floating inches over the green lapping water, there's this Walt Disney island, small, perfect, here a little bay, there a little machair, over here a little hill, on the horizon the Aegean little islands of Tiree and Coll, down there a little abbey, and oh, look, swaggering around there's a very big tall man looking like Prospero after a bad night.

The big man is of the clan MacLeod, a Highland aristocrat who had more Kirk Moderators in his ancestry than the Mackenzie clan had sheep-stealers (and that's a lot). He is in himself a field of paradoxes. A soldier in the 1914 Great War, awarded France's croix de guerre for courage, who became Scotland's most famous pacifist. The fashionable preacher in Edinburgh's west end who gave up a glittering career to espouse the poor and unemployed in the industrial west of Scotland. A passionate believer in Christian involvement in the heat and battle of politics who centred the greater part of his life on a Hebridean island. The rugged individualist who founded and anchored himself in a community on that island. A blisteringly aggressive preacher who could melt the hardest heart with a lyric prayer or split open the sourest face with a comic crack... oh yes, that's the gallus figure muttering to himself, or God, or the grass, outside the abbey.

Nobody can forget their first row with George MacLeod. Mine is over the abbey music. That is why I'm on the island. I've been asked to run the abbey music for the three-month summer season. I am no sooner on the island than with all the subtlety of a Scotch terrier catching sight of an ankle, I decide that the whole style of the Iona music needs to have teeth sunk into it. The singing should be in unison, not four-part harmony. It should be robustly brisk, not sentimentally lingering. More Reformation and modern tunes, fewer Victorian hymns. Out with Crimond and St George's Edinburgh. This modest programme of reform leaves George speechless—but not for long. The Scotch terrier finds towering over it a massive bulldog with quivering jaw. The MacLeod face vibrates. The body shakes with outrage. Then, the voice. "Do you realise that at the very moment we're putting up a scrawny wail at the behest of your latest whim, there is a Community man bathing in the River Zambesi singing the twenty-third psalm to Crimond at the top of his voice, confident—CONFIDENT—that here on Iona we will be supplying the other parts?"

Three months later, it is my last night on the island. Late in the evening the boss calls me to his private lair in the abbey. He glowers at me as if I'm some sort of disease. "Sit down," he growls. Clearly I am to be skinned alive and fed to the seagulls. But instead of reaching for a scimitar he reaches for a bottle and pours each of us a gigantic whisky. "I hope you're happy," he says. "During your stay here you've upset and divided the island, the Community, the associate members, the friends of Iona, half the visitors, and probably all the kings in their graves. Above all, you've upset me. Are you by any chance free to come back next summer and create more mayhem?"

He lifts his glass. "Drink up. Here's to mayhem. At least you've got stickability." I've treasured that compliment all my life. That is how George made disciples.

But that isn't enough. He doesn't want disciples, he wants something more disturbing. Friendship? Love? Such psychological parameters make him uncomfortable. What he is pursuing, always pursuing, ceaselessly as the sea-tide pursuing, is the Presence. The extra. The crossing of boundaries.

So half-way through the second whisky, he says, "Actually, I owe you an apology. Two months ago I was walking past the abbey in the evening. The wind was getting up. There was foam on the waves running up the Sound. Then mixed up in the wind I heard Columba's monks. It wasn't, of course, it was your choir practice in the abbey, and I realised what you were up to, getting us to sing in unison. Harmony is what you expect of upholstered Victorian angels. Unison expresses the unity of the creation across time and space. My apology is that I should have told you then that I understood."

To George, Columba and his monks were as real as wind and waves in the Sound. One evening, the following summer, he nabs two of us, myself and I think it was one of the guides, and urgently rushes us to the tiny St Columba's shrine. A team of archaeologists have dug up some bones. George is convinced these

are remains of a Columban monk which have lain outside
consecrated ground for one and a half millennia. It is a matter of
commanding importance that we commit these remains and pray
for the soul of the monk now. Crushed into that tiny shrine, really
little more than a cupboard in the outside wall, there in front of us
is that hulk of a man on his knees, with us on ours behind him. He
prays. The minutes cease, the twentieth century falls away. We are
on a voyage through time and beyond time. With the focus of a
priest of any religion or a scientist in any laboratory wrestling with
unseen forces and unresolved concepts, George intercedes for an
unknown spirit. With difficulty we return to the present, George
thanks us for accompanying him, we return to our tasks, the matter
is closed.

Except that later, the archaeologists give it as their opinion that
we had prayed over the remains of a sheep. Yes, some people did
laugh. "That's George," they said, "carried away by a Celtic
fantasy." But we did not laugh. We had been there. And it was no
fantasy. In the matter of souls, in the soul of matter itself, we had
been involved in some real transaction. Yes, George at one level,
had maybe got a fact wrong. But what is a fact? It is a fact that I
had been caught up in a struggle between strong forces, between
light and darkness, and the power of that prayer had affected
something, somewhere. There had been another Presence. A
boundary had been crossed.

Nobody could ever forget their first involvement in a
confrontation between a MacLeod and a Viking. One of the
week's visitors to the Community is a Great Dane. This Danish
pastor's arrival coincides with a drought. At the end of supper,
George rises. Neptune rising from the deep is as nothing compared
to George rising at the refectory top table. He stands there,
vibrating, a cross between a Horse of the Apocalypse with
toothache and Churchill preparing to fight Hitler on the beaches.
"We have a crisis. The well is running dry. Visitors may think it a
miracle that Iona, which is nine-tenths composed of water, is

surrounded by water, and for half of this summer has received water from the heavens in abundance, can run out of water, but the miracle is that the well was discovered in the first place. Nobody is to use a drop of water unless absolutely essential."

After supper I'm on the rota for washing up. So is the Great Dane. As a good Scandinavian he is hot on hygiene. As a Viking he is into power. As a Dane he is into planning. He takes command of the sink. In a trice he has completed a complex scaffolding of sloping trays, wooden boards, plates and pans. "The point," he explains, "is that for good hygiene you should rinse everything three times." With a flourish he turns on both taps.

Enter left, George Fielden MacLeod of Fuinary. He stands in mute disbelief, observing jets of water cascading everywhere. It turns out later, by the way, that our Viking had left the refectory to go to the loo before George made his announcement. He is therefore in a state of invincible ignorance. Picking his jaw off the floor, George advances on the sink. Smiling benevolently the Dane explains, "You see, good rinsing."

The rest of us hide behind our dish towels. Peering over the top of mine I see Scotland's leading pacifist pawing the ground, smoke and fire queuing up to issue from his nostrils. Then George does his magic. Putting his arm around the Dane's shoulder he says in the friendliest voice, "It is a great honour for us to have you here. The others can wash up. Come and tell me about the peace movement in Denmark." Exit hygienic Viking with peacemaking Celt. George pops a menacing face back round the door. "Every drop of that water, clean, dirty, filthy, goes into every pot, pan, jug, mug, egg-cup you can find. And put labels on saying "bottled in the chateau."

One evening, after supper, George announces with the weariness of Atlas with a broken collarbone, "At 7.30 this evening in the Chapter House a discussion will take place with our Anglican and Roman brethren on the subject of church unity and reconciliation." As he sits down he sighs loudly, and adds, "Volunteers, please, to join me afterwards in the mopping up of blood."

It isn't that George doesn't believe in the unity of Christians. He believes in the unity of everyone. But he doesn't think it is advanced by sterile church debate. His brain and heart are big enough to live with paradox. Depending on who is condemning him, he is known in his lifetime as the militarily decorated pacifist, the aristocratic socialist, the Catholic communist. Love your enemies is not for him a theory. George pursued love not in abstract principles but in criss-crossing Britain to plead for borstal boys in court.

Once, walking down Edinburgh's Royal Mile, I see through a cafe door the back of an Inverness cape. I walk in and sit opposite the world's greatest champion of the starving millions. He is with childlike enthusiasm digging into a banana split. I address my hero: "And two-thirds of the world is starving." He looks stricken. "I haven't eaten all day," he mumbles. There is a silence, while I quietly die. Pushing away the offending glass dish, he looks me in the eye. "You're right," he says, "they really are starving."

George MacLeod was a true seer. He saw things others didn't. He saw further into things. He saw into the past and into the future. He saw into souls. He was human, of course. Over issues big and small he could be petty, blind, deaf, stubborn. But on the whole, in him was as clear an access to the word made flesh as I'm likely to meet. And as many thousands would attest, I met it closest in worship and specially in the conduct of Holy Communion. When, leading up to the breaking of the bread, he spoke the great prayer, the central part of which he spent hours writing fresh for every Sunday, the earth moved. And heaven moved. And in some way they fused together. It wasn't just inspiring, it was shattering. An extra presence, a boundary crossed. A transubstantiation of matter and spirit in dangerous fission and fusion.

As his stupendous words mounted into a climax of clashing metaphor, it really was as if Christ was released in an explosion of light-energy. We can't compute how many lives were altered by that experience. In my second summer on Iona, the life of one visiting lecturer, a nuclear physicist, was changed. He threw away his lectures and delivered a blazing scientific and theological tour de force focussing on the Lipchitz statute of the Virgin Mary in the cloisters. That sculpture had one night given him a transforming vision, shared with Chris Adams, the stepfather of Douglas Adams of the *Hitch-Hikers Guide to the Galaxy.* Chris Adams' life was also changed and I've often wondered if something of that cosmic experience passed on to his son influenced Douglas Adams in taking the universe on board.

These Communion experiences make my last story all the more strange and difficult. As it is a very private story I have swithered about sharing it with you. If I've decided wrongly, George in his generous way will forgive me.

In my last year at the BBC, I got a message that George was willing to be filmed. This was during the Assembly and I went to his Edinburgh home the day before filming to discuss what he'd like to say. He was now in his nineties and frail. Making and pouring the tea was a painful effort but what he had to say was more so. Two nights before, he'd had a dream. In his loneliness he had turned to Lorna, his much younger wife, whose early death he was still grieving over. In the dream, she had given him the most tremendous scolding. "Oh George, stop all this self-pity. You've a lot to do. Just get on with it." He said in the forty-eight hours since that he'd felt released. He no longer needed Lorna's physical presence.

The morning after that encounter he'd been walking up the Mound to the General Assembly service of Holy Communion, and was suddenly stopped in his tracks by this devastating thought. "Why am I going to this so-called Communion? Am I really saying that Christ's presence is more real in bread and wine than in the whole of life? We don't touch God in dedicated bread. We touch reality everywhere. We should just get on with it."

I said, "Do you want to say that on film tomorrow, you who have made Holy Communion central again in Presbyterianism?"

"If I have made Communion central," he said, "then I have

failed. I only wanted to make love central."

The next morning he sent a message saying he would rather not do the filming. I guess he decided he had to cross that no-man's-land alone.

Nobody forgets their last seeing of George MacLeod. Mine was a year later. I saw him in the distance on the Mound. He'd obviously been at an evening Assembly meeting. He was standing totally alone, very bent. He hailed a taxi. With difficulty he climbed into it and was gone.

I stood looking at the spot where he'd been. Some words rang in my head. They weren't words of Columba, or of George, or of Scripture, but of Shakespeare: "What a piece of work is a man".

21
Paradise Regained

When in July 1988, in the Vale of Leven Hospital, my heart considered ceasing to trade, my brain countered with one unanswerable argument: I absolutely did not want to do to Stephen and Alice what my father had done to me. This request was answered in the affirmative. I have been reaffirmed beyond my deserving, though not theirs, by the bonus of seeing them grow into fascinating adults. I simply can't imagine children of whom one could be more proud. Thanks to my ticker for toughing it out.

What was beyond dreaming, let alone requesting, was all the other affirmations and reaffirmations that in those last fifteen years have broken through the ground of my being. It has amounted to a paradise regained. In that rhetorical leap I don't compare my modest narrative to Milton's, but each life has its potential paradise and loss of it, and every regaining of happiness is a miracle. Looked at in that light, my recent years have been packed with miracles, rebirths and new dawns. I won't identify them as constituting an Indian summer—Milton is an extravagance enough for now—and I haven't been to India, so I don't know for sure.

What I do know is where I have been in this period of growing older, if not old.

First I have been fortunate to be in a work place which, as in Peterhead, is my home. And I have been able in that environment to go back to the beginning and learn to write. I don't mean, of course, that I have learned to write, but I've had a chance to try. Nothing to do with writing courses, just the incredible luxury of time to do it. In essence it has led me to progress from rejecting one word before selecting a second, to rejecting nine before choosing a tenth. But how can one do that and not lose the flow? Ah! That's a question not only about writing or any art or any work, but about life, the art and the work of living it; and it's too late in this book to try answering. Anyway, it can't be answered. There is no formula. Jesus made that perfectly clear. There is no formula, there is only a way, and the way is called love: love of life, of art, of work, and of the extra dimension we limit by calling God.

Another place I have been able to revisit is broadcasting. Perhaps I should never have become entangled in that media world. Perhaps I should have been content to write, to preach, to play the organ, to be an engine-driver. But involved I became, and it has been a kind of epiphany for me to be invited back to party on the air not as a busy and problem-oriented operator but simply to communicate.

Johnston McKay, about whom I haven't written much because nearly everyone in Scotland knows him, or has heard him doing his brilliant, bluff, but searching interviews on *Personal Encounter*, was another of the talents I inveigled into the religious department; I had assessed him as having too large an ability to be trapped in the distinguished twilight zone of Paisley Abbey. In co-operation with a sensitive head of radio, Neil Fraser, Johnston was responsible for two historic achievements. In programme terms he carved out a three-hour Sunday morning radio sequence which has maintained a substantial audience for over a decade. Even more significantly, he succeeded in finally squelching into the past the claustrophobic tradition of male chauvinism and ecclesiastical orientation. He brought on a whole generation of female talent unencumbered by religious labels. In other words he made religious radio finally professional.

I've had the pleasure of contributing to that culture as an outsider yet an outsider sufficiently informed to rejoice over Johnston's angels. Mo McCulloch, who had begun in my time as a radio secretary, became under Johnston an award-winning producer. Ailsa Macintosh, wearing exuberantly a huge intelligence and talent, is the daughter of Farquhar Macintosh whose powerful debates with Kay Carmichael had so enlivened the Broadcasting Council. And Susan Mackay (no relation) had a piercing creativity which stretched me to my limit when I did a programme for Radio Four. It galvanised listeners all over England to send an avalanche of letters; a tribute more to her outstanding skills honed in the audio department than to any words of mine. She now wanders the world applying her energies to communication programmes in support of the prevention of disease.

Meanwhile, back at the ranch, I swoon every time I hear Erica Morrison on the phone. She is a newish religious producer and her voice is pure Stornoway, the place I failed to be born in. In protection of the male species I need to raise a cheer for Tom Dunlop, marooned in a sea of women. He is, with Father Bill Anderson, the most kindly and courteous producer I've ever had to deal with.

Now that Johnston has retired (from the Beeb, not from life or the church) his successor in charge of religious radio is Anna Magnusson. She is the less famous daughter of my old friend Magnus, but she has two (at least) formidable assets: a large slice of the overwhelming Magnusson charm; and a brain of forensic power. On the television side, Anne Muir carries on a charismatic tradition of people-centred programmes and Stuart Miller, now freelance, brilliantly angles TV worship in such a way to make it meaningfully watchable.

To me it matters that in a diversity of forms the torch is carried on. I hope all these names haven't created the impression of a dutiful list. I do think it's important that, coming out of the past, I pay tribute to the present, to give hope for the future. The future is never guaranteed, it has to be fought over. Already, the post I occupied for sixteen years has ceased to exist. The hyper-thin, mega-skilful and super-sensitive Andrew Barr has ridden into history as the last head of religion in BBC Scotland. Together with the controller John McCormick he enabled religion to ride the John Birt revolution. Well, it was called a revolution; I see it as a calamitous period of human destabilisation and cultural vandalism, accompanied by a wholesale assault on the English language. The Birt regime ruled by fear and its thought police terrorised in jargon.

The interfacing of regime changes in religion and politics was the theme of an Easter TV documentary I was commissioned to write and present for Channel 4 which took me to the café in Prague where the poet Vaclav Havel still, as president, mixed with the citizens, and to the Garden of Gethsemane in Jerusulam where Donald Swann described how on one occasion Jesus "turned up". In terms of my personal pilgrimage, one was as poignant as the other.

Apart from writing, preaching, broadcasting and events in our wider family as nephews, nieces, and the generation after that have coloured in the human landscape, this most recent period of my story has produced three major strands about which I am going to say far too little; not because there is not much to say, but for the opposite reason: each could fill a book.

The first would make an entertaining book because it is about old friendships marvellously rediscovered and new ones astonishingly made. Of the latter, the most astonishing was one which surfaced in the summer of 2002 when an American female voice left a message on my answer phone. Karen McKinnon (she explained) was a poet who lived up a mountain in New Mexico. In the Holy Week of 1962 (she further explained) we had met on a train between Edinburgh and Newcastle (where else?). She was twenty-one and I was twenty-nine and I had asked her, "What is writing for?" As she was married five weeks later she hadn't got round to answering the question. But now, forty years on, she had an answer, based on a career teaching, writing and publishing poetry. Writing a memoir, she told this story and set about finding me. She was told I was dead—a namesake—but by chance in St Giles bumped into Jo Penney, an elder who said he'd heard me do *Thought for the Day* and he assumed that was done live, not dead. Karen and I have conducted a long and earnest correspondence ever since. And the answer? She writes: "To stay alive."

Then there is Sam Salter. We have for several years been conducting a far from earnest correspondence since he wrote about a Radio Four programme of mine and I wrote a funny letter back. His reply was more funny than mine, so from then until now we have competed in amusing each other. He is a theoretically retired Anglican vicar who is my age plus a little, lives near Grantham, and entertains my wife. It is alleged that I entertain his wife. The two pairs have never met, and it is still an open question as to whether we dare risk it. It takes a lot for someone to intimidate me but I am in awe of someone who in his teens piloted bombers over Germany, was chaplain in a famous public school, and has written that fundamentalists are more infallible than the Pope and more devious than the mafia.

I am even more in awe of Ben Saunders, because he plays the organ more brilliantly than I ever could. We met when he was Herrick Bunney's last assistant and we discovered an amazing amount in common from both our connections with Herrick and Bill Minay. Though still a cub, he has been the music deputy at Blackburn and Chester Cathedrals and now runs the music at Leeds Roman Catholic Cathedral. Over several years, thanks to his hospitality, I've heard more wonderful music entirely free than at any time since I was a music student. Also Ben makes a mean pasta.

All that's been fun. Someone who has been the source of a lot of fun is Kenneth Roy, at first by allowing me to write in *The Scottish Review*, and then by setting up the Institute of Contemporary Scotland, with its devastating and prophetic offshoot, the Young Scotland Programme. The Institute was the most significant single enterprise created in the Scotland of my time, unless you reckon the parliament to be significant. (Yes, of course it is, but it's a lot less fun.) I could write a book about ICS, but I'll leave that to Kenneth.

And the other book that has to be written, not by me, is the one my wife has to write. After putting herself always last after me and the children, Elizabeth launched a formidable new career and for a decade and a half has been running the Dyslexia Institute in Scotland and fighting for the disadvantaged against many entrenched educationalists. It's been a punishing task but an utterly rewarding one which has changed many lives. She does more practical human good in a week than I've done in a life.

Talking about fun and doing good is not incongruous. One of the world's most unusual festivals is the Avanti! Summer Sounds festival, where the players for many years had no fee and now only a nominal one. At the heart of its philosophy is the belief that it is the work that matters, not the institution. That chimes so much with so much work I have experienced in Scotland, where institutions struggle to be born or to survive. A Scottish National Theatre is about to be born, though a huge opportunity was missed years ago when that towering man of the theatre, Tom Fleming, was ready to take it on. But for him it has always been the work that matters, not the status, and next to Peterhead, and Southwick, the Christian community where Elizabeth and I have encountered most fun and the doing of good is the little ecumenical church at Canonmills in Edinburgh unobtrusively led by Tom, illumined by a modern peripatetic college of preachers. In that community, laughter and tears co-mingle in an honest search for ways of living in hope.

Harry Whitley treated his St Giles assistants as princes. He nourished not only soul and brain but stomach. In my period of apprenticeship he would sometimes invite me to the New Club to chew a chop with him after Sunday evening worship. That usually signified yet another distressing set-to with the Edinburgh Establishment, and he wanted to talk it through with someone before facing his family. But more regular and uplifting were the monthly lunches he gave us assistants at the Howgate Inn, a famous howff south of Edinburgh which at that time did a handsome Scandinavian table.

There we replenished the body corporal and spiritual, putting the world and St Giles to rights with a heady cocktail of the uproarious and the serious. As he drove us (very carefully) home, it was amazing to find that with infinite craftiness he had lured us into another month of new commitments. In return one found oneself replete with a fresh supply of *bon mots*. One such soundbite (probably directed at us) was: "Anyone who is absolutely sure he is right is not only a fool but in the modern world a dangerous fool".

I have never thought otherwise, but if there are two decision I ever made which I dare to say were absolutely right, one was to ask Elizabeth to hitch up with me and the other was to present Helensburgh to her as the sole nominee for the site of our home.

During my three-month convalescence after the heart attack, when I wasn't allowed to work or to drive, I made some interesting discoveries. First, that if I put one foot in front of the other and repeated the manoeuvre for a while, it came to pass that in some magical way I had transferred myself from one part of Helensburgh to another, and that for no extra charge I had been able to inspect an exceptionally beautiful town in great detail. The effect was such pure pleasure that I vowed never again to go on four wheels. After all, the Strathclyde Passenger Transport system could move me electrically to Glasgow in forty-five minutes and Scotrail's separate West Highland sprinters could lift me over the roof of Rannoch to the end of the Road to the Isles. Alas, I broke the vow, but in my post-Beeb recuperation period I've been able to combine two legs and four wheels, thanks to the four legs of our dogs.

As a family our particular paradise, never lost, has been Glen Fruin, reachable by car in seven minutes. On our first evening thirty years ago, we drove to its western summit to gaze at the Faslane base far below in the Gareloch, then over range after range of hills, the Arrochar Alps, the tip of Ben Cruachan, and far to the south the dreaming peaks of Arran. Every spring, the four of us would set out in a competition as to who would catch sight of the first lamb in the glen and in recent years it has been a *sine qua non* of my week to take our collie several walks by the Fruin Water gurgling through the centre of the glen. Chelsea, like Nell before her, enjoys symphonies of sniffing wild scents, and I (at weekends it is with Elizabeth) enjoy hearing the cuckoo and the lark and watching the dipper skim, the heron stand, and the swallows swoop. For fifteen years Stephen and Alistair, his friend from schooldays onwards, have spent every midsummer night walking through the glen.

For me, Helensburgh has been a profound consolation, its thirty years of settled order and beauty filling up the gap which yawned when I was forced to leave my homeland on the North Sea, and in particular it has been a benediction to watch my son's evolving commitment to the town he loves, serving it as secretary to its Community Council, and the countryside he loves, working in it with the Wildlife Trust.

Helensburgh has offered other consolations. A beautiful church to worship in, with a fine organ and choir, led by one of Scotland's best organists, Walter Blair, and focussed by David Clark, possibly the most level-headed minister I've ever met wired up with a dry humour honed, I daresay, by Rotary and golf course. Sharing community joys and sorrows by playing the organ in Walter's absence has kept that old thread of my life in place. And my mother, who loved the Clyde (her father was Free Church minister in Brodick), was grateful to spend her last years with us and then in the Helensburgh Church of Scotland home, Clyde View. Her last view was indeed of the Clyde before she died quietly of bronchitis in her nineties against a burning red sunset.

Symbiotically, while we still guard the hinterland of the Clyde, my daughter Alice, a hundred and twenty miles to the south, has for some years stood over (she is tall) the Solway. Our connections with the lovely lands of Galloway go back nearly forty years when Harry and Elizabeth Whitley began renovating a glebe cottage in a small remote glen which runs down to the Solway and from which the peaks of the Lake District can be seen floating so mystically one can imagine them populated by poets, not tourists. This has been our second home, summer, autumn, winter, and spring. Granny is still there, to welcome us amidst her prodigal flowers and orchard. Our grandson Calvin thinks he owns it, as well as thinking that he owns Elizabeth, Alice, Stephen, and Mrs Whitley, all constituent parts of a paradise which, being only being five, he does not realise will one day be lost.

The tapestry of one human life is large, that of a family larger, that of a country vast. And that of a planet? Apart from six years in London I've lived all my life in Scotland, yet I don't know how much I understand about this carbuncle. "Carbuncle" is not rude. If you add the Cairngorms and Grampians to the Alps of Argyll, Ardnamurchan, and Kintail and then, for sheer dazzlement throw in Torridon, Suilven, and Ben Loyal, you have a conspicuous aggregate of carbuncularity, and since size isn't everything, would you dismiss the hills strolling across the Borders and Galloway, the strong ridges of Shetland, and the misty shapes of Barra and Skye? If I have omitted Ben Nevis that is only because tolerance of tourism has its limits and my limit begins to be reached as I approach Fort William, batting off caravans, backpacks, buses, and midges, unless, of course, I'm crossing Rannoch Moor on the train which sneaks behind the Nevis massif to connect with the steam run to Mallaig, in which case, as romance clouds the brain, one's arms open out to the world: "Yes, come and clutter our space; we have lots more space where that came from".

Of course it's not just about size. Scotland is a small country. Small is not just, in the argot of the sixties, beautiful, it is in the micro-fields of physics and biology in the twenty-first century, real. As a boy I knew every sand dune nestling in the arm of the two-mile Fraserburgh bay. I knew the curvature of each hollowed-out dune as exactly as a surgeon will consider every polyp; he considers it because it is there. What is there is what is.

It is the thereness of Scotland that has moved me from beginning to end. It is the thereness of word and sound and mood and picture and people that has invaded my brain like an army of occupation. It is the thereness of all this otherness that has tantalised me with the concept of God. It is all these therenesses towering into infinity and yet burrowing down into intimacy that have identified the hereness that is me. As Martin Luther almost said: "Here I am: I can be no other."

Luther said something else: "The first duty of the preacher is to entertain."

Scotland has been sublime entertainment. If I haven't conveyed some of that in these pages, then I've been whistling in the wind. The land entertained me, and the sea and sky. People entertained me—what a procession! Not just the amusing people like my aunt Etta, and Iain McGlashan and Graham Cairns-Smith at Fettes and other friends since, and Alice and Stephen, and Elizabeth, and all our cats and dogs, and Chic Murray and Stanley Baxter, George MacLeod, Donald Dewar, and John Smith, the funniest Prime Minister we never had. But also, at a level so mysterious I won't attempt word descriptions, I've been entertained by the people and events swimming towards me in deep places, dark places, bitter places, places of search and struggle, surfing in the veins of the sub-conscious, pressurising the heart. Stress and difficulty have entertained me as a householder answers a knock on the door and admits a stranger to a risky encounter. This is life; it's hell and heaven and many things in between.

For a nation as well as a family, a person, life is a fearful risk. The itinerant Palestine preacher is said to have said, "I came so that you could have a more abundant life." This means "I came to give you courage to explore a deeper danger." That's why the Jesus project is so scary for those who try it. How many do? As distinct from the many who mouth it. Not that I despise the mouthing or writing of words, in art or argument or preaching or personal encounter. Our ability to do this is one of the extraordinary carbuncles that has grown out of our brain. Talking is work, as much as doing things is.

The late Vernon Sproxton, film-maker and broadcaster, was a blacksmith as well as a wordsmith. In the forge in his Yorkshire village he liked to weld things as much as he liked to weld film in the cutting room or words in his study. He was fascinated by what he called "the is-ness of things", the is-ness of a dog, a cat, a tree. A dog is not like a cat or a tree. But also it is not a clone of another dog: that is true of every country and every part of every country. What is the is-ness of a Scot? Each Scot is different. Yet Scots are recognisable. I do not know every village and town in Scotland, or every city street, but I know many of them. Each is itself and many of these selves have spoken to me.

When I worked in broadcasting, I kept a vow that I would never go furth of my homeland to make a programme. Exploring foreign parts was taken by many producers to be a perk of the job. It wasn't for me a matter of saving money, it was a principle. As what I was always trying to do was reflect or dig out a tiny particle of the essence of what being human on this planet was about, if that couldn't be done where I was, then it wasn't worth looking for anywhere. Did that make me a little Englander when I worked in London, or a little Scotlander when I worked in Glasgow? Was I being parochial when I turned down jobs in Geneva and the USA? Yes, but was it bad to be parochial? The point of human identity is that where one stands is for oneself the centre of the universe. Infinity is at work in a finite being. Scotland is not a place. It is an aggregate of places and people and moments each of which can touch infinity.

I cannot therefore be a nationalist, because that is to over-define that reality. Isms ring-fence is-ness. Ring-fencing may be a useful device in finance, but not in living. Whether in asylum-seekers' detention centres or in religious bigotry, cutting out human beings or ideas is the enemy of life and love. I am not a Beethovenist, a Shakespearist, or a Burnsist. I may sometimes sound like a Goddist, but I try not to.

I am not a chauvinist, a feminist, or an ageist. So I can't be a Scotist. In fact I can't empathise with any concept which views reality as an entity defined by images of power. I am deeply suspicious of the words power and glory, and of what they are taken to represent. What they are taken to represent varies, of course, which is why one views them with such ambivalence. It is probably built into the evolutionary process as we lurch from swamp to Valhalla that individuals, clans, nations, movements, and ideologies, struggle with a basic conflict between force and wisdom.

But who is to say what is wise? You don't need to ask what force is, as you lie on the ground, bleeding. Historically, force seems to have won; but then, I'm no historian, nor am I a philosopher, and I'm not sure how much I'm a Christist (however that is defined), despite my cultural setting. What I am is someone brought up in a Scottish manse, with a religious background, brought up in a country called Scotland: a country which is still torn between the desire for wisdom and a hunger for glory, all charged up by a frustration about having less power than we want and deserve. How's that for a statement of the obvious?

Lest I sound holier or at least humbler than thou, let me say I am as torn as the next mouse. Take the Scottish Parliament. I cried like any onion operative during the first opening when Winnie Ewing with the authority of an archangel cataclysmically summoned the parliament from its three centuries of sleep, Tom Fleming spoke the magic words about an old and new song, the parliament sang like linties about brotherhood, and the greatest Scottish political utterance of my lifetime was spoken by Donald Dewar, the first First Minister. That day I cried with the relief of a wound finally binding after the tearing and stitching of too long a pain; it felt like a healing of Scotland in celebration of a shadowy old glory clasping a modern acceptance of power. I wasn't torn that day, but now?

I'm a faithful viewer of BBC Scotland's coverage of "Holyrood". Now that I'm liberated from the job hamster wheel, it is for me a democratic obligation to attend to what I can see on the TV of the goings-on on the Mound; but it is at this point that I have a problem. It manifests itself in a malfunction of the eyelids; they tend to be swayed by the force of gravity. If I could afford to take them to a privately financed initiative hospital, I might be advised that I would have to grin and bear a natural ageing process: the hinge mechanism holding the eyelids in the open position showing signs of metal fatigue. A cynic, on the other hand, might say I was just bored. But maybe that's OK. People in the parliament are getting on with honest modest work, not performing for glory.

And yet. The nearest I get to defining Scotland is that it is my part of this glorious planet. It has given me everything, at first life, then entertainment and glorious beauty. I can imagine myself fighting to save the earth from those that would despoil it or remove civilisation, even life, from it. Scotland is part of the planet I stand on, breathe on, pray on. There is, I trust, time for this lovely land and its new parliament to grow into the future, to learn, to breathe, to be civil and above all to be inspirationally entertaining. That is, as far as I am concerned, the bottom line. How can the gap between power (a.k.a. brute force, otherwise known as bullying) and glory (a.k.a. sentimentality) be bridged?

By art. We need that prism to recognise reality. To touch truth we need to be moved. Sometimes to cry. Sometimes to laugh. It doesn't happen a lot, in Westminster, Brussels, the United Nations, or sadly, Holyrood. Of course, as well, conscientious representatives of the people need to work, plodding away at practical minutiae. But so does everyone, in his or her work. We need more, however. Well, I need more. I need people who risk exploring the trapdoor to infinity which I saw in my childhood when the winter clouds parted to reveal through the blizzard the stars. That's a dangerous voyage, but it's one our planet is making every day and night. We, who are hitch-hiking through the stars on this fragile globe, should voyage dangerously in harmony. I want leaders and companions who strive to represent the subversive and multi-brained soul of my planet and of my native land.

Scotland may have to be more free from its big buddy across the border, in order to be more freely part of a diverse world. But independence of any kind is a chimera. Not only is no man an island, no living thing is. In the mysterious diffusion of time and space, the universe sparkles everywhere.

Epilogue

Gaining, losing. Losing, regaining. Living, dying. And after that? The mortal cycle. The haunting, goading immortal dream. This is the stuff of preaching. The most delicate privilege of these last years has been my reclaiming of the pulpit. I didn't, with rare exceptions, preach while I worked at the BBC. I knew I hadn't the ability or the strength to give my all to broadcasting and to Sunday worship. I interpreted my work as my worship, and indeed my Sundays were often spent working. The sheer relief now of being needed, usually in rural parishes, to bring words that matter to communities large or tiny has given me, I hope, a lightness of touch with a directness of message which people have seemed to appreciate. I have certainly appreciated the people, as has Elizabeth who has nearly always accompanied me.

I've delivered orations in the Old Parish Church of Montrose, a kirk whose grave exterior, dominating the fine main street, implodes into an interior of wild theatricality. James Weatherhead's ministry there has been followed by a ministry as faithful as flamboyant: that of the wee boy who whispered to Elizabeth, vis-à-vis me, that he was on our side, but not to tell anyone. He has in his adult life been on God's side and telling everyone. Laurence Whitley recalls his father, not only in luminous pulpit language, but in his tight-rope walk between humour and deep emotion. He is also one of the best *Thought for the Day* speakers Radio Scotland has ever had.

In Killearn, Balfron, Drymen, Milton of Buchanan, Lochgoilhead, Carrick, Balquhidder, and other more or less remote places, the summer journeys have been idyllic, the winter ones sometimes harsh. But in every place, as in our own West Kirk here, and the tiny cathedral of Southwick on the Solway, I have found what Moderator after Moderator says after a year's tour of Scotland's parishes. There—there—where it matters, communities are in good heart. Men and women of wit, intelligence, humour and courage, are enduring the wounds of living, suffering, and dying with a weave of faith and doubt that transcends all cheap pessimism. Dave Harned was right. George MacLeod, Harry Whitley, Bill and Millicent Macdonald, my father, they were all right. Love can win. The human evidence is all around, if we have eyes to see and ears to hear.

At night, if I can't sleep, I sometimes go to the window and, if it is clear, look beyond the street lights to the space beyond. It becomes more and more difficult to get there, because earth's light pollution is blotting out the cosmos. But from the glebe fields by the Solway one can see the fields of stars. There they are, the revolving galaxies. Inside the cottage behind me is my little family which one of these days I will have to leave. But for now they're here to cherish. My heart beats for them, but my heart also reaches out to the family who left me, father, mother, Alan, Catherine, Etta. My heart reaches out so far it thins to invisibility. They, and my friends that have gone, have been travelling beyond death for years. They must have gone very far by now. I don't find words, but I yearn that somewhere in the mystery of universes, wherever they are, in whatever form they are, they could be touched by the unconditional love I feel for them.

The intensity passes. Is it real? Do they exist anywhere? How at one moment can one be surrounded by faith and see everything fit together, and at another moment feel so utterly lost in aloneness and unknowingness?

That uncertainty is how it always has been, and always must be, no doubt.

Index